PASSIONATE Prayer

BRENDA WALSH

with KAY KUZMA

PASSIONATE
Prayer

3ABN BOOKS
PO Box 220, West Frankfort, Illinois
www.3ABN.org

Pacific Press® Publishing Association
Nampa, Idaho
Oshawa, Ontario, Canada
www.pacificpress.com

Designed by Mark Bond for BONDesign, Inc.
Cover design resources from iStockphoto.com
Photos in this book are provided by the author

Copyright © 2007 by
Pacific Press® Publishing Association
Printed in the United States of America
All rights reserved

Additional copies of this book are available from two locations:
3ABN: Call 1-800-752-3226 or visit http://www.3abn.org
Adventist Book Centers: Call 1-800-765-6955
or visit http://www.adventistbookcenter.com

3ABN BOOKS is dedicated to bringing you the best in published materials
consistent with the mission of Three Angels Broadcasting Network. Our goal is to
uplift Jesus through books, audio, and video materials by our family of 3ABN
presenters. Our in-depth Bible study guides, devotionals, biographies, and lifestyle
materials promote the whole person in health and the mending of broken people.
For more information, call 616-627-4651 or visit 3ABN's Web site:
http://www.3ABN.org

Library of Congress Cataloging-in-Publication Data

Walsh, Brenda, 1953-
Passionate prayer / by Brenda Walsh ; with Kay Kuzma.
    p. cm.
ISBN 13: 978-0-8163-2214-5 (paper back)
ISBN 10: 0-8163-2214-7 (paper back)
1. Prayer--Christianity. 2. Spiritual life--Christianity. I. Kuzma,
Kay. II. Title.
BV210.3.W35 2007
248.3'2--dc22
                                                2007009942

11 12 13 14 · 5 4 3 2

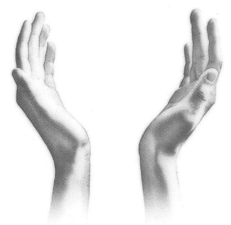

DEDICATION
To Jesus and My Family

With a heart full of thanks and praise, I humbly dedicate this book, first and foremost to Jesus, the joy of my life. I am overwhelmed with Your amazing love for me. Everyday You are teaching me that prayer is the breath of my soul. What a glorious privilege it is to enter Your throne room at any time of the day or night! My thanks and praise go to You, my powerful and loving God. It is my prayer that everyone who reads this book will have a desire to know You personally as their Lord and Savior. Thank You my precious heavenly Father, for the promised blessing in Jeremiah 29:12: "Then you will call upon Me and go and pray to Me, and I will listen to you." I love You with all my heart and just as You are listening to me, by Your grace, I am listening to You.

One of the special gifts God has blessed me with is my praying family. It means so much to know that they are ever ready to lift up any need or problem in prayer. For this reason, I also dedicate this book to my loving Christian parents, sisters, brothers, grandmother, and aunts who know what it means to pray passionately and to trust God for His will to be done.

To Mom and Dad, James and Bernice Micheff. Thank you for teaching me to pray when I was just a little girl. There is no greater gift you could have ever given me than to introduce me to Jesus and to model how to come close to God through prayer. I love you both with all my heart and am looking forward to spending eternity with you in heaven. By God's grace, I will be a star in your crowns.

To my sisters, Linda Johnson and Cinda Sanner. It has meant so much to me to have you for my prayer partners. Working together in ministry is a joy and a privilege for which I thank God. I love how we can come together in prayer and leave every burden at Jesus' feet. Thank you for your love and support and for always being there for me. I love you more than you could possibly know.

To my brothers, Jim and Ken Micheff. You both are so dear and precious. Your love and dedication to God's work continues to inspire me. Thank you for your unconditional love and for the encouragement you have given me throughout the years. Any time I have come to you with a crisis, your first words are "Bibby, let's pray about it." That has always meant so much to me and has been a great source of strength. I love you both very much, and I'm so blessed to be your sister.

To Aunt Myrtle Coy. From the time I was a little girl we have always shared a very special bond. I know I can count on you to be there whenever I need you. You have become a very treasured prayer partner, willing to pray for whoever is on my prayer list. That has strengthened the bond between us even more. I love you deeply and am looking forward to spending eternity with you.

To my Aunt Elizabeth Barra. The day you were baptized was such a special day, not only for you but also for my grandma, as you are her youngest sister. I know Grandma prayed passionately for you and that all the angels in heaven rejoiced when you fully surrendered to Jesus. I want you to know how very much I love you and I'm looking forward to what God has planned for us when we get to the new earth! What a day of rejoicing that will be!

In memory of Grandma Helen Micheff. I wish everyone could have known my precious grandma. She was the ultimate prayer warrior, and her love of God was revealed in the way she lived her life. Because she walked daily with Jesus, her character reflected that of her loving heavenly Father. She had the most giving and unselfish heart, always thinking of others. I'm so homesick for heaven. I want to see my Savior first of all—and then I want to see my grandma.

My Praying Family

"Mom and Dad,"
Pastor James and Bernice Micheff.

The Micheff family. Back row, standing left to right: Jim Johnson, Julie and Janie Johnson, Jimmy and Jack Johnson, David Sanner, Joel Sanner, Michael Coffin, Becky Coffin, Jason Coffin, Linda Kay Walsh, Bernice Micheff, me, Tim Walsh, Jim Micheff, Jamie Micheff, Jenny Micheff-Truby, Garrett Truby, Crystal Micheff, Ken Micheff. Front row, seated left to right: Linda Johnson, Catie Sanner, Cinda Sanner, James Micheff, Gail Micheff, Jody Micheff, Jason Micheff, Tammy Micheff, Jeremy Micheff.

The Johnson family. Left to right: Jim, Linda (holding Janie), Jimmy, Jack (sitting next to his mom), and Julie.

The Sanner family at Catie's graduation from Highland Academy. Left to right: Joel, Catie, Cinda, and David.

The Jim Micheff, Jr. family. Sitting on the ground: Jody Micheff. Sitting on the bench: Garrett Truby, Jenny Micheff-Truby, Gail Micheff. Kneeling: Jamie Micheff. Standing, left to right: Jim Micheff, Jason Micheff.

Back row, left to right: Tammy Micheff, Crystal Micheff. Front row, left to right: Ken Micheff, Jeremy Micheff.

David, Michael, Becky and Jason Coffin. This photo was taken on Michael's first day of school. Becky is such an incredible mother. I'm so proud of the woman she has become . . . and so thankful for my grandchildren!

Tim, my husband, and Linda Kay can talk for hours about politics, science, business—basically anything going on in the world around them.

My youngest daughter, Linda Kay, and me. She has a quick wit and a sparkling personality and is so much fun to be with.

*Jason and Michael—
two of the incredible
joys in my life.*

*My precious Aunt Myrtle Coy and
me. We have always been close but
prayer has bonded us even more. I'm
looking forward to spending eternity
with her in heaven.*

*Aunt Elizabeth Barra is my
grandma Micheff's youngest sister.
She is a wonderful prayer warrior
and loves Jesus with all her heart. She
will always be close to my heart!*

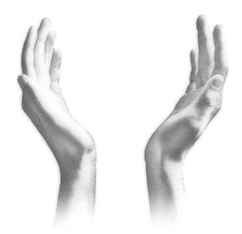

ACKNOWLEDGMENTS
Thanks Sincerely

My heartfelt thanks to so many people without whom this book would not have been possible.

To my precious husband, Tim. Thank you for choosing me to be your wife and for all the love you give me every day! You have always encouraged me to do what God wants me to do, even if that means time away from you. I'm looking forward to spending eternity with you in heaven! I love you with all my heart.

To my girls, Becky and Linda Kay. You have enriched my life in ways that you could never imagine. Being your mother has filled my life with so much joy! I'm so very proud of the women you have become, but I want you to know that no matter how old you are, you will always be "my babies"! I love you both very much.

To my grandsons, Michael and Jason. There are not enough words to describe the depth of my love for each of you. You are the light of my life, and I cherish every moment we spend together! You have filled my heart with so much love and happiness, and I thank God for you! I am so blessed to be your "Grandma."

To those who have shared their stories—Polly Aho, Julie Archibold, Kari Avery, Susie Babineau, Ray and Jackie Brosseuk, Sherri Childress, Sally Conklin, Sherry Helveston, Gordon and Dona Klein, Margie Leach,

Jan Nourollahi, Angela Piecarczyk, Debbie Rapp, Greg and Gena Reynolds, Ellie Santangelo, Ivan and Denise Wolfe. I love every one of you, and I want you to know that you have blessed my life immensely! Now, because of your willingness to share your stories, others will receive a blessing too, and be drawn closer to Jesus. I thank you from the bottom of my heart!

To my production assistants, Brenda Abbott, Sonia Gott, Virginia Gustin, Deanna Whitehouse, and Denise Wolfe. How can I possibly convey the love and thankfulness in my heart for each of you? I am so thankful to God for bringing you into my life, and I thank you for the long hours each of you spend helping with *Kids Time*, Micheff Sisters Ministries, and whatever project God has for me. Thank you, also, for your help with this book. Truly, you are an answer to prayer, and I know there will be souls in the kingdom because of your efforts! I pray passionately for you, and I love you all!

To my treasured friends, Binda (Bonnie Laing), Bonnie Shuris, Carole Derry-Bretsch, Cheryl Olson, Cheryl Giardina, Dona Klein, Jan Nourollahi, Janice Wasmer, Julia Outkina, Lois Somerville, Marie Macri, Mecca Conaulty, Mildred Lippert, Mollie Steenson, Nancy Sterling, Peg Bernhardt, Rita Showers, Sally Burchfield, Shelley Quinn, Susan Owens, and Truby Bowen. We share so many precious memories, and I thank God for the gift of your friendship. Thank you for always being there for me through fun and laughter as well as the tears—and especially for your prayers. You truly are blessings in my life. I love you dearly.

To Mark and Conna Bond. I know without a doubt that when God brought you into my life it was a *divine appointment!* You have the most precious family, and I love all of you so much. Thank you for all your hard work on *Kids Time*. I know God is using your efforts to win souls for the kingdom! God has blessed you both with incredible talent, and I'm thankful that you are using it to bring honor and glory to Him! Thank you, Mark, for the beautiful cover design you have created for this book, as well as the work you have done for all my other books! I look forward to being neighbors with you and your family in heaven.

To Bobby Davis. Thank you for the many hours spent editing this book. I know as a 3ABN editor you consider it "your job," but we both know you go way above and beyond, never expecting any praise. You are an incredible writer, and I know there will be souls in the kingdom because you allow Christ to work through you. I know I can always count on you to tell it to me straight, and I love that about you. You are a special and treasured friend.

To Russ Holt and Tim Lale. "Thank you" doesn't begin to express the thanks in my heart for all your efforts to make this book the best it could be! You have a standard for excellence like none other, and your business style truly reflects the character of Christ. I appreciate Pacific Press and its dedication to spreading the gospel around the world! I thank you from the bottom of my heart for your integrity, honesty, and Christian professionalism.

Last, but not least, to Kay Kuzma. Thank you for all the endless hours spent helping me edit this book. Even when you had your own projects to work on, you still took time for me! This book would not have been the same without you! God has blessed you with so many talents, and you unselfishly share them with others, always giving of yourself. You are a precious and treasured friend. Thank you for your honesty, support, wisdom, and guidance—but most of all for your Christian love. I love you very much.

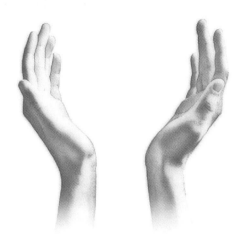

CONTENTS

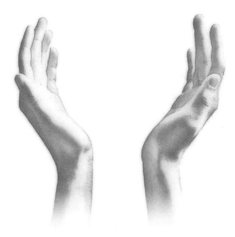

FOREWORD
by Kay Kuzma

I've always been intrigued with prayer. I've always prayed because that's what my mom taught me to do. But my prayers haven't always been answered. I haven't always gotten what I wanted.

So, I've wondered, *How does prayer work? Why does it work? Why doesn't it work? Why do some people get miracles and others don't?* If only I could understand God better.

Then over the years I began to realize that God never asked me to understand Him. The only thing He requires is for me to trust Him. To ask and to believe.

But it wasn't until I began to work with Brenda on this project that I started to understand another dynamic to prayer that my mother never taught me. And that's the spirit, the intense desire, the strong emotion, the passion that Jesus wants me to bring to my love affair with Him.

Why pray? It's not to move mountains. It's not to get a miracle. It's not to ace a test or find my keys or get rid of a sore throat—as important as these things may be. *It's to get to know Jesus better.* It's to fall more deeply in love with Him. It's to become one with Him so that His will becomes my will. Brenda calls it *passionate prayer.*

Passionate prayer and Jesus are synonymous. After all, the most intense emotion that anyone has ever experienced in this world was

Jesus sweating blood and praying to His Father right before He was brutally killed, "Father, not My will, but Yours." It was Jesus calling out as He felt the oneness of His relationship with His Father being ripped away, "My God, why have You forsaken Me?" It was Jesus pleading, just before His heart broke with love for His prodigal children, "Father, forgive them!"

That's why the suffering and death of Jesus is commonly called "The Passion"! Jesus was passionately in love with His Father. Their love was so intense that the separation killed Him. And at the same time, Jesus was so passionately in love with us that He was willing to endure the separation so we could be saved.

Jesus didn't just pray. He prayed passionately! And so should we!

Prayer is not just words and requests and praise. Prayer is a relationship—a love relationship with the most incredible Lover this world has ever known. Our God! And when we passionately call out to Him, He's not going to let us down.

This book is Brenda at her best. It's Brenda glowing with the love of Jesus, shouting with joy, and exploding with praise! And it all happens as a result of *passionate prayer*.

May Brenda's passion for Jesus become your passion. May you be inspired by the stories in this book, not just to pray—but to pray *passionately* and to trust passionately that He will open the windows of heaven and pour out on you so many incredible answers to your prayers that you will be totally amazed at the depth of His love!

INTRODUCTION
My Prayer—God's Promises

Dear heavenly Father, please use me in a special way today to bring others closer to You. Make me a blessing in someone's life. I ask for wisdom to know Your will, and strength and courage to carry it out. O Lord, I want to be a powerful soul-winning tool for You! Thank You for being the awesome God that You are. I love You. In Jesus' precious name I pray. Amen.

Every morning I passionately pray this prayer. And I have experienced the most amazing answers! So amazing that I can no longer keep them to myself. I just have to shout it to the world. God is so good! He is so faithful. Imagine, the God of the universe using me to share His love with others!

When I go to bed at night, I may be dead tired, but I'm joyfully praising God for the way He has led me through the day, even though I might not yet understand exactly what He has done or is in the process of doing. He has answered so many of my prayers that there is no doubt in my mind that He is busy working out His will through my willingness to be used by Him.

For years, I missed many witnessing opportunities because I didn't know how to pray. I wasn't praying and asking God to use me in a mighty way to bring others closer to Him. I failed to realize that God won't force Himself on me. I must invite Him into my heart to work through me. And when I move over to the passenger seat and let Him take control, I'm in for an incredible joy ride!

You'll see what I mean as you walk with me through the pages of this book. Over the years God has given me so many miracle stories that I can't possibly tell them all. But I have chosen a few of the most amazing to share with you so that your faith will be strengthened and that you, too, will have the burning desire for the intimate relationship with Jesus that He talks about in John 15:7: "If you abide in Me, and My words abide in you, you will ask what you desire, and it shall be done for you."

Imagine! It's that simple. If we just live every moment of our lives in Christ and maintain an open invitation for Him to live in us, there is no limit to what He will do for us! That's His promise. And the way to experience His promise is through prayer.

I am passionate about prayer. I pray all the time. Prayer has become my way of life. I pray with anyone who will pray with me. I pray about everything. I pray for everyone who needs a miracle. I just love to pray. Why? Because that's how I get to know Jesus better.

I believe Jesus. He has personally told me through His Word, "Brenda, I will give you whatever you desire if you do two things: First, abide in Me and invite Me to live in you. And second, Ask!" Read John 15:7 again. Isn't that what Jesus says? And if He is saying that to me, He is saying that to you, too! What a promise!

Why is Jesus willing to do this for us? Who are we to deserve this awesome pipeline to the treasures of heaven? Read on. The next verse makes it clear: Jesus is willing to do this for us because it glorifies His Father.

Now here's the part I love best. You've got to keep reading in John 15 to find it. Just a few verses later (verse 11) Jesus explains, "These things I have spoken to you, that My joy may remain in you, *and that your joy may be full*" (emphasis added).

I don't know about you, but I love to experience that warm fuzzy feeling of happiness and contentment. I love to smile! I love to laugh! I love to burst out with shouts of joy and screams of delight when great things happen. And that's exactly what I've experienced since surrendering my life to Jesus. Almost every day, I'm infused with an explosion of joy over what God has done through me, around me, and for me! Someone I've talked to catches a glimpse of God's extravagant love. Someone is healed. Someone is encouraged. Someone decides to give his life to Jesus. Someone prays for the first time. Someone's faith is renewed. It's exhilarating! It's awesome!

I have experienced the fullness of His joy by willingly doing what He wants me to do. And it all happens because of prayer: *Passionate Prayer!* I know without a shadow of a doubt that if you will fall in love with Jesus Christ and passionately pray, you too, will experience God's amazing answers.

With the joy of Jesus,
Brenda Walsh

CHAPTER I

MY JOY RIDE WITH JESUS

Call to Me, and I will answer you,
and show you great and mighty things, which you do not know.
—Jeremiah 33:3

I haven't always prayed passionately! I was a great external Christian—just going through the motions. It wasn't that I was a bad person. My heart was always seeking to help others, to witness for Christ, and to serve wherever there was a need. Because I was involved in so many church activities, others probably thought I was leading a Christ-centered life. I was a Sabbath School leader, at one time or another, in every children's division from cradle roll to early teen. I coordinated elegant fellowship meals every week, served on nominating committees, was the social committee chair, was on the church board, and spent Sabbath afternoons singing in nursing homes. I raised funds for disaster relief, played the organ every Sabbath, and baked cookies for members too discouraged to come to church. But all the while I was what you might call a "dormant Christian." My heart was in the right place, but the main ingredient in my spiritual life was missing. I wasn't really connected personally with Christ.

Oh, I understood that Jesus loved me, that He died for me, and that He had saved me, but I didn't fully comprehend the depth of His love—for me. And the worst part of all, I didn't even realize that something was missing.

I thought I knew the Lord. I prayed every day. I said all the right words and *hoped* Jesus would answer, but I never prayed really *believing* with absolute certainty that He would. That is, until the day God used cookies to show me how much He loved me! When I finally understood how important I was to my Lord and Savior, I fully surrendered my life to Him. And my life has never been the same since. But I'm getting ahead of my story.

I grew up in a loving home. There were five of us kids—three girls and two boys. And since Dad was a preacher, I can't remember a time when our family wasn't in ministry. In fact, I will go so far as to say that I can't remember a time when I didn't love Jesus. We had family worship in our home every morning and every night. My parents truly believed in the power of prayer! And we experienced some incredible miracles. I believe it is because of the prayers of Mom and Dad that all five of their children are in full-time ministry today.

Then came that awful time when at eighteen years of age I foolishly married a man I didn't know or love. The violence that followed almost cost me my life.

That experience shocked me into the reality of renewing my relationship with God. Thankfully, He used my sister Linda to help me and my infant daughter, Becky, escape this man's demented control over me. At the time, I prayed passionately for deliverance—"Lord, save me!"—because I was in desperate trouble. And in His goodness and mercy, He did. But I still had no concept of what a complete life of prayer was all about.

A few years later God orchestrated events in my life to allow me to meet Tim Walsh, a distinguished passenger on an airplane, who later became my husband, friend, and soul mate. What a wonderful loving father he has been to Becky and Linda Kay. I could not be more blessed than to be Mrs. Brenda Walsh! Then came the busy years of child rearing as we followed my husband's jobs—first to San Jose, California, and then to Boston, Massachusetts. All this time I played the role of a good Christian wife and mother. And I was! But I had no idea I was missing the exhilarating joy that only an intimate relationship with Jesus can give!

My total surrender to God and my dedicated commitment to do His will started in 1991. Tim and I were living in the Boston area, and our girls were doing well in school. Tim had a great job and was able to provide well

I'm so thankful God has blessed me with such a wonderful husband. Tim is my best friend, soul mate, and incredible prayer partner!

for our family. I was thankful I didn't need to work outside our home so I could be a full-time wife and mother. This also gave me time to help wherever needed at church. Life was good!

We decided to take a few days off and go down to see my family, most of whom worked at Little Creek Academy near Knoxville, Tennessee. My sister Cinda and her husband, Joel, lived only a few miles from the school, so it was an automatic Micheff family reunion whenever the Walsh family arrived!

That weekend, our childhood friend, Danny Shelton, president of Three Angels Broadcasting Network (3ABN), just happened to be at the church we attended. After Danny's inspiring sermon about witnessing, we all gathered around the dinner table to enjoy wonderful conversation and my mother's delicious food. I found myself spellbound as Danny related experience after experience of sharing Christ with people. He even told of individuals who gave their hearts to the Lord on airplanes!

That afternoon I should have been exhilarated as I listened to all those incredible witnessing experiences. Instead, I had the most empty feeling inside. *Why isn't something like this happening to me?* On the way back to Boston, I was so quiet that Tim asked if I was feeling well. Not really. That empty feeling had turned into a raw ache for Christ. Instead of interacting with the girls and Tim, I was praying, *Lord, why don't You use me like that?* Danny had so many witnessing stories he didn't have time to share them all. *Why don't I have even one story? Lord, I've been serving You all my life!* And then I came under conviction and honestly questioned, *Have I really been a willing vessel, eager to do what God wanted me to do, or have I just selfishly done what I wanted to do—or what I have been taught?*

I literally prayed all the way home, *God, use me*, and continued to pray each day throughout the next two weeks, *Let me be a blessing in someone's life today.* Every waking moment I prayed, *Lord, give me a soul-winning story—like You gave Danny.* Yet nothing happened.

Then it came to me, maybe there was something in my life that was keeping God from answering my prayer. I asked God for a cleansing from sin and from every unrighteous act. I claimed the promise in 1 John 1:9, "If we confess our sins, He is faithful and just to forgive us." I agonized with the Lord. I pleaded for Him to answer my prayer.

That's when I first began to pray passionately for God to use me. I asked, *Lord, why aren't You using me?* I knocked on the gates of heaven: *Lord, I'm here; I'm willing to be willing. Please use me. It's been two weeks, and I still don't have a story to tell.* I even asked, *Lord, if it's not too selfish of me, just give me a sign that You **will** use me when You're ready.*

MY SURRENDER

The next morning, the girls were at school and Tim was at work. I hadn't even gotten dressed or fixed my hair when the overwhelming urge came upon me that I should bake some cookies. We had a huge butler pantry with large bins of flour, sugar, and all the ingredients for almost any kind of cookie. *I know what I'll do*, I said to myself, *I'll make some oatmeal cookies for Tim. In fact, I'll make a double batch.* While those were baking, I thought, *Linda Kay doesn't like oatmeal cookies, but she loves ginger snaps. Maybe I should mix up a batch or two of those.* When those were ready to go into the oven, I thought about Becky. Peanut butter cookies were her favorite. And before I knew it, I had made a double batch of those, too. But I didn't stop there. I started looking through my cookbooks, and each recipe seemed to be equally enticing. Soon my kitchen was full of every kind of cookie you can imagine. By now it was afternoon, and I was still in my pajamas. I had become irrationally obsessed with making cookies.

By the time Tim walked in after work, there were stacks of cookies all over the house. It wasn't until he asked if we were going to have a party that I came to my senses. *What have I done? Why have I done this?* I had no idea. I individually wrapped each cookie in clear wrap, placed them in plastic bags, put them in the freezer, and forgot all about them.

Two weeks later, on a Sabbath morning, I went into the pantry and without thinking, took all the cookies out to thaw. Then I forgot about them until later in the afternoon. Why had I taken them all out of the freezer? I didn't know. But my mom had taught me that it wasn't good to refreeze food, so I knew I had to get rid of them. That's when the thought came to me that maybe I could take them to a soup kitchen. I didn't even know if there was a soup kitchen nearby. *Who would know if there is a soup kitchen in town?* I called the police station and found out that there was a soup kitchen in Clinton at the Methodist church, right across from the police station. They began serving at five o'clock every afternoon.

I looked at my watch. If I hurried, I would have just enough time to deliver the cookies before the meal began. Now here is where the story really gets interesting.

When I arrived at the church, only one woman was there, and she was wringing her hands. An emergency had come up, and the people who usually served the food had merely dropped off everything and asked her to serve it. Since she had never done anything like that before she had no idea where to begin. "And the worst thing of all," the lady lamented, "is that they forgot the dessert!"

"I'll help you," I volunteered. "I've got cookies."

"But you don't understand how many people eat here. We will need hundreds of cookies."

"Don't worry," I assured her. "I have more than enough cookies."

It wasn't until after the people were served and I had given away the last cookie that I realized what had happened. My hands started trembling. God had used me in a powerful way. *Oh Lord,* I prayed, *You knew two weeks ago when You had me bake all those cookies that the people providing food for this soup kitchen today would forget the dessert. What an awesome God You are!*

My eyes were opened, and I could see that God had a wonderful plan for my life, and I felt His closeness. That's when I realized just how much Jesus personally loves me, Brenda Walsh! It was at that exact moment that I fully surrendered my life completely to Him. *From now on, I'm going to serve You fully and completely, and I'm willing to do whatever You ask.* I praised God for allowing me to be there at just the right time to organize the food service at the soup kitchen—and to have all those cookies. But most of all I praised God for answering my prayer to be used. That commitment changed my life from a ho-hum existence to a vibrant, abundant life in Jesus.*

Ever since I said Yes to Him, life for me has been a whirlwind affair with God. I talk to Him continually. And when I pray, I pray fervently. I pray with passion. I pray believing. I've experienced so many miracles that I can't begin to record them all. And I've learned an important lesson: As long as we are willing to be willing to do God's will, He will use us!

Matthew 7:21 has become my life script. " 'Not everyone who says to Me, "Lord, Lord," shall enter the kingdom of heaven, but *he who does the will of My Father in heaven*' " (emphasis added).

KIDS TIME

It was not long after the cookie experience that I was asked to host and produce the *Kids Time* television program for 3ABN. At the time, I wasn't qualified. I had never been a television producer. Nothing I had done in life had prepared me for this challenge. The Lord had given me success in a variety of other areas. I was a registered nurse and had my own floral and interior design business. Singing, playing the piano, and oil painting were my creative outlets. However, my television experience was limited to singing with my sisters on my dad's television show, as well as doing vegetarian cooking programs with my sisters that aired on 3ABN. But that was it! Being *behind the camera* is a whole different ball game!

That's why, when I was asked to produce *Kids Time*, even though my daily prayer had been, "Lord, use me," my immediate reaction was, "I can't do that!" I knew nothing about what it took to produce a good television program. Plus, I lived in the Boston area, more than a thousand miles from 3ABN!

On the set of Kids Time, *taping praise music with Emily Traversy. Left to right: Emily's mom, Linda Traversy, Sonia Gott,* PraiseTime *production assistant/recruiter, and me with Emily.*

As soon as I said, "I can't," it was as if God spoke to me. *"Do you really want to serve Me or do you want to do just what you want to do?"* Once again, Matthew 7:21 came to my mind—that only those who do the will of the Father shall enter heaven!

I fell on my knees. *Lord, I'm so sorry. Your plan is perfect. I just have a hard time always seeing what Your plan is for my life. If You want me to be a producer, I will—if You show me how. But I have to know without a doubt that it is Your will for me. Give me a sign. Give me ideas about what I could do to make a quality children's program, because right now I'm clueless!*

I had so many ideas tumbling out of my head that I couldn't sleep for three nights. On the third night I was so exhausted that I prayed, *Lord, I'm so tired. Just shut off my mind so I can get some sleep.* And that's when it hit me, God had answered my prayer! By then I had Post-it notes hanging everywhere with enough ideas to produce

fifty programs! I *knew* God wanted me to produce *Kids Time.* The last thing I remember before falling asleep was claiming Philippians 4:13, "I can do all things through Christ who strengthens me."

That experience strength-

The set of Kids Time *where the Bible stories are taped.*

ened my relationship with God. Once again I surrendered the driver's seat of my life to my heavenly Father. I don't even get out of bed in the morning without praying, *Precious Lord, please use me in a special way and make me a blessing in someone's life. Give me a divine appointment and lead me to the person You want me to witness to today.*

Riding with Jesus has been one incredible road trip! God led me to *Kids Time,* where every day I have the privilege of introducing children to Jesus and letting them know how much He loves them. Then, just when I was feeling comfortable with television production, God asked me to share my story of domestic violence, which I had never ever intended to share. He did it by impressing me to write the book *Battered to Blessed.* That was way out of my comfort zone! Although I had many creative outlets in my life, writing books was not one of them. Because of that book, God began using me more frequently at women's retreats where I am able to give a message of hope to abused and battered women around the world.

But that wasn't all. Doors of opportunity soon began opening for me to speak not only to women, but to people of all ages and from every walk of life. They need to know God has a plan for each of them and that if they will totally surrender their lives to Him, He will use them in incredible ways. God now has me speaking not only to churches, retreats, and schools, but also teaching students of evangelism about the power of prayer and making presentations to non-Christian organizations, as well!

Sixteen years ago, I would have thought, *It's impossible!* But now I know the truth of Mark 10:27: "with God all things are possible"!

In 1991 I felt God's calling on my life and responded, *God send me!* And He did. He is giving that same call to you today. His commission is clear: "Go therefore and make disciples of all the nations, . . . teaching them to observe all things that I have commanded you; and lo, I am with you always, even to the end of the age" (Matthew 28:19, 20).

He has ordained each of us to be "ministers." God doesn't *need* us to finish His work, but in His love He allows us the privilege of witnessing for Him because He knows it will bring us the greatest spiritual and emotional high we can ever experience. This is His way of giving us the abundant life that He promised in John 10:10.

And here's the good news: When God calls us for a specific task, He will always provide what we need to accomplish it. Whether it's finances, opportunities, strength, courage, or holy boldness, His promise in Philippians 4:19 is clear: "And my God shall supply all your need accord-

My sisters and I traveled to Russia where we gave a concert. Julia Outkina, director of 3ABN Russian Television Network, translated as Pastor Vadim introduced us.

"The Micheff Sisters" on the 3ABN kitchen set, getting ready to tape a cooking program. Left to right: Brenda, Cinda, and Linda.

ing to His riches in glory by Christ Jesus."

Not only does God have an individual ministry for me to witness for Him, He also has called me to a ministry with my sisters—The Micheff Sisters—singing, recording CDs, speaking, and cooking. Yes, cooking! We demonstrate a healthier way to eat via a cooking program on 3ABN and have authored two vegetarian cookbooks. What great joy it brings us to go wherever God leads us! There is no greater happiness or personal satisfaction than serving Jesus!

Just when I thought life with Jesus couldn't get any better, my sisters and I experienced an incredibly stimulating spiritual prayer-powered weekend that I must tell you about!

My sisters and I write a recipe column for Vibrant Life *magazine. We enjoy sharing culinary history and our cooking talents with readers. This photo of us with* Vibrant Life *editor, Charles Mills, was taken during the magazine's annual 5K Fun Run, an outreach project drawing runners from across the United States.*

ONE INCREDIBLE, HOLY SPIRIT–FILLED WEEKEND

My sisters, Linda Johnson and Cinda Sanner, and I had been asked to be the keynote speakers at a women's retreat in Liberty Hill, South Carolina. It was going to be held at Nosoca Pines, a beautiful youth camp nestled in the woods beside Lake Wateree.

Linda had flown from Wisconsin to Knoxville, Tennessee, where

Cinda and I live, so the three of us could drive together to our destination six hours away. Before pulling out of the driveway, we stopped to pray, asking God to protect us as we traveled and also for a powerful Spirit-filled weekend. We prayed earnestly that God would bless and touch the hearts of the women who came and that they would be drawn closer to Him. We asked Him to use us as mighty soul-winning tools.

Cinda drove, and I sat up front as the navigator. I came prepared with step-by-step maps I had downloaded off the Internet. And should we get lost, I could call my husband instantly using the speed dial on my cell phone. Tim can help anyone get anywhere. In fact, my whole family calls Tim when they're lost!

"Did you remember our music tracks?" Linda asked.

"Yes, I have them right here. Are you ready to practice singing?" We were being stretched at this retreat as we were supposed to sing for all the meetings. This meant that we needed every spare minute to practice. When three people sing together, it is especially important that all three voices blend and that we also sing the same words at the same time. For this to happen takes lots of practice! I took one of the CDs from its case and loaded it into the player. We spent the next six hours singing, sharing what we felt God wanted us to do at this retreat, and praying for the women who would be attending.

The time passed quickly, and before we knew it we had arrived at the camp. We easily found our cabin even though it was almost midnight, and soon all three of us were fast asleep.

The next day we finished final preparations for our presentations and then had a wonderful time meeting the women as they arrived. Cinda had a seminar in the afternoon on Christian entertaining, and then the three of us gave a cooking demonstration similar to what we do on our television program. The women loved it because they got to sample everything we made!

In the evening, I gave my testimony about my life as a battered wife in my first marriage and how God had saved me. I was able to share that it is never God's plan that anyone be mistreated or abused and that Jesus is the only Healer of hearts! Afterward, Cinda and I sang a song that Danny Shelton wrote, "The First Moment of Eternity." This song has so much meaning, and hearts were touched by the words: "The first moment of eternity will be worth all the trials down here, and when I hear the King of all ages say, Come home, child; Come home to stay."

After prayer, many of the women joined us around the piano, singing songs until we all were too tired to sing anymore. I am always physically drained after giving my testimony because in order to tell my story I must relive each painful detail. That night was no exception. I fell asleep talking to God and thanking Him for the blessings He had already poured out!

One of the added delights of the weekend was having my friend Debbie Rapp stay with us in our cabin. Debbie is the Women's Ministries Director for the Carolina Conference, and we had become friends the moment we first met. I was excited to spend time with her again, and I wanted my sisters to get to know her, too. Debbie's friend, Marlene Schmidt, also stayed with us, and what fun we had laughing and swapping stories! In the evening, it was good to talk over the day's events and relate some of the testimonies that others had shared with us. It was obvious God was working in the hearts of the women present.

Sabbath morning, Cinda gave the early morning worship presentation on God's amazing love. She shared how God had helped during some of the darkest moments in her life and how He had carried her through. Cinda also emphasized how important it is to make Jesus your very best Friend.

Then Linda led out in the Sabbath School portion of the program. She emphasized the power of prayer and the importance of giving our burdens to Jesus. Various women in the audience read different Bible texts, and then we raised our voices in songs of praise. What happened next was a spiritual feast. Anyone who was carrying a burden was encouraged to stand and share it with the group while those sitting closest were asked to embrace that person during prayer. Each petition was then presented to our heavenly Father as I played softly on the piano.

The first lady stood up and shared how she and her daughter were estranged and had not seen or spoken to each other for a year! Linda then asked if there was a volunteer who would like to pray for this woman. A lady from the back of the room stood up and came forward. All those sitting near this woman stood and embraced her as the volunteer asked God to heal the wound and bring reconciliation. She prayed specifically that the Holy Spirit would impress the daughter that her mother loved her supremely, and more importantly, that Jesus did, too.

Then another lady stood and presented her need, and the same process took place. This happened over and over again. The next hour became a prayer service such as I had never experienced. I could feel the Holy Spirit in that room! It was awesome! The time went by so quickly; we didn't want it to end. So many people stood that there wasn't enough time for all 425 women to share their individual burdens. When Linda closed the service, she asked the ladies in the audience to softly say the name of their loved one out loud as she prayed the last prayer:

Our precious heavenly Father, thank You for loving us so much that You gave Your only Son to save us from our sins. Not only did Jesus pay the price for our transgressions, but His gift opened the door to Your throne room. We come into Your presence through our Lord and Savior, lifting up to You our families and friends who need Your healing touch. We claim Jesus' blood for them. As these names go up before You like a cloud of incense rising like smoke of the most beautiful colors, we thank You that You have heard us and will answer our prayers according to Your will. Thank You that it is always Your will to save our loved ones. We praise You and love You and ask everything in Jesus' name, Amen.

I spoke for the worship service on the importance of prayer and letting God use us the way He wants to use us. I talked about how we need to step out of our comfort zones and fully trust God to lead in our lives. There is no greater joy than serving Jesus. But He won't force Himself on us. We must let Him in before He will work in us and through us.

In the afternoon, Linda's seminar, "Finding the Joy," continued the theme of God's will, not our will, being done in our lives. Only as

we let Jesus live in our lives moment by moment will we be able to find true joy. Joy has nothing to do with the choices our children make, our professions, or our relationships with husband and friends. Joy is a gift God gives us when we allow self to die. It is only when our hearts look beyond ourselves that we can

Women at the Nosoca Pines camp, kneel to pray during the "Crushing of the Rose" ceremony.

see others through Christ's eyes. It is then that we are able to share His love with the lost and hurting. When people fully grasp God's love, that is our Lord's joy! That is how we find real joy!

Later that evening, when the women entered the gymnasium for the vespers service, the mood was set with dim lights, and on the stage was a brightly lit cross with a crown of thorns hanging from it. Just below lay a scarlet robe. Each lady was given a long-stemmed red rose and then took their seats while I softly played the piano. When Cinda sang "Beneath the Cross of Jesus," Linda quietly made her way up the center aisle barefoot and dressed in Bible costume to reflect the character of Mary Magdalene. She knelt at the cross until Cinda had finished her song. The room was still, and we could feel the Holy Spirit's presence.

Then "Mary" gave her testimony of what Jesus had done in her life—how His love had changed her forever and how she was now free. When she realized that the cost of her freedom had been paid with the blood from her precious Lord and Savior, Mary fell at the cross and wept. It was at the cross that she began to grasp the depths of His love.

Linda Johnson portrays Mary Magdalene as I play "Near the Cross" softly on the piano.

As Mary stayed kneeling at the cross, Debbie Rapp gave a call for each lady present to surrender all and come to the cross. Christ had paid not only for Mary's sins, but for the sins of each person. We then sang the song, "Above All," by Michael W. Smith:

Crucified, laid behind a stone,
You lived to die rejected and alone.
Like a rose trampled on the ground,
You took the fall, and thought of me . . . above all.

As we sang this song, each woman walked to the platform with her rose in hand. Reaching the cross, each crushed the rose until the petals fell on the ground, and then she laid the lifeless stem there as well. Many knelt at the cross in prayer beside Linda before returning to their seats so that the next lady could do the same. I watched the faces of the women as they filed past the piano. Many were openly crying; others wept softly, wiping the tears from their eyes. This "Crushing of the Rose" ceremony was so very meaningful and heart touching. It symbolized Jesus our Savior, the Rose of Sharon, who gave His life so that we might live. He paid the ultimate price with His blood.

Debbie Rapp, Carolina Conference Women's Ministries director, started the "Crushing of the Rose" ceremony with prayer. My sister, Cinda, is sitting next to Debbie.

The next morning while getting ready in our cabin, Debbie warned us not to be disappointed if not many women stayed for the final meeting. "In the past, many have left right after breakfast because they have a long drive home," she said.

We assured her that if there were only one person in the audience, we knew God would have a message just for her! You can imagine our surprise to see that almost every seat was filled! God obviously had something special planned.

As I was walking toward the platform, a woman stopped me. Her face was glowing. "I've got to tell you what God did for me last night! It's a miracle. It's an absolute miracle!" I must have looked a little startled because she quickly asked, "Do you remember me?" And without giving me a chance to respond, she added, "I'm the one you prayed for yesterday. I'm the first one that stood wanting prayer. I'm the one who hasn't had any contact with my daughter for over a year. Remember?"

She took a quick breath and plunged on. "I can hardly believe this, but God has already answered my prayer! Last night, after the program, my cell phone rang. It was my daughter, and she's coming home! I had no way of reaching her. I didn't even know where she was. Can you believe it? Less than twelve hours after we prayed, she called me! Prayer really works! It really works! I don't know how to thank you enough." We hugged and praised the Lord and hugged again. I was filled with thanksgiving to our precious heavenly Father that He had granted this woman an answer to her prayer so quickly.

What a way to begin the morning! I thought. *It can't get much better than this!* But I was wrong.

The meeting started. I spoke about God's plan for our lives and how His plan is always better than ours, but that we can't begin to know God's plan for us if we haven't fully surrendered our heart and life to Him. To do that, we need to know Him as our personal Savior. Prayer is our connection with God, and unless we have a love relationship with our heavenly Father, we will not enter the kingdom of heaven. It isn't enough, I stressed, just to be a "good" person. We have to *know* Jesus. And every time we pray we are advancing God's purpose for us. God is calling each of us to surrender all selfishness and pride at the cross and follow Him. He longs for us to come to Him, not just when we are in trouble, but for praise, honor, and worship. Jesus wants to be close to us, and He desires that we have oneness with Him.

Sometimes people ask, "Why should I pray? God knows what I'm thinking anyway." This is true. God knows our thoughts, but He responds to our prayers! Everyone can pray. If you can *talk* you can pray; if you can *think* you can pray. You don't have to pray a long beautiful prayer full of eloquent and fancy words. The most powerful prayer you can ever pray consists of just three words: "Jesus, save me."

Then I asked my sisters to join me, and we sang, "Have Thine Own Way Lord." While we were singing, we experienced something that I had never experienced in my life. First one person and then another throughout the audience stood to her feet. Tears were rolling down their cheeks as one by one they made their stand for Jesus.

It was nothing short of miraculous! I could hardly continue singing as tears flowed down my cheeks as well. I looked over at my sisters and could see they were struggling, too! It was incredible! *An altar call by the Holy Spirit!* I had not made a call for the women to come forward, yet here they stood! The Holy Spirit's presence was so strong in that room that I could feel it. It was awesome! Being a preacher's daughter, I have witnessed many altar calls in my lifetime. I have played the piano and organ for many evangelistic meetings; over and over again I have played "I Surrender All" as the preacher pleaded for people to come forward. But that day there had been no pleading, no long drawn-out urging, only hearts responding to the calling of the Holy Spirit!

After the meeting was over and we were reluctantly saying our goodbyes, a middle-aged woman approached me with this story. "I'm quite sure my new daughter-in-law consented to come to this retreat only so we would have a chance to spend time together. But God has been working a spiritual transformation in her all weekend. She told me that she is giving her heart to Jesus. She wants to have a closer relationship with God. Isn't that wonderful?" Praise the Lord! God is so good! This was just one of many testimonies we heard that day—and continued to hear in the weeks that followed.

I will never forget the Carolina women's retreat. It was one incredible Holy Spirit–filled weekend! We had called on God before we started driving there, and we continued calling on Him during our time together, and He showed us great and mighty things, just as He has promised to do (see Jeremiah 33:3). It's a humbling, joyous, exhilarating experience being used by God, whether it's baking cookies, producing children's television programs, or witnessing firsthand the awesome life-transforming power of the Holy Spirit. But the greatest feeling of all is the overwhelming love of Jesus I feel when I know I'm right in the middle of *His will* for my life. Every time my heart responds to the calling of His Spirit, I am flooded with His love. There's nothing quite like it this side of heaven. I call these experiences "Holy Spirit hugs"! And it's all the result of passionate prayer.

---

* You can read the entire cookie story in my book *Battered to Blessed* or see it on video from 3ABN by calling 1-800-752-3226.

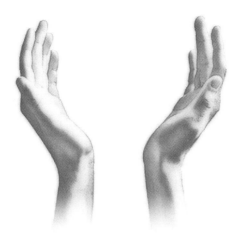

Chapter 2

Margie's Mission

And this gospel of the kingdom will be preached in all the world
as a witness to all the nations, and then the end will come.
—Matthew 24:14

Lee Jamieson is one of the best Sabbath School teachers I have ever known. He is always well prepared, knows his Bible backward and forward, and he doesn't do all the talking. He likes to throw out a thought or a question to the class that will generate discussion, and when there are opposing views, he ties it all up with Scripture. I was a member of his Sabbath School class for more than twenty years, although most of those years I was leading out in children's divisions and unable to attend on a regular basis. But when I had the privilege of sitting in his class, I always walked away spiritually fed. Now that is what I call a good teacher!

It was on one of those rare occasions when I was sitting next to my husband enjoying Lee's class that I noticed Margie Leach, a fellow church member, arrive a little late and slip into an empty pew across the aisle, leaning her head trying to listen. Now Lee's class was the most popular class in the church, and it filled up fast. This particular Sabbath was no exception. My husband, Tim, and I scooted down the pew and motioned for Margie to come sit by us. She shyly shook her head, indicating that she was fine where she was. Knowing how hard it is to be a part of a group discussion sitting apart from the group, I refused to take no for an answer. Again I motioned for her to come and sit by me. Fearing I would make a scene and embarrass her, she quietly came over and scooted in beside me. She whispered a quiet "thank you," and then we both joined in the class discussion. When class was over, Margie took a bookmark from her Bible and handed it to me. "Here. I'd like you to have this as a special thank you for including me today. I really couldn't hear too well over there, but I just didn't want to make a fuss. That was so very sweet of you."

The bookmark was absolutely beautiful! It was laminated on both sides and had a Scripture verse on it. And to top it off, the edges had been trimmed with special scissors making a decorative border around the entire bookmark!

"Can I buy more of these?" I asked. "It is absolutely beautiful! I just love it."

"No, you can't buy them. My sisters and I make them. It's our mission project. Mom makes them, too."

"You made this?" I could hardly believe my ears. It was so professionally done and it certainly didn't look handmade!

"Yes, you could make them too, if you wanted to."

Suddenly I remembered the prayer I had been praying every day for the past week. My sister, Linda, had recently moved to Wisconsin where her husband had accepted a job as the manager of Camp Wakonda, an Adventist youth camp. Linda didn't know anyone yet in the new area, and all the other positions at the camp were filled, so there was nothing for her to do. She was bored and wanted to feel useful. I had been praying for a special ministry just for my sister. When Linda told me that the most important activity of her day was watching the raccoons on her porch, I knew she needed serious prayer! She is not the kind of person who can sit around and do nothing!

"Margie, my sister is coming to visit me next week, and I know she is looking for a ministry where she can witness for Jesus. Do you think you could teach her to make these?"

"Sure, I'd be glad to. I'll even give her the supplies that she'll need. My mom and I can both help her. It's so easy that she won't really need much help. Just give me a call, and we'll make plans to get together!"

I was so excited that I could hardly pay attention to the preacher. All the way home I was still marveling at how God had answered my prayer. This was something that I knew Linda could get excited about, and I could hardly wait for her visit.

When Linda arrived the next week, I told her all about my bookmark experience, but she wasn't as excited as I thought she'd be.

"Brenda, I'm not crafty like you and Cinda. I'm not sure I can make these. Look at how beautiful it is." She was holding the bookmark Margie had given me.

"Sis, Margie assured me that they are easy to make. We can at least go over and see what she thinks is easy!"

Linda laughed. "Sure, we can at least go look, and I have a feeling you've already told her we're coming."

"You know me pretty well! As a matter of fact, she's expecting us this afternoon!"

"Looks like I never had a choice!"

Linda and I had a good laugh over that. Sure enough, ten minutes after Margie showed us how to make the bookmarks, Linda admitted that they were pretty easy to make.

"I can make these, and I love the fact that I can choose my own Bible texts and pictures. This will be so much fun. I can give them to my neighbors and church members and anyone else I meet, for that matter!"

"Yes, and you'll find that it's rather addicting—giving them away," Margie said. "People love them and are shocked when they find out they're free! This is a ministry for us; we're just trying to do our part to win souls for the kingdom."

The two "Margies"—Margie Leach (daughter) and Margie Holden (mother). Both have the love of Jesus in their hearts. They called themselves the "M&M Sisters."

At some point in the conversation I mentioned that I was going to Europe with my husband and hated to leave Linda Kay, our youngest daughter, home alone. Even though she was in high school and could drive a car, I didn't feel right leaving her by herself.

"You should have my mom come and stay with her!" Margie offered. "I'm sure she wouldn't mind at all! Here, I'll write down her number, and you can give her a call. Her name is Margie, too, only her last name is Holden. When we are together they call us the "M & M sisters"! It's rather funny, actually. Mom named me after herself, so I feel pretty special. You'll love her, by the way. She is something else."

Margie Holden and my daughter, Becky. Margie absolutely adored Becky and my other daughter, Linda Kay—and they loved her, too! We adopted Margie as an official member of our family.

Margie loaded us up with enough bookmark material to make hundreds of bookmarks, and Linda was ecstatic! I could almost see her mind working, imagining all the possibilities for witnessing! All the way home I was silently praising Jesus for answering my prayer.

That night I gave Margie Holden (the mother) a call and fell in love with her on the phone. We made arrangements to meet in person the next day, and from the moment we met I knew we would be friends for life. That is just the kind of person Margie was. She loved Jesus so much and was the most unselfish person you would ever want to meet. She agreed immediately to come and stay with Linda Kay and was careful not to label herself as a "babysitter" since Linda Kay felt she was too old for one of those!

Margie casually asked which countries I would be visiting in Europe. My husband had several offices there, so we made that trip quite often. I mentioned the various countries we would be in and didn't think anything else about it.

The night before we were to leave, Margie came over and moved her things into our guest room. While I was helping her get settled, she removed a small package from her suitcase and handed it to me.

"These are for you to give to people on your trip."

A look of surprise flashed across my face. I opened the package and couldn't believe my eyes!

"Why, there must be three hundred bookmarks here!" I exclaimed.

"Three hundred and fifty to be exact. I didn't know how long you would be in each country, but there are some in each of the different languages."

I was amazed. There were Scripture verses in French, German, Italian, and Hungarian—all the countries I had told her I was going to be visiting! I was totally shocked and filled with so much love for this special lady! I ran over and gave her a big hug.

"Oh Margie, you couldn't have given me a better gift! How can I ever thank you?"

"You don't need to thank me. Just give them out and keep sharing Jesus!"

In each country I went to, I passed out bookmarks to everyone I met, whether it was the hotel clerk, the ticket agent at the metro station, or the person next to me on the train. Amazingly, not one person refused them. Many were so happy to get the bookmarks that they wanted to pay me.

"Oh no, you can't pay me. This is a gift for you. Besides, if you paid me, it would steal my blessing!" I told each person the same thing, since it seemed to work pretty well the first time.

They, in turn, would smile and thank me again before I went on to the next person. *Margie was right,* I thought. *This is addicting!* I loved watching the smiles on the faces of those receiving a bookmark.

When Tim and I returned from Europe, Linda Kay and Margie had totally bonded. In fact, Margie Holden could have moved in with us and Linda Kay would have loved it! Our whole family loved Margie.

At that time in my life, I was managing three businesses. I owned and managed an occupational health nursing agency, did contract work for an interior design firm, and owned a floral business. I was the largest supplier of air-dried roses in New England and would dry between one thousand and three thousand roses a week. The roses would dry to beautiful bright colors that were so vivid that people often asked if they were fresh. Many would reach out and actually squeeze the head of the rose and draw their hand back in surprise when they felt the dryness of the flower. It had taken a lot of work to perfect the natural drying process, but the effort had paid off! The roses were absolutely stunning and lasted much longer than the popular freeze-dried rose.

Margie was always the first to help me with my roses. We often talked about how beautiful the flowers would be in heaven! I can't wait for Jesus to come!

Margie made it a habit to come over and help me with the roses. She loved flowers of all kinds, but more than anything she just loved helping people.

Soon she was going with me to the Boston Flower Market each week to pick up my fresh roses, and we became close friends. We had long spiritual talks, sharing various witnessing experiences. She especially loved the contacts made through her bookmark ministry.

"Brenda, these are not just bookmarks. These are soul-winning tools! When you give a bookmark, it is a *foot in the door* to tell someone about Jesus. As soon as they see the Bible verse, it tells them two things. One, that you are a Christian, and two, that you care about them."

Sometimes I would dry 3,000 roses a week. Margie would stay for hours putting the dried roses in individual plastic sleeves, ready to sell to wholesalers.

"I agree with you, Margie, and I know God is going to reward you for all your efforts. There will be stars in your crown because of these bookmarks!"

"Well, I'm not worried about collecting stars, just winning souls!"

I loved that about her—the way she was always so humble. We had so much fun together. I would go with her to the place where she picked up bookmark material, and she showed me her style of making the bookmarks. We shopped, went out to eat, made witnessing calls, and did so many other things—always leaving a trail of bookmarks behind us. If I traveled at all, Margie would stay at our house. In a short amount of time, we became closer than friends; we became family. She would introduce me to people as her daughter, newly adopted! Anytime I needed anything, Margie was there.

Margie always kept me supplied with bookmarks to give away. Each week I would pass through the Massachusetts turnpike tollbooth on my way to the Boston Flower Market. As I paid the toll to the attendants, I also handed them a bookmark, smiled and told them to have a good day. Once in a while the attendant would be someone to whom I had already given a bookmark, and they would be excited to see me again. Once, a man held up five bookmarks, but he was still excited to get another one! But I wasn't prepared for the reaction of one booth attendant that I hadn't seen before. As soon as I handed her the bookmark, she grabbed it from my hand, waving it wildly in the air. She stuck her head out of the window yelling to all the other booth attendants down the row. "I've got the bookmark lady! I've got the bookmark lady!"

Then she looked back at me and tried to catch her breath! "I'm so excited. Everyone here has gotten a bookmark from you, and most of them have more than one! I'm the only person who hasn't received a bookmark. I've wanted one of these bookmarks for so long. The others even tease me when we're taking our coffee breaks, and they all share the Bible verses. Sometimes they even trade with each other to get the verse they like best! But you have never come through my booth until today! I don't know how to thank you! This is wonderful, and I want you to know that you have made my day!"

"Well, God is impressing me to bless you even more. Here, you can have all of these."

I handed her a stack of bookmarks—probably twenty or twenty-five bookmarks.

"Oh my goodness! All of these are for me? Are you sure? Why, I would have more than anyone else! Wow! This sure will give me trading power! Thank you so much!"

"You're very welcome! I hope they will be a blessing to you!"

All the way home, I was thinking of that lady and how God's timing is so perfect. I had no idea that she would be the only one not to receive a bookmark, but I knew that God always has a plan! After that, I made sure I rotated which lane I went in at the toll booth and instead of dreading the long line to pay tolls, I actually anticipated the pleasure of having yet another witnessing experience. That's when I began praying specifically for the person receiving the bookmarks. I could see firsthand the Holy Spirit working on the hearts of people receiving this special gift.

When I went to Japan for two weeks, Margie made three hundred bookmarks in Japanese. I had so much fun giving them out to everyone. The concierge at my hotel had shared with me just how to properly present the gift.

"Hold the bookmark with two hands to present it to people. This will immediately say that this gift is special. If you hand it to them with only one hand, this signifies that it is not an important gift, only a casual one."

"Thank you so much for telling me that. I had no idea. Is this how you do it?"

I handed him the bookmark with two hands and bowed my head slightly.

"Yes, that is perfect. You are indeed a fast learner."

I smiled at him again and thanked him for his advice. I remembered all day to do just as he suggested, and people seemed excited to receive this "special" gift. However, I was puzzled at how they looked at them. Everyone's reaction was the same. They would first look at the picture, and then they would turn the bookmark upside down and smile! How very odd. As soon as I went back to my hotel that evening I went to see the concierge again. I related the day's events and how perplexed I was at everyone's strange reaction.

"Oh, that is easy for me to explain to you. I didn't have the heart to tell you this morning, but all of the writing is upside down. They must turn it around so that they are able to read the message that is written."

I began to laugh out loud.

"What did I say that was so funny?"

"Oh, it's not what you said. I was just thinking about my friend, Margie, who made these. I'm sure she'll get a good laugh out of this!"

When I got home and told Margie about my "Japanese bookmark experience," we both laughed and laughed.

"Well, I guess you are going to have to go back there again, and this time, I'll get it right! Of course, I might have to take lessons to learn the Japanese language first. So, on second thought, you might want to wait a few years before you book that next trip. It might take me a while to learn Japanese!"

When I began to produce the *Kids Time* program, no one could have been more supportive than Margie. She immediately volunteered to make bookmarks for every child that wrote to "Miss Brenda." Even when the letters increased from fifty a week to almost three hundred a week, she didn't bat an eye.

"Just tell me when you need more bookmarks, and I'll send them! Honey, I'll make these bookmarks for you until I die—or until Jesus comes, whichever comes first!" She would laugh and give me a hug. Margie didn't have a selfish bone in her body; she was always thinking of others. She raised six children—five girls and one boy—and had instilled in each of them the joy of helping others. Her five daughters, Polly Aho, Margie Leach, Susie Babineau, Ellie Santangelo, and Sally Conklin, were all involved in the bookmark ministry.

Susie started it first. She has a talent working with crafts. Susie had saved a pile of seed catalogs that had come in the mail, and someone else had given her a stack of colored paper. She looked around her craft room and asked God to give her an idea of what she could make with the supplies she already had.

It was then that she had the idea of printing out Bible verses on her computer and making bookmarks. She cut out pictures from the seed catalogs to decorate each one—beautiful pictures of flowers, trees, and fruit. Then she saw a stack of old greeting cards and began cutting out the pictures from those as well. When she showed her sister, Polly, the finished product, her sister was overwhelmed! The bookmarks were absolutely beautiful!

Polly took them to her church and passed them out to everyone. Before long, not only were all of Susie's sisters involved in this project, but her mom, Margie, as well. You might say they had caught the "bookmark fever"! Everywhere they went, they passed out bookmarks. The bookmarks found their way into nursing homes, hospitals, community service centers, shopping malls, and just about anywhere Margie and her daughters happened to go. People's reactions to receiving these special gifts were invigorating! They could see firsthand how God was blessing this ministry. Soon they began holding classes at the Southern New England camp meeting to show others how to make the bookmarks. Creative juices were flowing. Boxes were placed at various churches for people to donate their used greeting cards, magazines, calendars, and seed catalogs. Other church members volunteered to cut out the pictures to just the right size. Before they knew it their bookmark ministry had grown so fast that it had far surpassed their wildest dreams. It wasn't long before people going on mission trips contacted Margie and her daughters, wanting to take some bookmarks to the mission field. Now, the bookmarks were making their way around the world, all because one family wanted to do their part to witness for Jesus!

One night, while I was driving home from 3ABN, I received a call from Margie on my cell phone. This was not unusual as we often talked during my six-hour commutes.

"Hi, Sweetie, how are you doing? Are you driving back from 3ABN right now?"

"Yes, I have another hour, and then I'll be home. What's the matter? Your voice sounds a little funny."

"Well, nothing really. Why don't you give me a call when you get home; I want to share something with you."

"There's no need to wait till then. Please go ahead and tell me what's the matter. If you don't tell me, I'll get a speeding ticket racing home just to find out what it is."

She laughed at that and agreed I would probably do that very thing.

"Well, all right then. Now I don't want you to worry; everything is going to be OK. I went to the doctor this week, and he ran some tests, and—well, it wasn't good news."

"Margie! What did the doctor say? Please tell me. You're going to be OK, aren't you?"

"Well, Honey, the doctor told me I have liver cancer. I'm not sure what the doctors are going to do about it, but I'm in God's hands so I'm really not worried."

"Oh, Margie, I'm so sorry! How could this happen? I can't believe this. Are they sure? Are all the tests back? I think you should get a second opinion."

My eyes were welling up with tears. Not my precious Margie. *Please, dear Jesus, not Margie!* I decided to get off at the next exit and pulled into a gas station.

"Now, Honey, don't cry. It really is going to be OK. But the truth is none of us know how long we have to live on this earth. I don't know how much time I have, but we need to talk about the bookmarks."

"Bookmarks! Are you serious? Margie, I don't care about the bookmarks; I care about you! Forget the bookmarks."

"Now, Brenda, listen to me. You've promised those kids a bookmark when they write to you, and that is really important to me. I'm going to work extra hard to get ahead so that maybe after I'm gone you'll have some to last you a while. Please don't worry about a thing. Everything will be OK, I promise. Now, I need to go, but I'll talk to you again soon. I love you, Sweetie."

"I love you too, Margie. Before you go, can I pray with you?"

"Why sure. I'd like that very much."

"Precious heavenly Father" I prayed, *"I come to You tonight with such a heavy heart. I am lifting up Margie to You right now, as she is in need of Your healing touch. You know the discouraging diagnosis that she received, and yet we know that nothing is impossible with You. Precious Lord, if it be Your will, I am praying for a miracle for Margie—that she*

will be restored to health and that all traces of cancer will be gone. But I also am praying that Your will be done in her life. We don't know the end from the beginning, but You do, so I am trusting her into Your precious arms because there is no better place for her to be! I know You love her more than I do, and I am accepting whatever plans You have for her life. Please give her the strength and the courage to face whatever is before her, and more than anything, keep her faithful and close to You. In Your name I pray, Amen."

"I love you, Margie, with all my heart. You mean so much to me."

"I love you too, Honey. Don't worry now. Remember we are leaving it in God's hands."

I hung up the phone and sat there in my car crying like a baby. Surely God would heal Margie. I couldn't bear the thought of not having her in my life. After I dried my eyes and pulled myself together, I headed home. I picked up my cell phone and called everyone I knew who was a prayer warrior, and pleaded for them to pray passionately for Margie.

God didn't answer my prayer the way I wanted Him to. Over the next several months, Margie bravely faced the side effects of chemotherapy and homeopathic remedies, as well. She began to lose weight, and I wasn't prepared for what I found when I came out to speak at the Southern New England camp meeting and saw her for the first time since she had been diagnosed. She had dropped several dress sizes, and her face was sunken, but other than the outward appearance, she was still my same old Margie.

I hugged her warmly, not wanting to leave her embrace. She started talking about the bookmarks right away, wanting me to know that she was making a stockpile for me should the Lord take her. How I got through that conversation without bawling my eyes out, only God knows. That was the last time I was to see her.

Just a short time later, I called her on the phone, and no one answered. This was unusual because Margie rarely left the house now. I waited an hour and then called her again. Still there was no answer. I couldn't shake the feeling that something wasn't right. I began praying for her immediately. Not able to have any peace, I felt impressed to call her daughter Margie, and there was no answer there either. Next I tried her daughter Sally, and again no answer. I really can't explain it but somehow I *knew* that something was terribly wrong. I began to call all the Boston area hospitals asking for a patient by the name of Margie Holden. Finally, I dialed the hospital in Leominster. I spoke to the operator as though I knew that Margie was there, even though I didn't have a clue whether she was—or whether she was in *any* hospital, for that matter.

"Hello, can you please connect me to Margie Holden's room?"

"I'm sorry ma'am, but she is in the intensive care unit. I can connect you to the nursing station there, if you'd like."

My heart started beating faster, and I felt like I could hardly breathe. *So, she is in the hospital after all! And it must be serious because she's in ICU.*

"Yes, please. I'd appreciate it." I managed to get the words out.

"Hello, ICU. May I help you, please?"

"Yes, this is Brenda Walsh speaking, and I'm trying to reach Margie Holden. Is it possible that I could speak to her?"

"Are you a family member?"

"No, not technically, but I couldn't love her more than if she was my own flesh and blood. Can you tell me how she is doing?"

"I'm sorry, but I'm not allowed to give out patient information unless you are a family member."

"Can I just talk with her for a few minutes?"

"No, I'm sorry, you can't talk to her. She is not doing well. That is all I can tell you. You'll need to talk to one of her family members, and perhaps they can give you more information."

"Please, I'm a registered nurse, and I understand completely about the rules of confidentiality. I don't have to know her condition, but I really *do* need to talk to her. I know in my heart that she doesn't have long to live and this may be my last chance to say goodbye. I am begging you; please don't take that chance away from me. I know she would want to talk to me. I am pleading with you to please allow me the chance to talk to her one last time. I love this lady with all my heart!"

"Well, let me go ask her if she wants to talk to you. One moment, please."

A few moments later I heard Margie's weak voice on the other end of the line. She sounded as if every word were an effort to speak.

"Hi, Honey, I should have known you would find me. I don't think I have much time left now. The doctors said there isn't anything else that they can do."

"Oh, Margie! I love you so much! I want you to know how very much Jesus loves you, too, and it's going to be OK."

Before I could say another word, Margie interrupted.

"Honey, I'm not afraid. I know that when I die, I will be sleeping until Jesus comes again. And when I awaken, the next voice I hear will be His voice. I'm looking forward to that day. So don't cry for me. It is the people who don't know Jesus that should be afraid to die because they won't be saved."

"Margie, you are so brave, and I thank God for bringing you into my life. I am a better person because of knowing you. Let's make a plan right now that when we get to heaven, we'll meet at Jesus' feet!"

"That's a date, Honey; that's a date. Brenda, I want you to know that I couldn't love you more if you were my own daughter."

"Oh, Margie, I do know that, and I love you so very much, too! Goodbye for now, my precious Margie."

I hung up the phone and sobbed. I couldn't imagine not talking to Margie while I was driving on the road or having her call me just to tell me she was praying for me. Later, as I lay on my bed thinking about my own loss, I thought of Margie's children and how they must feel. I began to pray for each one by name, asking God to give them the courage and strength to face the loss of their mother. I asked God to comfort them and keep them close to His heart.

A little while later I received a call from her daughter, Margie Leach. She told me that just four hours after I had spoken to her mother, she slipped into a coma and not long after that, she fell asleep in Jesus. We cried together on the phone, and when we hung up, I threw myself on my bed crying again. This time, I wasn't crying for Margie; I was crying for myself and for the tremendous loss for everyone who knew her.

I said a thank-you prayer for all the special moments that God had allowed us to share, and I especially thanked God for giving me the chance to say goodbye to Margie. I knew that was a special gift God gave me, knowing how much it would mean to both of us to speak one more time. Then I asked God to lay His hand on Margie's bookmark ministry. I asked Him to bless every bookmark that she had ever made and that they would make a difference in someone's life and influence their decision to choose Jesus. I pleaded passionately for souls to be won for God's kingdom because of Margie's bookmarks and the life that she lived on this earth.

So often people feel that there isn't anything they can do to be a witness for Jesus. They feel justified in leaving it to those more talented, more educated, more blessed. But the truth is, God just wants all of us to be willing, obedient, and joyful—and He will take care of the rest. Margie wasn't a highly educated woman, nor was she wealthy in the material things of this earth. But Margie was indeed a rich woman in spiritual terms because of her love for Jesus and her willingness to let God use her however He saw fit! On this point, Ellen White wrote,

When the master of the house called his servants, he gave to every man *his* work.

With a loving spirit we may perform life's humblest duties "as to the Lord." Colossians 3:23. If the love of God is in the heart, it will be manifested in the life. The sweet savor of Christ will surround us, and our influence will elevate and bless.

You are not to wait for great occasions or to expect extraordinary abilities before you go work for God. You need not have a thought of what the world will think of you. . . .

The humblest and poorest of the disciples of Jesus can be a blessing to others. They may not realize that they are doing any special good, but by their unconscious influence they may start waves of blessing that will widen and deepen, and the blessed results they may never know until the day of final reward. They do not feel or know that they are doing anything great. They are not required to weary themselves with anxiety about success. They have only to go forward quietly, doing faithfully the work that God's providence assigns, and their work will not be in vain (*Steps to Christ,* pp. 82, 83).

Margie was a humble servant of God whom He used in a mighty way to win souls for His kingdom. Her bookmarks have crisscrossed the globe to every continent. She made bookmarks in fourteen different languages, and God is still rewarding her efforts. Men, women, and children from around the world have given their hearts to Jesus because of her soul-winning efforts. And the effects from those contacts are still being realized today.

Not long after Margie's funeral, I received a call from her daughter Margie. "Brenda," she told me, "my sisters and I got together and talked about this, and we want you to know that for as long as you are doing *Kids Time,* we will supply you with bookmarks. We know that would mean a lot to our mother. She loved you so much, and she loved the *Kids Time* ministry. This is something we want to do in her memory."

"Oh Margie, I don't know what to say. Thank you so much. Yes, I know how much this would mean to her. Thank you so very much. I will treasure every one." I couldn't stop the tears from rolling down my cheeks.

"You're very welcome. We want to do this for her. By the way, I have mailed you a package, and you should get it any day now."

"Thank you, again, Margie. Please give your sisters a big hug for me and tell them how much I love them."

"I'll tell them. Goodbye now."

The next day a package arrived, and I couldn't wait to open it. I burst into tears when I opened the box to find over *one thousand* bookmarks that Margie had made personally before she died. There was a short sweet note inside: "My dearest Brenda, I'm sorry these are all I have right now. Please use them to keep on sharing Jesus. I love you very much, Margie."*

---

* I wish each of you could have met Margie. You would have loved her. Margie did one more thing for me that I thought you should know about. When I made the *Cookie Lady* video for 3ABN and needed a person to play the role of the woman at the soup kitchen, Margie volunteered. You can see her today in that video. Her memory lives on—and so does her bookmark ministry.

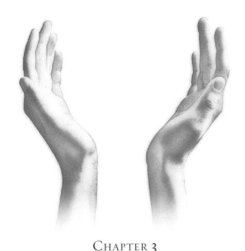

CHAPTER 3

A RELUCTANT MISSIONARY

And let us not grow weary while doing good,
for in due season we shall reap if we do not lose heart.
—Galatians 6:9

Once passionate prayer becomes a part of your daily lifestyle don't be surprised if God occasionally brings circumstances into your life to prepare you to do greater service for Him. Once you are so in love with Jesus that your highest priority is to do His will whatever that might mean and your primary heart's desire is to share Jesus' love, you'll be willing to follow Him wherever He asks you to go.

No one wants to go through tough times. We don't pray for God to test us with trials, persecution, pain, poverty, or physical affliction. Being pushed out of our comfort zone can be scary, disturbing, and sometimes downright appalling. And yet God knows what it's going to take in each of our lives for us to become the person of priceless character He can use to bless others.

Almost every Bible personality who we applaud for their faithfulness to God—and who God used in mighty ways—had to endure horrendous calamities, heartache, and suffering. Take the apostle Paul, for example. Here's what he says: "We are pressed on every side by troubles, but we are not crushed and broken. We are perplexed, but we don't give up and quit. We are hunted down, but God never abandons us. We get knocked down, but we get up again and keep going. Through suffering, these bodies of ours constantly share in the death of Jesus so that the life of Jesus may also be seen in our bodies" (2 Corinthians 4:8–10, NLT).

Every time I used to read that passage, I would think, *Well, that might have been good for Paul and his companions, but I don't want to be crushed, perplexed, hunted down, or knocked around.* I wanted to grow spiritually; I wanted to be used by God in whatever capacity He wanted me to serve, *but I didn't want to have to suffer to get there!* I was very happy living in my comfortable home in Bolton, Massachusetts, with warm water, electricity twenty-four hours a day, pleasant smelling bathrooms, a well-stocked pantry, a rat-free neighborhood, and my air-conditioned car to take me over smoothly paved streets to wherever I desired to go. And then the call came from my brother Kenny asking me to go with him on a mission trip to the Dominican Republic.

THE CALL TO MISSION

Kenny has always had a big heart for mission work. As a pastor in

Tammy and Ken Micheff work side-by-side in ministry. They have a passion for mission work— saving souls for Jesus!

Michigan, he would regularly organize mission trips so his church members could complete needed building projects, provide medical and dental care, and do evangelism in poverty-stricken places where people were hurting. He's been to places like the Mississippi Gulf Coast after Hurricane Katrina hit, and to the

Bahamas, Honduras, Haiti, and the Dominican Republic—to name a few. In fact, he and his family had been to the Dominican Republic several times. I cringed as his son Jeremy described the rats, spiders, lizards, and cockroaches that flourished on that tropical Caribbean island!

Although I was impressed with all the good these mission trips accomplished, never once did I think, *Wow, I wish I could be a part of something like that!* I thought mission work was a wonderful idea—for someone else! My family is well aware of my aversion to unsanitary conditions, dirt, and creepy crawly things like rats, lizards, and cockroaches. So you can imagine my surprise when I received a phone call from my brother suggesting I consider going with him to the Dominican Republic.

"Kenny, you can't be serious. I'm not the one who goes on mission trips. I'm sure you can find a nurse to go with you that enjoys that sort of thing!"

"Sis, I'm very serious. I've tried to find another nurse, but I don't know anyone else to call. We have only two doctors and one dentist—that's it. I wish we had fifteen nurses, but at this point I'd be happy with one. We *have* to have a nurse, and the trip is only two weeks away. I know you have a current passport so that's not a problem. I really need you on this trip! I know I'm begging, but I'm desperate! Come on, Sis! It'll be fun!"

"What! Are you nuts? I know all about the 'fun' you had on the last trip. Rats the size of cats and cockroaches the size of mice! No thank you! That's not for me! You seriously need to find someone else. I'm not going, so you might as well save your breath."

"I thought you told me you wanted to be used by God? Is that true or not?"

"Yes, of course that's true, but you are not God!"

"No, I'm not, but how do you know that God isn't impressing me to ask you? Why don't you just pray about it before you say no? You can do that, can't you?"

"Sure, I'll pray about it, and if it's God's will, I'll go. But God has promised that He'll never give us more than we can stand, so I *know* God would never ask me to go to the Dominican Republic!"

"Well, why not lay your fleece out before the Lord? You know that we've been saving all year to go on this trip and that everyone has to pay his own way, right?"

"Yes, I know that. What does that have to do with me going to the Dominican Republic?"

"If I were to raise the money for your trip, would you take it as a sign from God that you should go?"

"Are you talking about all the expenses? That's a couple thousand dollars, right?"

"Yes, I'm talking about raising *all* your expenses."

In my mind, raising more than two thousand dollars in only two weeks was not even remotely possible. Feeling quite sure I had nothing to worry about, I made the deal. "Sure, if you can find the money—and I'm talking *all* the money—then I'll take it as a sign from God, and I'll go!"

"Thanks, Sis! I can't ask for more than that. And if it's not God's will, then I wouldn't want you to go anyway. Let's just take it to the Lord in prayer." Kenny then prayed a short prayer asking God to make His will plain.

Feeling quite sure I had nothing to worry about, I went about my tasks, cleaning the kitchen and putting away the supper dishes. What I didn't know was that as soon as my brother hung up, he called my sister Cinda and told her all about our conversation, ending with, "So, if I can raise the money, Brenda is going to the Dominican Republic."

Cinda burst out laughing at the mere thought of me on this trip. "Just a minute, Kenny, I want to ask Joel something." Kenny listened as Cinda called to her husband, "Hey, Joel, how would you like to send Brenda to the mission field? Kenny just talked her into agreeing to go if he can raise the money for her trip. I'm sure she's feeling pretty confident or she never would have agreed."

"Brenda, in the Dominican Republic? On a mission trip? Oh yeah! This I'd love to see! Just ask Kenny how much and where to send the check." By now, Joel was howling with laughter. "I'd sure love to see her face when he makes *that* phone call!"

Kenny had heard every word and was so excited that God had answered his prayer so quickly. He had hoped Cinda and Joel might contribute something, but to pay for the whole trip was even better than he had wished.

"One thing, Kenny," Cinda added, "you have to promise not to tell Brenda who donated the money. Just say it was an anonymous donor. You can't tell her, promise me?"

"I promise; I won't tell. Thanks so much. This is one phone call I can't wait to make!" Kenny eagerly dialed my number and waited for the phone to ring. "Hello Sis, are you sitting down?"

"No, should I be? Oh no! Kenny, don't even joke like this. You're not going to tell me what I think you're going to tell me! It's not possible!"

"Well, that's exactly why I'm calling. After we hung up, I made one phone call, and your trip is completely paid for!"

"What did you say? Who would do such a thing? You're not serious! Kenny stop teasing, you almost gave me a heart attack!"

"I'm not teasing! I'm very serious. The donor wants to remain anonymous, but has given the full amount. So start packing! You're going to the Dominican Republic. And by the way, I need you to collect donations of medical supplies that you can bring with you—so pack light! You know lots of doctors, so that should be no problem. I've got to run. I'm so excited that you are going, Sis! God is so good! We'll have a great time. I just can't wait to see what God has planned."

My knees suddenly went weak, and I felt queasy all over. I pulled out the kitchen chair and sat down, trying to comprehend it all, *O Lord, surely You didn't intend for me to go someplace where You know I can't possibly survive? Oh please, let the phone ring and have Kenny tell me he's joking!*

But the phone didn't ring, and I began to accept my fate. To me, it was more like a death sentence. I knew it would take serious time on my knees for me to become a willing and cheerful participant in this mission adventure. *O precious heavenly Father, I have no idea why You would choose me to go on this trip. You know my heart, and You know that I want to serve You. But You also know my weakness. Please make me willing to be willing because this is definitely not something I'm excited about! When I committed my life to You, I promised to be willing, obedient, and cheerful in doing whatever You had planned for me, so I'm asking You to make me not only willing, but joyful. Please use me in a special way to win souls for You. I'm sorry for my reluctant attitude, and I am trusting You wherever You lead me. Thank You, Jesus, for hearing and answering my prayer.*

The next morning I prayed again that God would create in me a "clean heart and a right spirit." Then I began calling every doctor I knew asking them to donate medications I could take to the Dominican Republic.

By that afternoon, the medical supplies began rolling in! One doctor even contacted a pharmaceutical company that donated a whole case of parasite medication. At the time, I had no idea just how valuable this would prove to be. There were other supplies, such as dressing materials, antibiotics, pain medications, and syringes. It was amazing how it all happened so quickly. I knew God was already answering my prayer.

But most surprising, the more I prayed and prepared for the trip, the more I realized I was no longer feeling resigned to my fate. I was actually excited about what God was doing! By the end of the week, I had so many medical donations I couldn't accept any more. Now I was praising God, not just for the medical supplies, but for His gift of joy that He had put into my heart in spite of the anxiety I felt every time I thought about the rats and the cockroaches. The Bible says, in Philippians 4:19 "And my God shall supply all your needs," and He certainly was doing it for me.

After Kenny told my sister Linda that I was going to the mission field, she immediately said she would have to go to support and protect me! Bless her heart, she doesn't like bugs anymore than I do, but she was thinking of me! Little did we know what God had in store for us. The next week passed quickly, and all too soon it was time to leave.

Our adventure started before we even reached foreign soil! Linda and I booked a hotel in Nashville in order to leave on an early morning flight. Cinda drove us there. Thinking everything was arranged, we were shocked to learn when we arrived at the hotel that our reservations had been canceled because of a big convention. *Now what were we going to do?*

Immediately we prayed! The only vacancy we could find in town was a rundown motel in a shady part of Nashville not at all close to the airport. Linda and I carried our luggage into the lobby filled with rough, tattooed, bearded bikers and truckers.

As I was checking us in, Linda started up a conversation with a big, unshaven, husky guy in dirty jeans and a "muscle man" shirt. Being the only women in the lobby (and probably in the entire motel), we were now the center of attention, and I didn't like it at all.

After what seemed like forever, we were finally given our room key. We had prayer with Cinda, said our goodbyes, and then headed to our room. Linda was impressed to learn a security guard patrolled the halls all night. That fact alone made me even more nervous. I couldn't imagine staying in a place that was so unsafe that a security guard was needed to walk the halls! I had no way of knowing that in just a short time, I would be looking back at this motel and wishing for something this luxurious!

Culture shock and our "guardian angel"

Our Dominican Republic adventure started the moment we got off the plane. It was like getting off on another planet. I was overwhelmed with culture shock. There were hundreds of people everywhere, the noise level was intolerable, and no one was speaking English. *Oh why didn't I take Spanish in school? Please, dear Jesus, help us through customs. Please let our boxes of medical supplies pass inspection, as You know how much they're needed. And keep us safe!*

We followed the crowd toward baggage claim and customs. The line went on forever. The wait in the hot, humid, non-air-conditioned terminal seemed endless. Standing next to me was a nice looking, tall gentleman who I thought might be an American. "Have you been here before?" I asked.

He nodded and said, "Yes, I took my medical training here, but I live in the States now. I have a practice in Detroit, but I come back once a month to visit my son."

"Does it usually take this long to get the luggage?"

"Oh, yes, sometimes longer. I think you can fly from the States to Santo Domingo faster than you can get your luggage!" We both had a laugh.

"By the way, my name is David Schultz."

"I'm Brenda, and this is my sister, Linda."

Linda and I explained about our mission trip, telling him all about the medical clinics we would be conducting in the villages. We chatted for the next thirty minutes until all four of our boxes arrived. David helped us get them on the carts.

"David, would you mind if we followed behind you in customs so you could interpret for us, if needed?"

"Sure, I'd be glad to help. Sometimes the customs agents can get a little testy."

When our time came, the customs agent didn't look happy to see all of our boxes. Taking a quick glance at the long line behind us, he gave the order to have the boxes opened and inspected. David spoke to him for a few minutes, and after that all questions were directed to him. In turn, he told us what was said and relayed our answers. "No, they are not selling the medicines." "Yes, they are part of a church group." "Yes, they are going to be helping in a medical clinic." "Yes, she has her nursing license with her." As the questions went on and on, the agent's mood seemed to get worse.

Three boxes were finally approved, but there seemed to be a problem with the fourth one. David told us the health inspector would have to come out and go through it personally.

By this time I was feeling guilty for imposing on David's time. He assured me, however, that he had nothing else to do since his son was still at soccer practice.

Twenty minutes later the inspector came and looked through the box in question. He then motioned for us to follow him to see the medical director. Linda stayed with our luggage while David and I followed the inspector down several long hallways to a small, dingy office.

The medical director was nowhere in sight, so the inspector picked up a form and shoved it toward David. Finally he motioned for me to write our names down on a logbook and told us that we could pass "this time." We followed him back to customs, and I retaped the boxes shut.

While we had been gone, Linda had made friends with some very eager porters, and we headed toward the exit. The second we stepped out the door, we were confronted with a mob of people shouting for friends and family who were arriving. Strangers were trying to grab our boxes, and our porter was yelling and pushing them away. Taxis were honking. Soldiers with guns were everywhere. *What have we gotten ourselves into?*

I was definitely out of my comfort zone and very, very thankful that I was not alone. Not only had God given me Linda to make this trip less scary, but in His foresight, He had directed a tall, kind American physician to act as our guardian angel!

My eyes scanned the crowd searching for Fred Flint, director of Bethel Mission, who was to pick us up, but I had no idea what he looked like or how to find anyone in this mass confusion. So many people were yelling and screaming that everything became a blur! David suggested we have the porter take our things to the curb so one of us could guard the boxes while the other looked for the director.

I'm standing here with David Shultz, the "guardian angel" God sent to help us when we first arrived in the Dominican Republic. Imagine—a perfect stranger staying with us for four hours! It was amazing.

Since Linda had met Fred previously and knew what he looked like, she agreed to search for him while I guarded the boxes. David stayed with me, speaking Spanish to the overly aggressive porters and instructing me to hold on tight to my purse.

Suddenly the medical inspector showed up and got into a heated discussion with David who then told me what was happening. "The inspector is demanding that you pay him for his help in getting your boxes through customs. He wants twenty dollars, but I told him that is too much. Now he has agreed to five. I think you should pay him."

I handed the inspector a five-dollar bill. He scowled at me and left as abruptly as he had arrived.

"Wow! I'm absolutely shocked! I've never experienced anything like this!"

"Get used to it. It's common practice here. I'm nervous leaving you girls by yourselves. It just isn't safe. Do you have a phone number of the man you're looking for? I could try to reach him on my cell phone."

"Yes, I have it right here. That would be great! Thanks so much!"

David called the number. When he hung up, he announced, "I have good news and bad news. The good news is that Fred is on his way. The bad news is that his vehicle broke down and he has no idea how long it will take to fix it or when he'll be able to pick you up. You'll just have to wait."

"Oh, David, you've already done so much for us. I couldn't possibly ask you to stay with us. I feel awful about keeping you this long. Please, go see your son. We'll be OK."

"No, I'm not going to leave you stranded like this. Who knows what could happen? Really, it's OK. I'll just make a couple of phone calls. I'm the one who would feel terrible if something happened to you. Besides, didn't you say your God sent me here to help you?"

"Well, I can't argue with that! We would still be back in customs if it weren't for you." David and I both laughed, and he admitted there was more truth in that statement than I realized.

About that time, Linda came back exhausted from her search. We quickly filled her in about Fred's bus breaking down. Although not happy about the news, she was glad to quit searching through the noisy crowd.

Three hours later, Fred showed up. True to his word, David had stayed with us the entire time! We thanked him over and over for all he had done for us, while he humbly insisted that it was "no big deal" and that he was happy to help! And we thanked God for this kind American physician. There is no doubt in my mind that God sent him to be our guardian angel! I had survived my first four hectic hours as a missionary!

From bad to worse

A group of volunteers from Maine was joining Kenny's mission team. They had originally planned to go to Guatemala, but due to recent political unrest that country was now too dangerous. Hearing about their plight, Kenny had invited them to join us. They were thrilled to have a place where God could use them. By now, this group had arrived at the airport and had found Linda and me. We gathered for a prayer of thanksgiving for the safe trip so far and asked for protection for the next part of our journey. Kenny and his church members would be arriving the next day.

We all piled into a rickety old bus, having no idea that for the next two hours we would be bumping along on what must have been the roughest dirt roads in the world. Once we left the city, the road conditions deteriorated drastically! Some of the potholes were as big as bathtubs, and other parts of the road looked like we were crossing the Grand Canyon! Linda and I hung on to our seats for dear life, as every now and then we would almost land on the floor. In fact, it was so bumpy that every few miles Fred would stop to tighten the lug nuts on the wheels.

One of those stops was right in front of a dilapidated shack where naked children were running around. My heart ached to think anyone lived in such poverty. Some of the folks from Maine gave the kids candy, and many took pictures. The mother was so happy that we were photographing her kids that she ran into the house to get yet another child so we could take her photo, too.

It wasn't long before we came to a village and pulled up outside a bakery. Fred suggested that it would be a good idea for everyone to use the restroom, as it would be some time before we'd have another chance. Linda and I were first in line, but we didn't feel like we had won any prize. There was no electricity and only enough toilet paper for one person, and the stall was so tiny you couldn't turn around. But the worst part was that the toilet didn't flush. The stench was so horrendous that I feared I would pass out! I think I set a world speed record for getting the job done!

BETHEL MISSION

By the time we reached Bethel Mission it was dark, and every muscle in my body ached from being jostled up and down on that crowded bus. As I looked around trying to determine where we would be sleeping, I heard excited screams. It was Linda and Stella jumping up and down hugging each other. *So this is Stella, whom I've heard so much about,* I thought. Linda had worked with Stella in Colorado several years ago and had related how wonderful she was. My daughter Becky had met her as well and had gone on and on about how "everyone loved Stella." I was happy that at last I would be able to meet her, too.

Stella came over and gave me a big hug and told me she would have known me anywhere! She was bubbling over with excitement, and I knew instantly why everyone loved her. She led us to the medical building and informed us we would be staying there with her. The "medical building" turned out to be a cement structure with cement floors, no screens on the windows, and walls that were not connected to the roof, leaving a twelve-inch space that was open to the great outdoors.

Since I had never visited a tropical country, I was not prepared for God's special creatures that thrive in this climate. Everything grows bigger there—especially the critters! We weren't there five minutes before I came face to face with my first Dominican Republic spider. It had big fat legs and a huge body that must have been at least three-and-a-half inches in diameter! Little green lizards were crawling on the curtains and everywhere else, trying to gobble up the huge cockroaches covering the walls. Unfortunately for me, the roaches outnumbered the lizards a hundred to one!

Hermes and Stella Tavera are now married and have three children. Today, Hermes is a pastor in Orlando, Florida.

But it was the rats I hated most! I never knew that rats could run up and down a stucco wall, but I can testify with absolute authority that they can! I stood frozen as I watched rats eight to twelve inches long running under the bed and up over the dresser. I was trying desperately to stifle a scream when Stella came and put her arm around me.

"Oh Brenda, you are so funny. Why are you trembling so? These little guys are harmless. Really, they are! They're no problem!"

Dear Jesus, please give me the courage You promised because I could sure use an extra dose right about now!

It was after my prayer that God reminded me how He had protected Linda and me from rats when we were little girls. Our dad sold religious books, and when sales were slow or nonexistent, so was the money. We were renting an old, rundown house that was infested with rats! We couldn't afford furniture, so all three of us girls shared a mattress on the floor. Each night during family worship, we would pray and ask God to protect us from the rats! Not once were we bitten, although many times I felt them run across my legs at night. We always gave God the credit for His protection and care. Now in the Dominican Republic, God was again giving me a lesson in the importance of trusting in Him.

Thank You, Lord, for reminding me that You are always with me.

As I prepared for bed, I was thankful for toilets that flushed and the shower, even though it had only icy cold water that nearly took my breath away. Linda and I slept with our mosquito nets over our beds. I prayed again, as I lay in my sleeping bag, that God would take away my fear and protect us from the rats and other creepy critters, and then I fell fast asleep.

I was soon awakened by the urgent tone of Linda's voice. "Sis! Sis! Are you awake?"

"Well, I am now. What's the matter?" I shined my flashlight in her direction, and there she was under her mosquito net, clutching her Bible for dear life!

"Brenda, how can you sleep at a time like this?"

"Well, I just prayed and asked God to take away my fear, and I trusted Him to keep me safe, so I went right to sleep." I couldn't believe I was encouraging Linda when she had come on this trip to protect me. I was amazed. *God must really be working a miracle in me!*

Since Kenny and his church group wouldn't be arriving until the next night, we had a full day before we would be starting the medical clinics. Stella asked if we would help out in the kitchen. "What about baking some cookies?" she suggested.

There were so few ingredients available that it was difficult to find a recipe we could use. "What about oatmeal molasses cookies?" Linda suggested as she searched through the only available cookbook. We tripled the recipe, which called for three cups of molasses. The dough was so black, sticky, and bitter that it almost made me gag! We managed to salvage it though by tripling the recipe again and this time leaving out the additional molasses!

When it came to adding the flour and sugar, we were in for the shock of our lives. As I was scooping up the flour, I noticed it was full of long, black, skinny bugs! I tried to avoid them. I tried to sift them out. But it was no use. The flour and sugar were stored in burlap bags because sealed containers were a luxury this mission couldn't afford. We soon accepted the fact that getting rid of the bugs was futile and finished the cookies—bugs and all! Actually the cookies turned out tasting great, which was a good thing because supper consisted of cookies and popcorn—nothing else! What little food the mission had was very precious and rationed carefully.

The kitchen was poorly equipped with very few utensils, pots, or pans. There were only two small, well-worn pot holders and no towels. Electricity was not available, so refrigeration of food was not an option. Any leftovers were stored on the counter and covered with a white lacy tablecloth. Oh how my heart longed to share from my own kitchen. I thought about all the extra gadgets I hardly ever used and wished I had brought them with me. It was amazing how the people there could cook for so many with almost nothing to work with!

When Kenny arrived with his church group, we had worship together and prayed that God would allow us to be a special blessing to

Stella and I are getting ready to cook for the crew. Food was rationed carefully, and nothing was ever wasted. The kitchen facilities sure made me miss my fully stocked pantry at home.

73

others on this mission trip. There were three main aspects that we would be focusing on: building a boy's dormitory, conducting medical clinics, and holding evangelistic meetings in the nearby town of Bayaguana. Linda and I would be involved in the last two projects.

MY MEDICAL MISSIONARY EXPERIENCE

The next day, twenty-four people, including Linda and myself, crowded into the back of a run-down pickup truck. It would be a two-

hour ride to our first medical clinic. Before we even arrived, I was black and blue and aching all over from being bounced around in the back of the truck. We would hit a bump, and someone would come flying into me just like a missile aimed at its target! *Bam!* Next it was someone's elbow in my ribs or jammed into my back! I longed for roads with pavement!

We're loaded up and ready to leave for a village two hours away where we will hold a medical clinic. Medical supplies went on the truck first, and then the crew. This was a lucky day for me—I had a box to sit on! Most days were standing room only.

When we rounded the corner into the little town, there was a long line of people waiting for us. We jumped out quickly to set up as fast as possible. The dentist, Ken Pearson, needed lots of light, so he set up his clinic outdoors. Dr. Knowlton and I set up in an open area with a roof. Villagers brought an old handmade table to serve for exams, and someone else brought a dingy cloth to cover it. Looking around at the people, I realized I'd never seen anyone like this. The adults wore clothing that was either three sizes too big or three sizes too small; the children were simply naked. Many people looked as if they hadn't eaten in weeks. Oh how I wished we had brought enough food and clothes for everyone! Seeing all this was almost too much to bear. I constantly prayed for strength not to break down and cry.

Disease was rampant, as is typical in poverty-stricken areas. We saw patients with AIDS, diabetes, venereal diseases, eye infections, hypertension, sciatica, and various skin diseases such as scabies and ringworm. Everyone suffered from parasites and malnutrition. What little food the people did eat consisted mostly of pork and rice, but no fruits or vegetables. No one had shoes, and the bottoms of their feet were thick with calluses.

At one point during the day, I took a break from seeing patients and started passing out candy to the children waiting outside. In minutes I was mobbed with so many kids pushing and shoving each other that I had to put the candy away before someone was seriously injured. How sad that these kids had so little—candy was worth fighting for!

By the end of the day we were all exhausted. We had lived through record high temperatures; no food, little water, no bathrooms—and we still had to endure the bumpy ride back to the mission. We were all on the truck patiently waiting for the dentist to come so we could go home. He was the last one to finish because every time he thought he was done, more patients showed up. Dental care was nonexistent, and so many people chewed on sugar cane that their teeth were literally rotting away! They had so much pain that all they wanted was for the offending tooth to be pulled! When the last patient was seen, the dentist packed up his supplies and headed toward the truck carrying the fruits of his labor—a bucket full of bloody teeth! It was disgusting! Unfortunately, because of superstitions, we were not allowed to leave this "treasure" behind.

After sweating all day and enduring the dusty ride home, I was looking forward to a shower. I didn't complain about the cold water. I even killed a cockroach in the shower without cringing! God *was* answering my prayer about bugs. I didn't like them any better, but at least I wasn't shaking in fear! That in itself was a miracle!

After attending the evening evangelistic meeting that Kenny was holding, we ended our day with worship. There were no songbooks, but the villagers and mission workers knew every verse to every song and joyously praised the Lord! When someone learned I could play the piano, a keyboard was brought out of storage. Now I could join the musical praise without knowing Spanish. One of their favorite songs, "Más Allá del Sol" ("Far Beyond the Sun"), became a favorite of mine. So many people in this country were caught in abject poverty that it was no wonder they found strength and hope in its message. Once these precious people accepted God's saving grace, they could then look up, not at the sun god of their ancestors, but to their "home, blessed home, far beyond the sun." That was why we were there—we were praying and working for souls so that we could all spend eternity together far beyond the sun.

Every day was the same—early to rise, a long truck ride to a different village, seeing patients until dark, another long bumpy ride back to the mission too tired to eat, evangelism meetings, worship, a cold shower, and then falling into bed exhausted.

SPIDERS, RATS, AND OTHER CREEPY CRAWLIES

I quickly learned not to shine my flashlight on the walls when I came home at night. Cockroaches came out in droves after dark and covered the walls. The first night when I shined my light, they started dive-bombing Linda and me, causing us to scream hysterically. Stella came running, and when she saw what was happening, she explained that cockroaches were attracted to the light. I decided it was much easier to cope with these unwanted guests if I didn't have to look at them. It was bad enough just knowing they were there. I rarely used my flashlight except when absolutely necessary! I also learned to lift the toilet seat prior to use because big black spiders love to hang out there. Some people might not quite understand this, but I never approached the bathroom without praying first!

I was not the only one struggling with unwelcome guests in our apartment. One evening before getting ready for bed, Linda was standing in the kitchen by the counter when out of the corner of her eye she saw a huge black spider near her hand. This not only produced a blood-curdling scream, but sent her scrambling on top of a kitchen stool, too terrified to move. I tried to talk her into getting off the stool, but to no avail. She was trembling and refused to be reasoned with. The next thing I knew, Stella and her boyfriend Hermes came flying through the front door. Linda's scream had been so ear-piercing that they had heard it from the other side of the mission compound. It wasn't until Hermes killed the offensive intruder that Linda left her perch.

That night, Linda and I prayed together for God's protection—not only from the spiders and bugs, but also from the rats. The week before, a volunteer had been going to the bathroom when a rat came up through the sewer pipe into the toilet and proceeded to bite him. He wasn't able to sit down the rest of his stay and he even flew home early for treatment. Linda wished we hadn't learned about that story.

Linda and I devised a plan to ensure a good night's sleep. Every morning when we awakened, we immediately rolled up our sleeping bags and placed them in large plastic garbage bags that we secured tightly. Seconds before going to bed, we removed our sleeping bags, not taking our eyes off of them for one moment. As an added precaution, we tucked our mosquito nets under our sleeping bags. This way we knew with absolute certainty there would be no unwanted guests when we crawled into our sleeping bags each night. This plan worked beautifully—well, almost!

I had just dosed off to sleep one night when suddenly I was awakened with the unmistakable feeling of something big crawling on me. I let out a blood-curdling scream and was so hysterical that every rational thought left me. I frantically tried to get out of my sleeping bag, but in my frenzied state I didn't realize that the reason my mosquito netting wouldn't set me free was because I was sitting on it. I had almost torn apart the net when two huge green lizards scampered out of my sleeping bag and across my legs, slithering through an open hole of the mosquito netting and out the door. I sat there hugging my pillow crying uncontrollably. Linda was by my side instantly with her arms around me, assuring me everything would be OK. Minutes later, our brother Kenny burst in the room, ready to do battle against our enemy.

Kenny has an incredible sense of humor and loves to tease, but one glance told him I was too distraught for jokes. After hearing about the *giant* lizards, he gave us a brotherly hug and prayed with both of us, and then he did something that I will forever love him for. He checked our beds and sleeping bags from top to bottom for any other critters that might be hiding there and after proclaiming them safe had us crawl inside, and then he lovingly tucked the mosquito netting under the entire mattress! He made this his ritual for the rest of our trip! Only a brother who dearly loved his sisters would do that, and I'll never forget his loving act of kindness!

DISCOURAGEMENT SETS IN

After several days passed, I began to get discouraged. I thought about the long lines of people who waited—sometimes for more than twelve hours—and then we couldn't see them because we ran out of time. Since there was no electricity, we were forced to close the clinic when darkness fell.

Sometimes desperation causes people to behave in ways they normally would never act otherwise. These people needed medical care desperately, and we were their only hope. When daylight began to dim and people realized they would not be seen by the doctor or nurse, they would begin to panic. One evening, this panic turned into a life-threatening situation. Every time we opened the door to let in a patient, the people would begin pushing and shoving to get inside while the door was open.

There were no windows or back door in the building we were using, so as more and more people pushed their way in, we began to fear for our lives. There were still several hundred angry people outside who, by now, were demanding to be seen. However, too many people were in the building already; it was so hot and stuffy we could hardly breathe. The only way out was through the front door, and if any more people pushed inside, we would all be trampled to death.

All of a sudden, the door began to give way from the pressure of so many people pushing against it. It opened just a crack. Stella and I quickly threw ourselves against it. We pushed and shoved but could not get it shut. Stella screamed for help, and a few men inside the building came and threw their weight against the door. However, we were no match for the strength of the crowd. I began to pray and ask God to please protect us and close that door! With one more heave, the door shut tight, and Stella quickly secured the lock. We braced the back of a chair under the doorknob and then stopped to catch our breath. It was over a hundred degrees inside, and it felt even hotter now with the extra people in the room. The stench of vomit, open infected wounds, blood, and perspiration was unbearable! But we couldn't take a chance and open the door to let anyone out!

Stella yelled firmly through the door telling the people to leave. "Go home! We will not see any more patients today. You have been too rowdy! The clinic is now closed. Please go home." Upon hearing this, the crowd protested loudly. We had to wait inside that hot room for over an hour until the people realized we were serious and began to wander away.

That night, as I was lying in bed, I felt overwhelmed. Once I began sobbing, it was as if someone had opened the floodgates, and I couldn't stop.

"Sis, what's the matter? Why are you crying?"

"I just want to go home. We've worked day after day until we're dog tired, and yet we haven't even made a dent when it comes to helping these desperate people. No matter what we do, it will never be enough! Do you realize that in no village have we ever been able to treat everyone who has come for care? Not even once! There has always been a long line of hopeless, disappointed, angry people when we pack up to leave.

I don't know what I am doing here when I can't even make a difference in somebody's life!" Another burst of sobs erupted.

Linda was quiet for a few moments and then said softly, "Brenda, do you remember the man who came into the clinic today who almost died? You know, the one who was having an allergic reaction—his tongue had tripled in size and was blocking his airway? He was gasping for breath, and after you gave him a shot, the swelling went down, and he couldn't stop thanking you. Do you remember?"

"Yes, I remember." I pulled a tissue from under my pillow and wiped my nose.

"Well, I think you made a difference for that man. And remember the lady who came in with a wound so infected that if it had gone another day without treatment, she probably would have lost her leg and maybe even her life?"

"Yes, I remember her; what's your point?"

"Well, I think you made a difference in her life."

One by one, Linda recounted various people I had cared for during the day, ending with, "I think you made a difference in *that* life!"

Linda's message was loud and clear, and as it began to sink in, I realized that even though I couldn't help everyone who came, God was using me to help the ones He directed me to. I blew my nose one more time and wiped my eyes. "Sis, thanks so much for reminding me that God's in charge and that He is using us. It sure puts things in perspective! I guess I'm going to pray for stronger faith and an extra dose of courage. Linda, I love you so much. Goodnight, Sis."

I then prayed a long prayer asking God to forgive me and pleading with Him to keep using me however He chose. I took a deep breath and fell peacefully asleep knowing God was with me each step of the way.

The next day, something very unusual happened at the clinic. Because I don't speak Spanish, I needed an interpreter, and Stella and Hector were helping me. Stella was still giving my instructions to the last patient, and Hector had taken a break, so I moved ahead in the line to a lady who was probably in her seventies but looked much older. I motioned for her to tell me where her pain was. With one swift movement, she pulled open her dress, at the same time spitting her dentures down into her bosom—slobbery saliva and all. I first looked down and then up at her face. She had her mouth wide open, her tongue sticking out as far as it would go, and drool dripping down her chin.

Apparently, a man in her village had died two weeks before, and because this lady didn't have any teeth, she had taken his dentures. However, they didn't fit properly, so now she had infected sores all over her gums. Afraid someone would steal the dentures from her, she kept them in her mouth in spite of the excruciating pain.

I gave her medication for the pain and infection and tried to explain she must give up the dentures. Stella tried to impress upon her that if she continued to wear them, the pain would only get worse. However, the way she was protecting those teeth, I have a feeling she didn't take our advice.

Linda Leaves Her Comfort Zone

God provided Linda with some excitement of her own. She had been helping Ken Pearson, the dentist, all day, and he had taught her how to pull a tooth all by herself. She was so excited that she grinned from ear to ear just talking about it! Now you would have to know Linda to realize what a feat this was. Cinda and I are the nurses in the family; Linda is not!

When I found out that I would have to function as a "doctor" in the Dominican Republic, diagnosing illnesses and dispensing drugs, I promoted Linda to be my nurse. She is not comfortable around sick people and gets nauseous at the sight of blood. One day a lady came in with a terribly infected wound. She had an eight-inch gash in her leg where a car had hit her the week before. Not able to afford a doctor, she suffered alone. Neighbors carried her to our clinic and waited six hours in the hot sun for her to be examined.

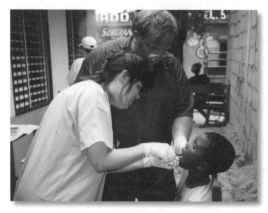

Dentist Ken Pearson guides and instructs Linda as she pulls her first tooth!

I took one look and knew the wound needed to be irrigated and washed. There were little pieces of gravel from the road imbedded in the wound. The smell was horrible because infection had set in, and she was burning up with fever. I looked at the long line of people still waiting to be seen and knew this patient would require more time than I had to give. Looking at Linda I told her how to irrigate the wound and before she could refuse, I quickly turned my attention to the next patient. A few minutes later I looked up to see Linda following my instructions perfectly, even though she looked as if she were going to vomit. I was really proud of her willingness to step up to the plate. Later she told me that she was praying for strength and courage the entire time!

MINISTERING TO THOSE IN NEED

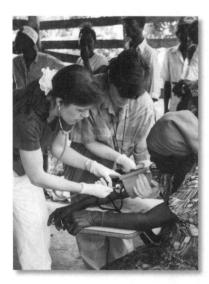

I taught Linda to take blood pressures, wash wounds, apply bandages, and other nursing skills. I was so glad for her willingness to step in and be my "nurse"!

One day had been particularly difficult. We had been at a very poor village, and almost everyone that day was suffering from typhoid. We had to wear masks for our own safety. It was hot, and we had been working so many days in a row, standing on our feet, that we were physically drained. Our emotions were raw at seeing so much heartache. But it was the suffering of children that affected me the most.

One ten-year-old girl's legs had been intentionally broken and twisted behind her. They were then tied in place until the bones healed in that position. This effectively turned her into a cripple so that even the most hard-hearted person would take pity on her and give her money. Her face was wracked with pain, and it hurt me just to look at her. She would now support her family by spending most of her days on the side of the road begging. What a high price to pay! Not only would she never walk again, but she would suffer this pain for the rest of her life. I wish I could say this was an isolated case, but sadly it was not. *Oh dear Jesus, please come soon and end this suffering, sickness, and heartache.*

After another emotionally draining day, our staff got into our "truck," which was really an old jeep with a truck bed built onto the back, and started to head home. We were waiting for a couple more of our staff when a few of us noticed several large boxes of clothing on the truck that we had forgotten about. I asked Hector to carry a box over to one of the buildings. As soon as I opened the box and pulled out the first article of clothing, a riot broke out. It is difficult to imagine the extreme desperation caused by abject poverty, and even after seeing it with my own eyes, it still seemed surreal. People started grabbing the clothes out of each other's hands: pushing, shoving, and knocking each other down. When we realized how uncontrolled and violent the crowd had become, we raced as fast as we could across the road to the safety of our truck.

"Hurry! Let's get out of here before we get trampled," one of the volunteers yelled. Dr. Knowlton was the last to swing his leg up over the side

Dr. Marvin Coy surgically removed an extra finger from each hand on this baby who was born with six fingers on each hand! His mother was so grateful. Hector helped translate for me as I gave "after care" instructions.

Dr. Marvin Coy sutures a facial laceration. I was amazed at how this child lay perfectly still and didn't even cry during the procedure.

of the truck as we took off, but we weren't fast enough. There must have been a hundred villagers chasing us, trying to grab on to the bed of the truck. They were desperate to get the other boxes of clothing before we left. One box of clothing, no matter how well intended, had now placed all of us in a very dangerous situation. I felt terrible because it had been my idea to bring the clothes that morning. Stella had tried to talk me out of it.

"Brenda, it just isn't safe. It is hard to explain, but it's very dangerous to give out clothing." In my wildest dreams I would never have imagined this nightmare! *Oh why didn't I listen to Stella who knows the culture here in this country?*

The villagers were frantic. Even though we were moving down the road, they were still hanging on to the truck trying to get inside. We literally had to pull their hands from the vehicle and shove them away. But for every person we managed to push away, there seemed to be five more hanging on.

Please, dear Jesus, let us get away and don't let anyone get hurt! Oh Lord, I am so sorry I didn't listen to Stella's advice this morning. Please forgive me and please help us!

In desperation, we picked up the heavy boxes of clothing and threw them over the side of the truck. It wasn't until the villagers could see there were no more boxes that they abandoned the chase. I watched in horror as they fought and tore the clothing from each other's hands. This was a most shocking example of what it is like to be this desperately poor! I shuddered to think of how many children and elderly persons may have been trampled in this frenzy over a few articles of clothing!

Dear heavenly Father, there must be a better way to do this. Please help me understand Your plan.

To make matters worse, we hadn't gone more than a couple of blocks when our truck came to a sputtering halt. The driver tried again and again, but it would not start. We all got out and started pushing, when all of a sudden it started. Everyone quickly jumped back on, and we headed off. But our jubilation was short-lived. Another block down the road, the engine died again!

Once more everyone got out to push, but this time the truck refused to start. Dusk was descending upon us, and we still had almost a three hour drive to get back to the mission. It didn't help that Hector, our driver, said it really wasn't safe for us to be there at night. We stood around the truck and first one and then another prayed that God would watch over us and provide a ride back to the mission. The men lifted up the hood and stared at the engine. To tell you the truth, I don't think they knew what they were looking at any more than I did.

"Well, I think we're going to need a mechanic, but I don't know how we will find one here." Hector shook his head as if this were a lost cause. But not Stella! We had prayed, and she knew God would provide. Without saying a word to anyone, she marched off toward a group of houses, with Linda and me following close behind. Stella spoke in Spanish to some men standing outside, asking them if they knew of a mechanic nearby—anyone who could help us.

One of the men nodded his head and started shouting down the street. Almost instantly, men appeared out of nowhere, each carrying a variety of tools. One man was obviously the respected mechanic of the village, and he began taking different parts from the engine of the truck and laying them on the road. I looked around at the faces of the members of our group and could see that I wasn't the only one worried. At one point the mechanic stuck his head down near the engine and sucked out gasoline then quickly spit it out on the side of the road.

One of the many times our vehicle broke down. On this occasion we were extremely grateful for the mechanic God provided to make repairs.

Linda, Stella, and I went behind the truck and joined hands. With our heads bowed, right there on that open road, Linda began to pray, *"Precious heavenly Father, You know the situation that we are in and how dangerous it is for us to be here after dark. Please place Your hand on this vehicle, and if it be Your will, Lord, fix this truck so that we can go back to the mission. Lord, we are trusting in You, and are claiming, Hebrews chapter thirteen, verse five, where You have promised never to leave us or forsake us! Thank You, Jesus, for hearing and answering our prayer. Amen."*

I'm still not sure what the mechanic did, but in just forty-five minutes the problem was fixed and we were heading home. The man charged us only fourteen dollars, and he seemed elated to get that. Stella explained it was more than he could make elsewhere in a whole week.

All the way home we sang songs and praised God for answered prayer. I thought about Philippians 4:6, 7: "Be anxious for nothing, but in everything by prayer and supplication, with thanksgiving, let your requests be made known to God; and the peace of God, which surpasses all understanding, will guard your hearts and minds through Christ Jesus."

Once again, God was giving me a lesson in the importance of trusting Him. We had prayed and made our petition known, and God had provided for our every need.

HELPING WITH EVANGELISM

After working long days in the medical clinics at the different villages, we raced to Bayaguana each evening, where Kenny was holding evangelistic meetings. Linda and I, along with our sister-in-law, Tammy, were in charge of the children's divisions. Our nephew and niece, Jeremy and Crystal, helped too. The first night of the meetings we had around a hundred kids. But every night the number increased until there were over five hundred attending. Linda told the continuing story of "Dookie, Sookie, and Big Mo," and Stella translated. Linda would get very animated, and the kid's eyes were wide as they took in everything she said. Each night when our bus rounded the corner, hundreds of kids ran after us, shouting "Big Mo, Big Mo!" I've heard Linda tell that story many times, but never to a more enthusiastic group of kids hungry to learn about Jesus.

One night there were more kids then usual, and during her story they began pushing to get closer to her because it was difficult to hear. Linda had to keep backing up as they pressed in tighter and tighter. All of a sudden Linda screamed, and her arms went wildly up in the air. She began stomping her feet and jumping all around. The kid's eyes went wild with excitement thinking this was all part of the story. So Linda calmed down and continued. As soon as she was done, Stella and Tammy

In the evening, we would all pile on the bus to go to the evangelistic meetings in Bayaguana, where my brother, Kenny, was preaching. My sister-in-law, Tammy, is sitting next to me.

started the kids singing, while Linda went running off with one of the young girls.

What had really happened was that as Linda kept backing up, she backed right up against the edge of a house and sank twelve inches down into a raw sewage pit! The neighboring houses didn't have running water; instead there were ditches dug around the perimeter of each home. When people needed to use the bathroom, they did their business in a bucket and then disposed of its contents in the ditch!

A little girl standing close to Linda saw the whole thing, and as soon as Linda finished her story, this girl took my sister by the hand and motioned for her to follow. She led her over a block away to her own home where she had a bucket of clean water. This alone was an incredible gift because houses didn't have running water, and water had to be carried long distances. Tenderly she bathed Linda's legs, rinsing off the disgusting human waste. Although it wasn't exactly breaking the alabaster box, it was an extravagant act of love!

CALMING THE STORM ON THE BUS

One day when Stella needed to go to Santo Domingo for supplies, she invited Hermes, Linda, and me to go along. We would be riding a public bus. Had I known what these buses were like, I might have opted to stay at the mission.

We stood on the side of the road for what seemed like hours before the bus arrived. Then as we entered, the driver ordered us to the very back. Stella and Hermes were told to sit on one side and Linda and I were to sit on the opposite side. At each stop, as more people entered, we were forced to squeeze together until we had four people sitting in a space meant for two. We were so packed in that Linda and I could hardly breathe. Once the seats were filled, a drop-down seat was pulled up in the aisle for more passengers.

I looked nervously at Linda and whispered, "I sure hope there's not a fire on this bus because without an aisle we'd never make it out. And the windows open only six inches!"

"This sure wouldn't pass safety regulations in the States," Linda agreed. Suddenly the bus came to a screeching halt! Someone in the back needed to get off. What happened next was most unusual. Everyone in the aisle seats got up and walked off the bus, allowing the person needing to get off to do so. Then everyone else got back on and did the "fill up and squish" process all over again. I had never seen anything like it!

Everything went smoothly until at one stop, the driver could see a lady in the distance running to catch the bus. He waited for her. For reasons that are still unclear to me, this made the whole busload of people angry. They started arguing and screaming at the bus driver and then with each other. Then, as if on cue, the aisle people got off the bus—still arguing. The driver was yelling at them, but since it was all in Spanish, Linda and I didn't have a clue what they were saying. The lady entered the bus and the other passengers all filed back into their places, and the driver took off again. But the fighting didn't stop. Instead, it escalated. Now people were standing up and loudly shouting at each other. The hostility and anger were intense. As people began pushing and shoving, I began to pray. *Dear heavenly Father, please protect us. This is not a safe situation. The driver could roll down an embankment because he keeps looking back at the angry people and not watching the road. And if people continue to riot, we're going to get crushed. Please quiet this crowd, just as You did the water during the storm.*

Immediately I felt impressed to sing. I leaned over to Linda and said, "Let's sing."

"What did you say?" The noise level was so loud now that it was difficult to hear.

"Sing! Let's sing!" I said, this time a little louder.

We started singing "Mansion Over the Hill Top," but after one verse I realized no one could hear us. I nudged Linda with my elbow and shouted, "Louder!" So we sang it again, this time at the top of our lungs. All of a sudden the crowd became quiet, and people started staring at us. I'm sure they were wondering just who these crazy American ladies were! By the time we ended the song, the bus was completely silenced, and every eye was on us. I glanced at Linda and then started the next song and the next in our normal voices. We sang for two hours—all the way to Santo Domingo!

When we got off the bus, people hugged and kissed us on both cheeks. They spoke to us, although we couldn't understand a word. When Stella and Hermes finally made it out from the back of the bus, I asked them, "What were the people saying?"

Hermes answered, "They say, 'Before singing, war. After singing, peace.' They say you sounded like the angels."

Linda and I thanked God for using songs of praise to quiet an angry crowd. Once again God had demonstrated His loving care and protection. I thought of 2 Timothy 1:7: "For God has not given us a spirit of fear, but of power and of love and of a sound mind."

God does not want us to live in fear, but to trust His love for us. He created each of us with a mind to think, and He gave us the gift of choice. It is up to us whether or not we choose to listen to His voice and feel His peace or to be burdened down with fear. He had impressed Linda and me to sing, and He used our voices to silence a crowd. God is so amazing!

Looking back

I had started this trip as a *reluctant* missionary. I was selfishly thinking of myself and my own comforts and fears. But when I prayed and asked God to make me willing to be willing, He answered my prayer and opened the windows of heaven, pouring out such blessings that there was not room enough to receive them!

That trip changed my life in so many positive ways. I didn't return the same person. Now I see mission service in a whole new light and am eager to go again. I now have more love and appreciation for those who are suffering and can't help themselves. Although I still have a strong dislike for insects and rodents, I know that I can trust that fear to Jesus! It doesn't mean I will never be afraid again, but I *can* go forward knowing with absolute certainty that Jesus will always be there for me to lean on and that I can depend on Him to help me through every situation! If things were always easy, we would never realize our need for God!

I no longer take simple pleasures for granted—such as warm showers, plentiful groceries, electricity, medical care, and so many other things. Even today, when I am driving down smooth highways, I say a prayer of thanks.

At the end of the evangelistic meetings, many were baptized. Here Kenny and Tammy are standing in front of the church where they held the baptism.

I believe that sometimes God allows us to experience hardships in life to perfect our characters. Revelation 3:18 says, " 'I counsel you to buy from Me gold refined in the fire, that you may be rich; and white garments, that you may be clothed, that the shame of your nakedness may not be revealed; and anoint your eyes with eye salve, that you may see.' "

I don't regret any of the things I experienced in the Dominican Republic, even though at the time they may have been challenging. Each one was a testament of God's grace and mercy. I praise God for allowing me to be His hands and voice to bring healing and hope to so many precious people.

I'm thankful that God called me to the Dominican Republic. I wasn't angry even when Cinda told me that Joel was the one who had paid for my ticket! I believe God used both of them to encourage me to follow His leading. Next time I won't hesitate. I'll go anywhere God asks me to go, and I will go willingly, obediently, and with joy in my heart, claiming Philippians 4:13: "I can do all things through Christ who strengthens me."

I'm no longer a reluctant missionary!

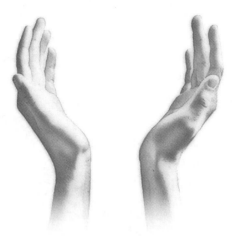

CHAPTER 4

BROKEN GLASSES, BROKEN DREAMS

Inasmuch as you did it to one of the least of these My brethren, you did it to Me.
—Matthew 25:40

I have never been the adventurous type, and even though I was raised in a Christian home, I never dreamed of being a missionary. Every time I heard someone give a mission story or tell of his or her actual mission experiences, I would shudder to myself and think, *I could never do that!* Of course it didn't help to hear about all the bugs, snakes, wild animals, or lethal scorpions!

So when I was asked to go on a mission trip to South Africa to help the thousands of AIDS orphans there, I went to the Lord in prayer. As long as I *knew* God was calling me to go, then I knew I had nothing to fear. I had learned that lesson ten years earlier when I went to the Dominican Republic. When I fully surrendered my life to Jesus, I promised Him that I would serve Him. And since then not a day has gone by that I don't ask Him to use me in a special way.

There are three very important things that are essential if you are going to allow God to use you.

1. Be willing. God will not force you to follow Him or serve Him. He will use you only if you ask Him to. First Chronicles 28:9 tells us to "serve Him [God] with a loyal heart and with a willing mind; for the LORD searches all hearts and understands all the intent of the thoughts. If you seek Him, He will be found by you."

2. Be obedient. Matthew 7:21–23 says that unless we are doing the will of our Father, all we do is for nothing. He'll say, "I never knew you." Wow! That's really powerful, isn't it?

3. Be joyful. We can be willing to allow God to use us, and we can even be obedient to His will, but unless we accept His gift of joy, we might as well do nothing! An attitude of, "Oh, all right, I'll do it, if I have to," just doesn't cut it! So you see, to *be willing, be obedient,* and *be joyful* are critical if we really want to be used by God! Psalm 5:11 makes it very clear: "Let those also who love Your name be joyful in you."

I began doing research on Swaziland, the area in South Africa that I would be visiting, and it didn't take me long to learn that AIDS was claiming the lives of 40 percent of the population and that the average life span was only thirty years! Unthinkable! Grandmothers were raising their grandchildren and children raising other children because of this horrible disease! And because so many families were without fathers or mothers to provide financially for their children, these kids were starving! I was shocked to learn that children often go days without a meal and that many sleep on the hard, cold ground because they don't have a bed or a blanket. Before I had even landed in the country, my heart was filled with compassion for their plight.

For several months before our trip I spoke in various churches and seminars to raise funds for the children, even going on live television to raise awareness of the enormous need. Other people were collecting money, too, and the funds started coming in as people opened up their checkbooks because their hearts were touched. Clothes, shoes, medicine, blankets, even eyeglasses were collected. Someone donated a million meals consisting of dehydrated soup!

In preparation for my trip I went to see my medical doctor to find out what vaccinations I would need. When I told him where I was going, he informed me that I could not have picked a more disease-ridden place.

"Don't you realize that Swaziland has the highest concentration of people infected with AIDS and HIV than anywhere else in the entire world?"

"Yes, that's what I've been told."

"Then why do you want to go there? Perhaps somewhere less dangerous would be a better option."

I smiled and let him know that I wasn't worried at all because I was doing what God wanted me to do! He just shook his head and said, "Well, if you're determined to go, then these are the vaccinations that you'll need." He wrote them all down on a pad of paper and handed it to me.

"How much will all these vaccinations cost?" I wanted to know.

"I'm guessing somewhere around six hundred dollars," he replied, "but I don't even have all the necessary medicines here. You'll have to go to the public health clinic. It won't be any cheaper there, however; it's the medicines themselves that are so expensive."

I processed what he said in a microsecond and quickly told him that the cost might as well be six million dollars because I just couldn't afford it! I was a full-time volunteer and hadn't had a paycheck in years. We depended solely on my husband's salary and were struggling as it was. I certainly didn't want to burden my husband by even asking him about it. The doctor then informed me that unfortunately my insurance would not pay for the vaccinations, but that it would be very foolish not to have the shots. He added that if I didn't get the injections, I should cancel my trip. I thanked him for his advice but assured him that I knew God would take care of me.

"If you don't do anything else, at least take the malaria pills. Malaria can kill you." He handed me a prescription, and I tucked it into my purse.

"Thanks," I said, "and I appreciate all your good advice."

"Then follow it because that's what you're paying me for." He laughed and added, "But I have a feeling you're going to do what you want."

All the way home I prayed. *Precious Lord, I know that if it is Your will, I don't need shots or pills to keep me safe because You can just speak, and it will be done. However, if it is Your will that I have these vaccinations, please provide the money since You know I can't afford it! Thank You for hearing and answering my prayer. In Your precious name, Amen.*

When I had finished praying, there was a peace inside me that whichever way God led, it would be OK. I really wasn't worried because I knew God *would* take care of me.

Several days later I received a letter in the mail. It was from a man in California who had watched the program about our Africa trip. As I read his letter, my hands began to shake, and tears rolled down my cheeks. The letter said, "Dear Brenda, I have been impressed to send a donation for your trip to Africa, and I'm especially impressed that you will need funds to take care of your personal needs. Please use this money for whatever you need to prepare for your trip. Please know that my prayers are with you."

Enclosed was a check for one thousand dollars! I could hardly believe my eyes! God had abundantly blessed more than I could have ever asked or thought! Now I would not only have money to pay for my vaccinations, but there would be enough for other things, such as insect repellant, a mosquito tent, and a sleeping bag. We even had to take our own toilet paper! I had wanted to bring some special treats to pass out to the kids—stickers and candies. Now there would be plenty of money for everything. God is so good!

The first thing I did was to get on my knees and thank God for His goodness. Then I called my generous benefactor to thank him for his kindness and generosity! He was so humble and gracious and tried to act as though he had done nothing, but we both knew God was in the midst of it all.

From the moment I first agreed to go on this trip, I began to pray that my sister, Linda, would go as well. Linda had been a great comfort to me in the Dominican Republic, working with me side by side. I knew she didn't have the money, and I couldn't afford to pay her way, but I also knew that funds would not be a problem if God wanted her to go to Africa. So, every day I made this a matter of prayer.

The first week in Africa, I would be in charge of the children's division at the Swaziland camp meeting. Over two thousand orphans were expected!

Dear Lord, You know how much work it's going to be to keep the attention of two thousand kids! This is not a selfish prayer; I really do need Linda to be there! If it's Your will, Lord, for her to go, then please provide the way. Thank You, Jesus, for hearing and answering my prayer.

Several weeks before we were scheduled to leave, God gave me His answer. At times certain events happen that are so meaningful, you will remember them forever. And what took place next is one of those times for me. I had just raced to the West Town Mall in Knoxville, in search of some skirts for the trip. I had been told that the women in Africa prefer dresses and skirts as opposed to pants. Not wanting to offend anyone, I was searching for some skirts that were on sale and in my price range. I had been side-tracked by a shop that was going out of business and was allowing myself the luxury of looking at all the merchandise and marveling at the good deals, even though I knew I couldn't afford them, when my cell phone rang.

"Hello, is this Brenda?" the voice on the other end asked.

"Yes, this is Brenda. How can I help you?"

"This is Bob Schaefer, and I wanted to talk to you about your trip to Africa. I think it could be dangerous for you to go there; don't you think you should stay home? I mean, kids around the world need 'Miss Brenda.' I think it is too much of a risk for you to go."

I assured him that I wasn't afraid and that I knew God would be with me. I pushed back uneasy thoughts of lions and tigers growling at my door at night!

"Bob, I have prayed about this trip, and I know this is something that God wants me to do. So I have nothing to fear."

"You are determined to go then?"

"Yes, I'm determined to go," I answered.

"Is your sister Linda going?"

"No, she's not able to go this time."

"Why not? I read in your book about how God has used your sister to protect you many times in your life. If you are going to Africa, then your sister must go with you."

"Well, I would love to have her come with me, but she can't afford to go. Everyone must raise the money for their own expenses—including airfare, food, and lodging."

"Then consider it raised."

I could hardly believe my ears. Surely he didn't mean that he would pay for Linda to go to Africa—did he?

"Bob, I don't even know how much the trip will cost, but I know it will be a lot of money. I'm guessing it will cost around two thousand dollars."

Bob didn't hesitate for a moment. "Tell me where to send the check," he said firmly.

My heart was beating fast, and I was oblivious to the people walking around me

Bob Schaefer has installed more than 5,000 satellite dishes so that others can hear the good news that Jesus is coming soon on 3ABN. He volunteers his time, expecting nothing in return. God impressed Bob to help me and my sister, Linda, with expenses for our trip to Africa.

as I stood motionless in the aisle. Taking a deep breath, I told him where to send the money and thanked him for his great, big, generous heart!

"I don't even know how to thank you," I managed to say. I was so choked up with emotion I could hardly speak.

"Don't thank me," he replied in a humble voice. "I'm just glad I can help. I want you to know that I'll be praying for you."

"God bless you, Bob. Thank you again; goodbye now."

It was almost surreal. Did I just hear a man say that he was paying for my sister to go to Africa? Why, I had never even met this man, and yet God had impressed him that Linda should go.

"Oh no, I had better call Linda quick!"

I dialed Linda's number and waited impatiently for the phone to ring.

"Sis, are you sitting down?"

"No, should I be?"

"Oh yes, I think you'll need to sit down for this one."

"Well don't keep me hanging, what is it? Are you all right?" She could hear the emotion in my voice, and yet I could hardly get out the words.

"Sis, you are going to Africa!"

"What are you talking about? No, I'm not!"

"Yes, you are! A man just called me from California, and he is paying all your expenses."

"Oh my heart! Are you serious? Brenda, stop teasing me like this! I am not going to Africa! You are so silly!"

"No, I'm serious! You really *are* going to Africa!"

When Linda realized that I was indeed serious, she began to panic.

"Brenda, I am really quite happy just staying here and praying for you while you go."

"Well, it looks like God wants you to do more than pray! He wants you to witness to those orphans yourself! So start packing!"

"Sis, I really need to pray about this."

"I know, but you have only tonight because tomorrow he is sending the check."

"I just don't know what to say except that I am completely shocked. Yes, I will pray about it!"

The next day Linda had made her decision. If God had provided the money as an answer to my prayer, then how could she refuse? You can imagine Linda's surprise when the check arrived to learn that not only had Bob paid for all expenses for the entire trip, but he had also included an extra amount of money which was enough to cover the costs of all her vaccinations and personal supplies! Linda was overwhelmed at how God had supplied her every need!

We began planning the children's program, talking about all the things that we would need. We would take Bible costumes and tell the stories just like we did on *Kids Time*. We made a list of action songs to teach the children and decided which mission stories to tell. Not knowing what to fully expect, we decided to be flexible and just go with the flow when we got there.

When we first arrived in Africa, I was overwhelmed with just how beautiful the country of South Africa actually is. I had imagined the terrain would be like a desert with elephants, lions, and tigers crouching in the bushes. I'm sure this mental picture was from all the mission stories that I had heard as a little girl. But I didn't see anything like that, although I did have a brief glimpse of monkeys hanging in trees. Instead, I saw rolling grassy hilltops and low mountain ranges with lots of green foliage. Linda was equally impressed. I had my camera out like the typical tourist, snapping photos and trying to capture all the beauty around me.

It was late when we crossed the border into Swaziland, and the night air was cold. A large group of children, dressed in their Pathfinder uniforms, were waiting to welcome us. Not knowing when we would arrive, they had waited at

A group of Pathfinders waited for hours at the Swaziland border to welcome us. This photo appeared on the front page of the newspaper the next day.

the border for hours. They held up a big welcome banner and even did a few marching routines. The press was there as well, and the next day Linda and I were on the front page of the local newspaper, surrounded by smiling kids. Wow! What a welcome!

When it came time to go to our motels that evening, we faced our first challenge. There had not been enough rooms reserved for everyone. We drove around from motel to motel trying to find a place to stay. By now, it was the wee hours of the morning, and I thought my eyes could not stay open another minute. Finally we found a motel with a vacancy. However, my feelings of relief were short-lived. When I walked into the room and looked around, every cell in my body screamed to go home! My old fears gripped me once more. The room was dirty, and the sheets on the bed looked as if several people had slept on them since the last time they had been washed. I started to put my suitcase on the cabinet and stifled a scream. "Sis, is that mouse droppings or bugs?"

Linda came over to get a closer look. "Both," she said with disgust. "But they're too large to be from mice; they look more like rat droppings to me. And those things right there are some kind of beetle—I think," she said pointing in their direction.

We were thankful for mosquito nets that sealed completely, keeping out not only mosquitoes, but larger insects and rats.

"Oh yikes! I'm so glad that we have sleeping bags and mosquito tents. At least we know there won't be any unwelcome guests in our bed." Again, I was thankful for the generous donation which had allowed me to purchase special tents for each of us that were completely enclosed. The netting was so fine it would keep out the tiniest flea.

Linda and I both laughed out loud. We would just have to chalk this up as "going with the flow." We struggled to get our tents set up, and I couldn't help thinking how our husbands would be having a good laugh if they could see us now! We did finally figure it out, and as we lay in bed listening to the unfamiliar sounds of the night, as well as the rats scurrying around the room, I thanked God for giving us our angels to watch over us.

"Sis, are you awake?" I asked.

"Yes, I'm awake."

"I just love Bob Schaefer!"

"I do, too!" We both started to laugh.

I had never met this man, but I loved him for his kind and generous heart! I couldn't imagine having to experience this alone. "Sis, I'm so glad you're here. If you weren't here, I would be in this room all by myself. I was just thanking God for you and for Bob."

The first week went by quickly; we were busy from morning till night. Each day was filled with eager children just waiting for the program to begin. There were two thousand children, and some days more than that. Many crowded around outside, unable to fit under the tent and escape the hot sun. The children loved our Bible stories and the costumes, but dressing up was difficult for those telling the stories as the heat under their robes was almost unbearable. Linda was in charge of "Story Time," and our friends, Mary Sukow and Pat Taylor, helped. They acted out the Bible stories, and the kids' eyes went wide with excitement. We had to use an interpreter because although many children spoke English, the

In one of the villages we taped a program for Kids Time. *All the villagers were quite fascinated. Moses Primo Jr. is behind the camera.*

More than 2,000 AIDS orphans attended camp meeting every day. They loved to sing and were the most well-behaved kids I have ever seen.

majority spoke only their native Swaziland language.

Linda also told the continued story of "Dookie, Sookie, and Big Mo." Oh, how the kids loved that story! She would always end at a very exciting part, and even when the program was over, kids would follow her wherever she went begging to hear about what happened to Big Mo. It was easy for me to understand that God didn't bring Linda on this trip just for me; He had brought her to Africa to touch the hearts of these special children.

I think their favorite part of the program was singing. I have never heard so many kids singing so loudly in all my life! We taught them songs, and then they wanted us to learn some of their African songs. I can only describe the music as absolutely beautiful. I imagine that's what the music will be like in heaven. These kids sang with such energy and enthusiasm, their eyes dancing with joy! It was like nothing I have ever heard before, and I wish I had been able to capture it on tape to hear over and over again, although it is seared in my memory forever.

Most of those children were orphans, and my heart ached as I looked at each precious face. There were so many thousands of them that it was virtually impossible for caregivers to provide anything more than their basic physical needs—mainly food and water. I thought about how God loves each of them and how hard it must be for Him to see so much suffering. *Dear Jesus, please wrap each one of these precious children in Your arms and let them feel and know how very much You love them. Help them to realize how special they are to You. Please use us in a special way to share Your love with them.*

More times than I care to remember, children would come and throw their arms around me and plead for me to be their mother. It was almost more than I could bear. There was one little boy in particular whose face I can still see in my mind. He always pushed to sit on the front row and hung on my every word. If someone tried to get in front of him, he would push or shove them away, fiercely defending "his spot." Each day, when the meeting was over, he would fight his way through the crowd for his hug, not wanting to let go. I am guessing he was around five or six years old—dirty and scantily dressed.

"Please, you must take me with you. Please be my mama. I love you, Auntie Brenda. I wish to live with you. Please take me to America." He had barely gotten the words out when there was a rush of children all wanting the same thing. I honestly wanted to adopt them all! I looked past the dirty faces, into the eyes of God's precious children. For a brief moment I actually contemplated what it would take to adopt that one little boy who had so successfully stolen my heart, but after praying about it I knew it was impossible. God had given me a world of children through the ministry of *Kids Time* on Three Angels Broadcasting Network, and it would not be feasible to focus on just one. As painful as it was, this was the reality. I can see why God commissioned each of us to help those less fortunate. I thought of Matthew 25:40: "Inasmuch as you did it to one of the least of these My brethren, you did it to Me."

I soon learned that God had not brought me to South Africa to minister only to the children. At the end of the week I was asked to share my testimony about being a battered wife and how God had rescued me from a life of pain and misery. About five thousand men and woman were all gathered under a gigantic tent. The man in charge explained that many women in the audience had been abused. "Our women suffer a great deal," he explained, "and they need to hear your message."

This was very unexpected; I hadn't planned on giving my testimony.

Lord, what can I possibly tell them? I've heard the women here suffer so greatly; they have surely endured more pain than I have. My experience pales in comparison with theirs. Precious Jesus, please give me the words that You want me to say and use my story to bless someone else. I don't understand why You want me to share my testimony, but I am willing, trusting You for strength and courage. Could You please give me a good interpreter so that the people will understand the message You want them to hear? In Your holy name I pray, Amen.

God answered my prayer with the most incredible translator. Even her voice reflected the same expressions as mine! Several times I looked over at her, and tears were streaming down her face. When the meeting was over, so many people wanted to share their own stories of pain and abuse that it was impossible to speak to them all.

One man came to me with tears. He beat his wife, he admitted, and he had never understood how terrible this was until he heard me speak. He asked for prayer because he didn't want to be that kind of man anymore.

Another woman told how her life was not worth living, how every day her husband beat and raped her, sometimes bringing other men home to abuse her, as well. She showed me the evidence of fresh bruises, burns, and cuts from a knife. She was sobbing and threw her arms around me. When she managed to compose herself a little, she looked into my face and said, "I don't know how to thank you. Before tonight, I wanted to take my life. Now, for the first time, I have hope. If Jesus can save you, then He can save me too!"

One after another, these women shared stories so horrible that I felt sick to my stomach. I handed out my business cards to those that could not wait in line to speak to me so that they could contact me later. What a horrible sinful world this is! Surely Jesus must come soon; the world can't possibly get much worse! That night, long after the others in my cabin were fast asleep, I lay in bed—safe inside my mosquito tent—and cried.

Lord, I prayed, *oh, how this must make Your heart break! I don't know how You can stand to look down on this world and see so much pain and suffering. Thank You for using me tonight to bring others the hope that they need to go on. Please always make me willing, Lord, to serve You even when it's something that I don't want to do. Please keep me in Your plan and use me in a special way to be a powerful soul winning tool for You. I love You so much, Jesus, and I thank You for the many blessings You have given me. I know I am not worthy! Please keep my eyes focused always on You and let me not get sidetracked by the evils of this world. I thank You for hearing and answering my prayer. In Your precious holy name, Amen.*

From 2,000 to 7,000 people came each day when we set up to distribute clothing. They stood for hours, hoping to go home with shoes, clothes, and medicine.

The second week we focused on the next phase of the mission. We had collected clothing and supplies to pass out to the orphans at various villages throughout Swaziland. Each day we were at a different location, usually at a school or public building. In some places five thousand to seven thousand people waited in line. They had been told that clothes and shoes would be given away, so they came in droves. Most had walked for hours to be there. Unlike our experience in the Dominican Republic, these people waited patiently in the hot sun for their turn. Amazingly, I didn't see any pushing or shoving—just a hopeless resolve that they must wait.

That first day was heart wrenching for me. It took several hours to open the bales of clothing and sort them into piles on the ground. Then fifty to a hundred people were let inside the gate for their turn to choose something to wear. Each person could choose one top, one skirt or pair of pants, and one pair of shoes. They had fifteen minutes

Here people are frantically rummaging through clothes in hopes of finding something their size before being rushed out the door. Any attempt to organize this mess was useless!

to find something and then they were rushed out the back door—but not before a volunteer worker marked a large X on their hand with a black marking pen to prevent people from getting in line twice.

I tried to help people find something in their size, but it was like looking for a needle in a haystack. Most people, unable in that short amount of time to find something that fit them, just grabbed anything so they could bargain with others when they went outside. Just watching the whole process made me feel sick to my stomach; there seemed to be no dignity for these desperate people.

To make matters worse, I soon realized that most of the people

The smile on this little girl's face says it all!

would rather have shoes than clothing. We had brought only approximately five thousand pairs of shoes, and these were gone the first day! I watched in shock as first one and then another individual pleaded for shoes. They would try to squeeze a size ten foot into a size four shoe, insisting that it fit perfectly. Somehow, some shoes had arrived with no mate, so we saw people walking away with one shoe on one foot and a different kind of shoe on the other foot. And the amazing thing was that they were smiling and happy—just to have shoes of any kind! My mind couldn't comprehend it all.

The next day, in the midst of all the chaos, one girl came to me wanting help finding clothes. She was especially excited because I actually found something that would fit her. As I led her to the exit line, she stopped and asked, "But please, Miss, where are my shoes? I must have shoes." I had to tell her that there were no more shoes. I was so very sorry, but there just hadn't been enough for everyone.

She then lifted her bare foot up for me to see, and I gasped as I looked at the most callused foot I had ever seen! The bottom had deep ridges that resembled the creases on the sole of a tennis shoe. I had never seen anything like it in my life. There were even some small stones and twigs caught between the ridges. It looked so painful, I winced. She was now pulling at my arm again, pleading for shoes. I shook my head once more, emphasizing that there were no more shoes. She then took the precious clothes that

Mothers carry their children on their backs in Africa. This lady was so grateful for the clothes that I was able to find for her and her baby, but she was terribly disappointed that the shoes were all gone!

were in her arms and thrust them at me, saying, "Please, I must have shoes. I have no shoes. The ground is so cold, and I walk many miles for water each day. You can have my clothes, just give me shoes."

This was more than I could take, but there was nothing I could do. I gave her back the clothing and led her to the exit line once more. As I walked away, tears rolled down her face as she continued pleading. I felt dizzy and sick at my stomach as I quickly pushed my way through the crowd to get to the side of the building where I couldn't be seen and burst into tears.

Oh Lord, I don't think I can stand to see much more of this. How much suffering has to take place before You come? Jesus, I don't understand, and I hate it that I can do so little to relieve their pain and hopelessness. I have been blessed with so much, and they have nothing! I know that soon I will return home to a nice warm house, a soft bed, and food to eat, yet these people have nowhere to go. They have no hope of a better life! Oh precious Lord, please show me what to do. Please give me the strength to carry on. I can't do this without You. Please show me a better way to help these people.

I had just dried my eyes, taken a deep breath, and was starting to make my way back to the distribution site to do whatever I could when I ran into Ray and Jackie Brosseuk. They had given up trying to help people find clothes because the day was ending and panic was setting in as those people still waiting in line could see there soon would be nothing left for them. In desperation they started grabbing whatever they could as we watched helplessly from the sidelines. Many had walked miles and miles, waiting in line for more than twelve hours, only to walk away empty-handed!

Ray and Jackie could see that I was upset and asked what was wrong. When I told them about the girl who so desperately needed shoes, they nodded with understanding. Then they shared with me the vision for ministry that God had given them. Ray, who was raised in a missionary family, had learned from his parents what worked and what didn't. Through trial and error, he and Jackie had discovered useful and dignified ways to help people in need.

They told me that for years they have shipped supplies to various countries—and they always go to that country and make sure the supplies go to the people who need them. They sit down with the church leadership of that particular country and ask, "What do you need, and how can we help?"

Once the clothes, food, or other supplies arrive, Ray and Jackie divide it between all the churches and let the church members sort it all out. This also allows the members the blessing of helping their own communities. After everything is sorted, the members take the items to the individual villages, letting the people get the sizes they need in a dignified manner. No waiting in lines or fighting for something they can't even wear! This helps members find other ways to help, as well, and friendships are formed. Later, evangelistic series are planned in the villages, and now people are willing to come. When personal contact is made, the people's hearts are open and receptive to hearing about Jesus, the Savior of the world.

"To us, this is not just about meeting people's physical needs. It is about meeting their spiritual needs, winning souls for the kingdom," Jackie said, wiping a tear from her cheek.

"That is why we do what we do," Ray added.

Wow, I thought, *this makes perfect sense!*

"I want to be a part of your ministry," I told them, "because this approach is something that I can wholeheartedly endorse! God has called me in a different direction, and I can't spend the time needed to do what you do. But I can help raise funds and build awareness of the need.

My sister, Linda, and I had the privilege of meeting the Queen Mother of Swaziland. She rules jointly with the king. Linda presented her with one of Margie's bookmarks.

When we get home, I'm going to do whatever I can to help you. What is the name of your ministry?"

"Partners for Others," Ray answered. "We would be thrilled to work with you, and I know God will do some great and mighty things."

The next day wasn't any better for me emotionally, but God had given me a renewed strength just to do what I could. Linda was helping first one and then another of the children to find clothes, and I

We also had the privilege of meeting with her royal highness, the Queen of Zulu. She told us that she loves Jesus very much and that she has a burden to help the people of her country learn of Him too.

decided to do the same. Linda had the same feelings I did about some of the problems we saw, but she had determined from the beginning just to help the best she could. So she rolled up her sleeves and got to work. I love that about her. And she always prays through every situation. She had been a big comfort the night before as I cried on her shoulder about the hopelessness of it all.

One boy, about twelve years old, was looking frantically through a pile of clothing that was mostly for girls. I walked over and told him I would like to help him. He got a big smile on his face and said, "Yes, thank you to help me." I could tell that he understood only a few words of what I was saying, so I gently took his arm and led him over to where I had earlier seen a large pile of blue jeans. His eyes lit up like a Christmas tree when I held up a pair of jeans just his size. He grabbed them and hugged them as if they were the most precious possession he had ever owned. Then I spotted a bright blue T-shirt—brand new, with the tags still on it. Sure enough, when I held it up to him, it fit perfectly! His eyes now danced with excitement, and so did mine just seeing his joy! I started to lead him to the exit line, but when he realized where I was taking him, he stopped and said, "Please, to fix my glasses?" He pulled a pair of glasses from his pocket.

I could see that the lenses were shattered like a broken windshield. I shook my head, saying, "I wish I could help you, but we have no more glasses. We brought only three hundred pairs with us, and they were gone the first day. I'm so sorry, but I can't help you."

All of a sudden the joy that had been in his eyes just moments before was gone. With a look of terror on his face he thrust his clothes into my arms. "Please! You must fix my glasses."

Again I repeated that I was unable to fix his glasses. Upon hearing this he flung himself on the ground and wrapped his arms around my legs. His body was shaking all over, and with tears running down his cheeks, he looked up into my face.

"I cannot see; I cannot see," he kept repeating over and over again. By now, he was so distraught that he was no longer speaking English but had reverted to his African tongue. Of course, I couldn't understand a word so I yelled for a volunteer to come over.

"Please, tell me what he is saying. I don't understand."

The lady spoke to the boy, and after hearing what he had to say, she looked at me and tried to explain.

"In Swaziland, most orphans do not go to school. To go to school, you must first pay—or no school. Sometimes an orphan will be fortunate enough to find a sponsor, but this is very rare. This orphan boy is one of the lucky ones who found a sponsor; he has been in school only two weeks. Someone stepped on his glasses, and now he can't see to read. The schoolmaster told him that he is not allowed in school if he cannot see. If he does not have glasses by tomorrow, they will give his seat to someone else. Every child knows he will not have a good life without education, so school is very precious to him. He will not be so fortunate again. This is his only chance. Now he will probably spend his life in the streets as a beggar or worse!"

"Isn't there anything we can do? Can I buy him new glasses? Is there a place nearby where I could buy a simple pair of glasses?"

"No, there is no such store. You would have to take him to the big city that is far away. Glasses cost more than two hundred dollars. That is why you do not see many people wearing such things. Besides, he would not be allowed to go with you. No, I'm afraid there is nothing for you to do."

The lady pulled the boy to his feet and spoke to him firmly. She took the clothes from my arms and thrust them back into his. Then she pushed him toward the exit line, and he helplessly obeyed and walked away. I can still see his shoulders shaking with sobs as he walked out of sight.

This was too much. Once again, I ran to a safe place to release my tears. My heart was breaking, and I could do nothing but pray for Jesus to come soon. I prayed not only for the people in Africa, but for all those around the world who are suffering. I also prayed for the boy with the broken glasses, and I prayed for his broken dreams.

Sometimes things are out of our control, just like when I couldn't help the girl wanting shoes or the boy needing glasses. Life in this world is not fair, and all my prayers weren't enough to fix it. Sin has caused these problems, and they won't go away until Jesus comes and sin is ended. Passionately praying for these people is one thing, but it's not enough. God needs every one of His children to be concerned and caring for others.

Jesus set the example here on earth when He said, "Blessed are the poor in spirit, For theirs is the kingdom of heaven" (Matthew 5:3). Jesus didn't cause the suffering that takes place in this world. Instead, He came to save us and put an end to the suffering that Satan and sin have brought into our world.

Chapter 5

Doomed to Die, Destined to Live

Every good gift and every perfect gift is from above.
—James 1:17

I stared out the window of the van and watched as the headlights lit up the rugged road on which we were driving. The word *road* seems a bit of a stretch because it consisted of dirt, gravel, and huge ruts and crevices twisting and turning in ways that could only have been created by nature. I was jolted out of my seat by the sudden slamming of the brakes.

"What was that?" I asked, more to myself than to anyone in particular.

"Just a great, huge lion!" our driver yelled.

"Really? Oh, no! Can he attack us in this van? Are we safe?" Every hair on my body was standing on end.

Violet started laughing. "I was just kidding. It was probably a dog or something."

Letting out a breath, I cautiously relaxed back into my seat, hoping she was right. Violet stepped on the gas pedal once again, but was still giggling. We had been in Swaziland, South Africa, on our mission trip for more than a week. It hadn't taken Violet, our driver, long to figure out that I was very uncomfortable with the words *lion, tiger, leopard,* or basically any other wild animal! She had a wonderful sense of humor and loved to tease me about it.

Tonight, she had caught me off guard, as I was tired from a long hot day. We had been distributing clothing and medical care to over five thousand orphans! That in itself was exhausting, but what was even more draining was the emotional heartbreak of seeing so much suffering—hungry, filthy children wearing tattered, worn clothing, most of them barefoot. The look of hopelessness in their eyes was almost more than I could stand.

After a long day of work, Dr. Rukundo had treated our whole team to dinner at a fancy restaurant. The room was beautifully decorated, and the food delicious and artfully prepared. However, I hardly touched my pasta primavera because all I could think of was those poor starving kids that I had been with all day.

Dr. Rukundo, an American doctor, was in charge of trying to manage the AIDS epidemic for all of South Africa. He was so grateful for the help we were bringing to the people in Swaziland that he offered

I am standing with Dr. Eddie Rukundo in the restaurant where he hosted our entire group.

to treat us to dinner. This kind man talked throughout dinner and shared some of his challenges working with this horrible disease. It is unimaginable how AIDS is destroying whole generations. Many children are left not only without their parents but without any living relatives at all! This is too much for anyone to comprehend.

Yet I had been out to the villages and had seen it with my own eyes! I was horrified as I thought of the orphaned children dying of starvation, malnutrition, and various diseases.

Most didn't even have clean drinking water. There were over a hundred and fifty thousand AIDS orphans in the country. Soon one out of six people in the nation will be a child under the age of fifteen who has lost both parents to AIDS. I shuddered when I heard those statistics. These victims have no money and no means to obtain it. They are literally starving to death. Thousands face this hopeless reality.

As we drove toward our bungalow, my mind drifted back to the lines of children earlier in the day, eager to receive their clothing. A particular face had seared itself into my mind. It was the face of a young boy, probably around eight years old, who had pleaded with me to be his mother.

"Please, Miss, please be my mother. I am all alone. You must take me with you to America. I will work hard; you will see. I can work very hard."

I tried to explain to him that I could not be his mother, but he wasn't listening to my words, only terrified when I shook my head no. With determination he flung himself at my feet and wrapped both hands around my legs. With tears streaming down his dirty face, he pleaded once again, "But please, you must be my mother. I have no one. Please take me with you."

I reached down and wrapped my arms around him and told him that I loved him and that Jesus loved him and that he was never really alone. Jesus was his best Friend, and he could talk to Him anytime he wanted to. "But who is Jesus?" he asked. He looked puzzled as if I were speaking foolishness. Before I could answer, one of the village ladies came running up and jerked him away by the arm. He screamed to me with outstretched hand, "No, no! Please don't let her take me!" But his words fell on deaf ears as the lady hit him with a stick, scolding him to stay back with the other children. I stood there horrified, helpless to do anything but watch, as he disappeared into the crowd of orphans.

Oh how my heart aches even now just remembering! *Why didn't I ask him his name?* I wondered. *Oh Lord,* I prayed. *It doesn't matter. You know who he is. Please be with him tonight. Somehow, dear Jesus, let him find out who You are and that You love him!*

The car came to a complete stop, forcing my mind back to the present. We were outside *Gibela,* the place where we were staying, waiting for the gate to open. The entire grounds were surrounded by a high electric fence. Theresia, the owner, had told me that at night the voltage was increased to keep out lions and other wild animals. Inside this protected area were several bungalows, or guest houses. We waited for what seemed forever before the electric gate opened and we could drive through.

"Thanks so much, Violet. I really appreciate you driving us everywhere. If we had rental cars, we never would find our way all around by ourselves! Most streets don't even have signs to tell what road it is."

She laughed. "I'm glad to do it. I enjoy being with you, and all too soon you'll go back to the States, and I'll miss you very much. But you'll forget all about me!"

"No I won't; I'll miss you, too," I said as I slammed the door to the van. My sister Linda had already left, and I now searched in the darkness, looking for her. I headed down the steep slope toward our room, when I noticed Linda standing by a parked car.

"Sis, come look. Hurry! It's a baby; come see the baby!"

Linda was so excited she could hardly contain herself. I poked my head inside the car window, and there was a woman in the passenger's seat—and right next to her, just lying beside her, was the most adorable little baby.

The woman introduced herself as Sonya and went on to explain that this tiny, little baby had just been found in a field by a young boy. She had been in a plastic bag with her umbilical cord and placenta still attached. The boy had been walking home when he saw the bag moving. He ran to tell his parents, who in turn notified the police. It was the police who had brought the baby to Sonya.

Sonya runs an orphanage, and she already had more babies than she could take care of. She had brought the baby to us because she knew there was a doctor in our group. She was also hoping that someone among the Americans would want this little girl.

Linda scooped up the precious bundle in her arms and carried her to the room where we were staying. Sonya followed close behind.

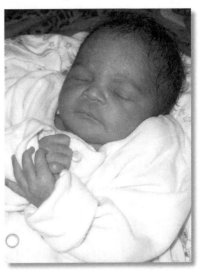

Word of the "baby in a bag" spread quickly, and it wasn't long until most of our group was crowded into our tiny bungalow. Everyone was in shock and talking at once. First one and then another insisted that they would adopt this little gift from God. We each took turns holding her, and as I held her in my arms and looked into her precious face, I marveled that she had lived through such an ordeal. *Why, she must be only a few hours old!* What a traumatic entrance into this world.

This photo of Keiara, the abandoned baby, was taken just a few hours after she was brought to us . . . rescued from a plastic bag!

Listening to Sonya, it became even more apparent to me that God had spared this little one's life for a reason! Sonya explained that throwing away babies is a common occurrence in Swaziland. In fact, so many babies were being thrown into the sewers that the Queen Mother decreed that mothers who would just leave their unwanted babies where they could be found alive, wouldn't be prosecuted for abandoning them.

Before you judge these mothers harshly, consider what they are facing. There is not enough food and clean water to supply the needs of the children that they already have. To listen to one more child's cries of hunger is just too much to bear. So, out of desperation, the mother chooses to end the life of her newborn, thinking that it is much kinder to end its little life as soon as possible, than to let it slowly starve to death. But since the Queen Mother's decree, more abandoned babies were being found alive. Even so, by the time they were found, a large number of these unwanted infants were dismembered and partially devoured by a wild dog or other animal or had simply died from exposure to the harsh elements.

I handed this precious bundle to Linda and stepped back to process what was happening right before my eyes. I watched as different ones took turns holding her, each declaring love for her and their plans to make her a part of their lives. Suddenly it occurred to me that Ray and Jackie were missing from this scene. Ray and Jackie Brosseuk had come on this mission trip with their three children and had even raised the funds for two of the containers of supplies we had brought with us. They had been involved in mission work for years. In fact, Ray, whose parents were missionaries, grew up living most of his life in various countries. Ray and Jackie had worked for a while in Fiji and had adopted a little girl there who was now five years old. I knew instantly that this little abandoned African girl was going to be the newest addition to their family! I can't explain how I knew. I just knew!

Quickly, I ran to the bungalow where Ray and Jackie were staying and banged on the door. The lights were out, and they were probably already in bed, but I didn't care. This was too important. Jackie and Ray both came to the door. They could sense the urgency in my knocking.

"Jackie, Jackie, come and see the baby! A baby girl has been found in a plastic bag in a field, and a lady brought her to us! Come quick; you guys have to see this baby!"

I turned and ran back toward my room with both of them following close behind. Jackie took one look at the little head peeking out from the bundle of blankets and then did something very strange. Instead of racing over and asking to hold the baby like everyone else had, she stood silently for a moment just looking at this precious baby. Then she turned and rapidly walked back outside. I quickly followed her and found Ray was already there, tears rolling down his cheeks. I looked first at Ray and then at Jackie, who was crying too.

Seeing the look of confusion on my face, Ray explained. "She looks so much like our little Katie. If we hadn't adopted Katie, her life would have been so different. She wouldn't have the opportunities she has now, and most certainly she wouldn't have known the kind of love that we give her. How can anyone leave such a precious baby alone to die!" Ray was so overcome with emotion that he could no longer speak, so Jackie continued.

"You see," she paused a moment and then went on, "we just love Katie so much. She's brought so much joy to our family that we can't imagine life without her. I don't dare hold that little one because I might not be able to let her go."

I gave them both a hug and told them I understood. I heard someone calling my name, and Jackie motioned for me to go. I could tell that they needed a moment alone, so I went back inside and began to pray. *Lord, if it is Your will for this little girl to be part of their family, then please work a miracle and let this all work out. I don't know why she was brought to us, but You do, and I believe that You have a special plan for her. I don't believe it was an accident that she was brought here tonight. Lord, if You want Ray and Jackie to adopt this precious little girl, then please give them the courage to come and hold this baby. Give them a peace that they will know You are with them. I am lifting up this special family that Your will be done in their lives!*

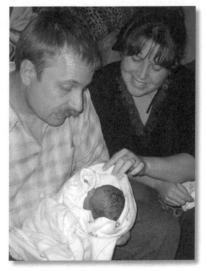

"Sis, I think this baby's hungry. Where is that can of infant formula that you bought?" Linda asked.

"I don't know. Isn't it with the rest of the stuff we are taking to the baby in the village tomorrow?"

"No, I don't see it anywhere," Linda replied.

Ray and Jackie are holding Keiara for the first time. The baby is only a few hours old.

"I'll look in the cupboard. Maybe someone put it with the rest of our groceries."

After several minutes of rummaging through the cans of food, I jumped up and shouted, "I found the formula!" but I could say no more. My mouth fell open, and I couldn't believe my eyes. While I was behind the counter searching, Ray and Jackie had come back inside and were now seated on the couch. Jackie was holding the baby!

Thank You, Jesus, I prayed silently. *Thank You for answering my prayer. You do have a plan for this child, and her new family is holding her right now! I just know it! You are such an awesome God!*

I was overwhelmed with what God was doing. Jackie and Ray were so filled with emotion that tears rolled down their cheeks as they smiled and cooed at the precious little girl. And the baby was responding. So much love was wrapped up in that moment, it is difficult to explain. A few minutes later, their eldest daughter, fifteen-year-old Cassandra, was beside them, and the joy on her face was evident! This little family had bonded instantly! It was nothing short of amazing.

Several people grabbed a duffle bag filled with infant clothing and began rummaging through it. Outfit after outfit was held up to her little body, but even the smallest of the clothes were too big. Grabbing the tiniest nightgown she could find, Linda said, "Well, we can make this work by rolling up the sleeves."

Jackie carefully undressed the little baby, talking gently to her the entire time. Like any new mother, she was counting the fingers and toes, making sure the baby was perfect. But where was that foul odor coming from? After careful inspection, Jackie determined it was not coming from the diaper area. It was the umbilical cord. Usually when a baby is born, the cord is cut right away, but in this instance the cord and placenta had been attached for several hours and was now rotten, creating a terrible smell. The baby was dressed in only an old tattered T-shirt, without a diaper of any kind. Several of us were thinking out loud as to what could serve as a diaper.

"Maybe you could use a washcloth," someone suggested. A wash-cloth proved far too big, but with nothing else available, it would have to do. Someone else shared a package of baby wipes.

I leaned over and whispered to Jackie, "You need to be careful to protect yourself because there is the very real possibility that she could be HIV positive. I don't want to alarm you, but being a nurse, I need to warn you of the danger of handling bodily fluids."

She nodded that she understood, and carefully Jackie cleansed her little bottom and then fastened the washcloth in place. It was so huge that everyone laughed. The baby was so tiny she could almost fit into the palm of one's hand.

I handed Jackie a bottle of hand sanitizer, and she poured a gener-ous amount on her hands. I couldn't help but think how sad it was that this tiny little baby could very likely be doomed to die. *But, God can work miracles, and we serve a God of miracles,* I reminded myself.

Jackie looked up at Ray and gave him a knowing look, and then Ray disappeared. It was the secret language that only a husband and wife share, speaking volumes without uttering a single word. An hour later, Ray returned with a box of diapers. He had driven almost twenty minutes over those bumpy, crevice-filled roads to find a market that would sell him diapers. The store was closing just as he pulled into the parking lot. The lights were already turned off, but Ray quickly banged on the door and pleaded with the shopkeeper to sell him some dia-pers. After listening to Ray's story of the "baby in a bag," the man's heart was touched, and he reopened his store.

By the time Ray returned, Jackie had the little one sound asleep. She had been fed, diapered, and now was sleeping like an angel. We were all thankful for the baby bottles we had found in the duffle bag. It was as if before we had even left the United States, God had already prepared for this very need.

Everyone was still gathered around in awe knowing something mi-raculous had just happened and that we were all a part of it. It was getting late, and now Ray was holding the little sleeping baby. He was gently stroking her cheek with one of his big strong fingers when I said, "Would you two consider taking this baby? I mean, making her a part of your family?"

Jackie looked at Ray who was still trying to fight back the tears as he held the tiny life in his hands. They both looked at me and nodded.

"Yes, if it's possible," Ray managed to say.

"Would you like to keep her for the night?" Sonya asked.

Jackie looked surprised to hear herself say, "Yes."

Ray quickly searched Jackie's face until Jackie assured him, "I'll be OK, Honey."

After that, it was a whirlwind of activity as everyone helped gather up the infant clothes, blankets, formula, baby bottles, and five more wash cloths. Gently, Jackie carried the little girl. But where would she sleep?

Cassandra quickly emptied Katie's smallest suitcase and placed a pillow inside. That night Jackie spent much of the time awake. Not because of Little Peach, as Jackie had begun calling the baby, for she woke up only twice in the night for food. Jackie was awake because she was praying that God would make it possible for this little one to be a permanent part of their family. In just a few short hours, Little Peach had managed to steal their hearts, and Jackie had fallen head over heals in love with her. Even the possibility of ripping her out of their lives at this point was unthinkable.

Katie was thrilled to hold this precious baby girl. She hoped the baby would become her sister. Keiara is two days old in this photo.

The next morning at worship, Ray shared with our group a new prayer request. He and Jackie lived in Canada, and because of that country's socialized health care system, strict adoption laws were in place. If this baby tested HIV positive, the Canadian government would never allow the adoption to go through. To make matters worse, the odds were not in the baby's favor. Swaziland has the largest population of HIV and AIDS infected people of any country in the entire world! India was second. We needed a miracle!

It was easy to see that this family had already totally bonded with this baby. Katie's eyes were dancing as she talked about her new baby sister. Even Kyle and Cassandra found it difficult to contain their joy at this new addition to their family.

"What will you name her?" I asked Jackie.

Jackie looked at me cautiously and said, "I'm not going to give her a name just yet. First, I need to know that she will be ours, and then we will give her a name."

I nodded my head that I understood the depths of a mother's love. Already, I knew that should the adoption not go through, Jackie's heart would be shattered! I began to pray silently. *Oh, Lord, please make it possible for this baby to be part of this precious family. I know You have a plan, and I am trusting You, Lord, that Your will be done in their lives. This little baby needs a home, and there is already so much love in this one. I'm praying for a miracle that this baby will be healthy! But I am not asking for anything that You cannot do, for You are a God of miracles! I pray that Your will be done. In Jesus' precious holy name, Amen.*

Dr. Rukundo had invited our whole group to visit his clinic and tour the Baylor Bristol-Myers Squibb Children's Clinical Center in the capital city of Mbabane where he worked. Ray and Jackie arrived earlier than everyone else and went directly to Dr. Rukundo's office. You can imagine how surprised he was to see them holding this tiny little baby and to hear all the details of how she had survived the first few hours of life, ending up in the care of this Canadian family.

When Ray explained how critical it was that this little baby *not* be HIV positive, the doctor just shook his head. "I'm afraid there's not much hope of that, but bring her in here and let me check her over."

Gently the doctor examined her and was surprised to see how remarkably healthy she was. He removed a very foul smelling portion of her umbilical cord. But other than that, he said she looked amazingly fit. She was given her first immunizations and weighed in at just five pounds three ounces!

"Can you test her now for HIV?" Ray asked.

"No, I'm afraid not. This hospital will not test a baby under six weeks of age."

Jackie let out a gasp. "How can we possibly wait another day, much less six weeks? We need to know as soon as possible if this baby can be ours!"

"Well, there is one thing we can do," Dr. Rukundo offered.

"What? Please tell us, all this waiting is killing us!"

"You must understand that it is a test that tells us whether *the mother* is HIV positive. The baby can't be tested accurately until she is six to eighteen months old. It is kind of complicated, but let me try to explain. If the test is negative, that will mean that the mother was negative and therefore that the baby will be negative. This is the best that we can hope for because then the baby will be perfectly healthy. However, if the test turns out to be positive, it means only that *the mother* is HIV positive. It does not necessarily mean that the baby will be positive, as well. There is always a chance that a baby born to an HIV-positive mother is actually HIV negative, but it can take up to a year or two to know that for sure."

Ray and Jackie sat there stunned at what they were hearing. "Let me get this straight," Ray said. "If this test comes back positive, then it could be two years before the baby would be cleared for adoption?"

"That's correct," Dr. Rukundo replied. "You will have to come back tomorrow and take her to a private hospital in Mbabane to perform the test."

Ray and Jackie were numb, trying to process everything they had just heard. "Thank you, doctor. We appreciate all you've done. We'll be there tomorrow."

Later, as Dr. Rukundo gave our group a tour of the hospital, Ray and Jackie's fourteen year-old son, Kyle, walked past an open door. What he saw inside made him sick to his stomach. Wanting to protect his mother, he cried out, "Mom, don't look!" But it was too late. In the open doorway, lying on a bed, was a child so emaciated by AIDS that it instantly made her nauseous. Holding her precious bundle even tighter to her chest, she prayed, *Oh no, this can't happen to this little girl. Please, Lord, not this baby! Please, dear God, save her!*

During the rest of the tour, Jackie refused to look inside any doorways for fear of what she might see. She shuddered at the mere thought of what it would mean if the test were positive. *This little baby could look just like . . . , but oh, no! I must not think of it. I must believe,* she told herself.

All Ray and Jackie could think about was how much they needed this little baby in their arms to test negative. They silently prayed for a miracle!

Linda and I had just finished our tour of the clinic when we saw Ray and Jackie sitting on a bench outside the hospital. Jackie relayed everything that Dr. Rukundo had said, ending with, "So you see, we need a miracle. The test just has to turn out negative."

"The good news is that we serve a God that is in the miracle-making business," I reassured them, "and I don't believe for one moment that God brought this little baby into your lives just to tear her away from you! God has a reason for everything, and right now we just need to trust Him."

"That's right, Sis," Linda agreed. "I believe that, too. In fact, let's just say a prayer for you right now."

We formed a circle, and I began to pray. *"O Lord, what an awesome God You are. I lift up Ray and Jackie and this precious little girl to You as we are in need of a miracle. If it be Your will, please let this tiny baby test negative for HIV. I know this is asking a lot when she is born in a country ravaged by AIDS, but Jesus, You are a God of miracles, and we know that with You, nothing is impossible. You have promised in Matthew chapter seven, verse seven, that if we ask it shall be given, and right now I am claiming that promise. We are asking and trusting in You because we know that You love this baby and that You know what is best for her. I pray, believing that You hear and answer our prayers. In Your precious holy name, Amen."*

Next Linda began to pray. *"Precious heavenly Father, we are so thankful that You have saved this little baby. We know You must have a special plan for her life. You alone have placed her in Ray's and Jackie's arms to love and care for her. Please bless her as she is tested tomorrow. Please make the tests come out in her favor. Lord, we are asking You to part the Red Sea for Ray and Jackie so that they will be able to adopt this precious little one and take her home with them to Canada. You are their only hope. Only You can cut through the red tape to make this happen. We are claiming Jeremiah chapter thirty-three, verse three, in behalf of this little one. You have promised to answer and show great and mighty things that we know not of. In Jesus' name we are asking, believing, and thanking You for Your answer, Amen."*

When Linda finished her prayer, we were all choked with emotion. We stared at this precious little girl for a few minutes, and then Linda and I took turns holding her. She was so tiny, so helpless, and so absolutely beautiful!

"God certainly has something special planned for you," I said to her softly as I stroked her curls.

Linda looked at Ray and Jackie and said, "God didn't bring her into your life without a purpose! I can't wait to see what God is going to do next."

Ray cleared his throat, trying to compose himself. "We believe that, too. Thanks so much for your prayers. Please keep on praying."

The next day, Ray and Jackie left early for the two-hour drive back to Mbabane for the test. They had to squeeze the baby's little finger so hard to get enough blood for testing that it actually turned black and blue.

"There, there, Little Peach. It's OK. Don't worry; it's all over now. Everything is going to be OK," Jackie spoke reassuringly to the baby.

Now the hard part began. Each minute that ticked by felt more like a year. Every member in our group was praying for this little baby whom we had now started calling Baby Hope. Ray and Jackie prayed almost continuously as did their children. Even little Katie prayed for a "good test for our baby."

The next day Dr. Rukundo called. Afterwards, Ray came out of their bungalow smiling from ear to ear. "Well, at least we have some good news. The doctor said that all the tests for hepatitis and the other diseases have come back negative. In fact, he said that she is amazingly healthy; all her blood work looks great. The only test we don't know about is the HIV test. We still have to wait a few more days for those results!"

Jackie had now joined Ray and was holding Baby Hope. "The doctor said for her to be so healthy is a very good sign. It means that the mother was not malnourished, which gives us hope that the mother was healthy!"

Ray continued. "This is very good news, very good news indeed. But we can't assume anything yet. We need to be patient and trust in the Lord. I have to tell you, though, that I believe God does have His hand on this little girl!" Ray could hardly contain his jubilation.

We gathered around for a thank-you prayer and continued to pray that the HIV test would be negative.

Two days later, our Swaziland mission was completed, and everyone was getting ready to leave. We gathered together for one last worship and prayer that God would indeed work a miracle in this baby's life.

Linda and I each vowed to make Baby Hope part of our daily prayer. So you can imagine how elated I was when Ray called from Africa just two days after we had returned home. Baby Hope had tested negative for HIV! I was screaming on the phone with excitement.

"Oh, and I thought you should know that we have named our little girl Keiara Thembi Dawn Brosseuk. *Keiara* means "little dark one,"

Thembi means "hope" in the Swati language. So her name means "little dark one, hope dawns."

I could hardly speak; I was overjoyed!

"Ray, thank you so much for calling. I can't tell you how wonderful it is to hear this news. Please give Jackie an extra hug for me and tell her that our God we serve is a God of miracles!"

"That's for sure. He certainly demonstrated that today. Yes, I'll tell her. Please tell the others for me, will you?"

"Absolutely! I can't wait to give them this good news!"

The next person I called was sister Linda, and we prayed together over the phone, praising and thanking God for His goodness.

Little did the Brosseuk family realize that this was just the first hurdle toward making Keiara part of their family. There were many heartbreaking challenges and struggles along the way, yet each one drew them closer to Jesus.

They literally put their lives on hold, changing their plane tickets and making arrangements to stay in Africa as long as it took for the adoption to go through. Their faith was tested each day, and God rewarded them greatly.

In just two months' time, all the paperwork was finalized, and the Brosseuk family headed home to Canada with their newest family member safe in their arms—legal in every way. God performed a series of miracles to bring Keiara into the Brosseuk family. The first miracle was that she had survived her cruel entrance into this world, saved from certain death. Another miracle, that she was completely healthy and HIV negative. Still yet an-

The Brosseuk family at home in Canada. From left to right: Cassandra, Katie, Ray, Jackie, Keiara, and Kyle.

other miracle was that she could be adopted outside her country. In the process of adopting Keiara, Ray and Jackie learned that in the last five years only two babies had been adopted *outside* the country of Swaziland, and that each of those adoptions had taken two years! It was nothing short of a miracle that in just two months' time she was legally theirs. And the amazing thing is that from the time she was just a few hours old, she was placed in the loving arms of her new family and never once spent a moment away from them. They were bonded in the heart from the

Official documentation stating that Keiara had been "dumped" (abandoned). This was one of the certificates needed to proceed with her adoption.

first moment they held her in their arms! Keiara Thembi Dawn Brosseuk was "doomed to die, but destined to live." Little Dark One, hope did dawn!

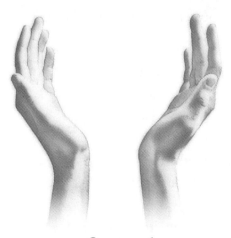

CHAPTER 6

WHAT FOR AND HOW MUCH?

It shall come to pass
that before they call, I will answer;
and while they are still speaking, I will hear.
—Isaiah 65:24

*I*t was one of those days when every cell in my body wanted to curl up on the couch and enjoy relaxing with a good book and a hot drink. But as I looked at the stacks of mail on my desk and the long list of things to do, I knew taking time off was a luxury I couldn't afford.

I was in the middle of producing sixty new *Kids Time* programs. Normally I would have been at 3ABN during the week, but we were changing segments, which meant three days off: one day to tear down the old set, one day to put up the new one, and one day to light it! With three days at home, I was determined to catch up on all the work that had piled up while I was gone. There were letters to write, phone calls to make, and two cases of videos to watch of kids who wanted to be on the program.

I was only an hour into my work, when the ringing of the cell phone interrupted my peaceful morning. "Hello, Brenda speaking."

"Hi Bibby, this is Jim. Are you in Tennessee today?"

"Yes, I'm home for three days and pretty excited about it! Where are you?"

"I'm at Southern Adventist University in Collegedale, recruiting students." As Youth Director for the Michigan Conference, Jim traveled every year to various colleges interviewing potential staff members. "Why don't you come down this afternoon and spend the day with me? It's been ages since I've seen you, and I miss you."

I looked at the stacks of mail in front of me and thought of all the things I *had* to do. There was no way I could afford to take a day off! "Jim, you'll be so busy interviewing, I wouldn't even get ten minutes with you! Remember last year, you barely had time to say hello?"

"I know, I know," Jim said, "but I'm sure it won't be like that this time! Of course you're busy, but all that work will still be there when you return! I really would love to see you."

Once again I surveyed the piles on my desk. Then I thought of my brother and how much I loved him. It was true; we both had such busy schedules, and it *was* difficult to find time to be together. *And family is important*, I reasoned.

"You're right; the work can wait, and I miss you, too. All right, I'll drive down this afternoon. Will you be at the same place as last year?"

"Yes, same place! I'm so glad you're coming, Bib."

When I hung up, I knew I'd made the right decision. I quickly made some phone calls that couldn't wait, and then drove the hour

Gail and Jim Micheff. My brother, Jim, is the Youth Director for the Michigan Conference; his wife, Gail, is the Associate Director of Family Life Ministries.

and fifteen minutes down I-75 from Knoxville to Collegedale, Tennessee. It was a beautiful day, and I actually enjoyed the ride. Before I knew it, I was at Exit 11 and had almost missed my turn.

I found my way to the student lounge and scanned the room. I saw other camp managers all doing the same thing my brother was doing—looking for the best students for summer camp staff. I didn't see Jim, but I did see my sister-in-law, Gail. She waved for me to come over. I gave her a warm hug, and we talked for a few minutes until more students showed up. She's a big help to my brother and was busy making appointments for students to talk with him. She had posted a sign-up page with an appointment every fifteen minutes. I walked over and casually glanced at the sheet to see if there were any openings. I thought I'd surprise Jim by putting my name on the list! But I was disappointed to see that the entire sheet was full.

A few seconds later, Jim stood up from behind his booth. He was getting ready to call his next appointment when he saw me. He waved and smiled and mouthed the words, "I'm so sorry," and then disappeared quickly for the next interview. I knew my only hope of seeing my brother was if someone canceled an appointment.

All afternoon I waited, but other than a quick "Hello," I never had an opportunity to visit with Jim. I spent my time talking with the students who were waiting for their appointments. I even had an opportunity to share Jesus with several who were there. But I only saw glimpses of Jim as he said goodbye to one student and greeted the next.

After standing in three-inch high heels for more than four hours, my feet were telling me it was time to go. There hadn't been even one cancellation! I waited until Jim was about to start the next interview and then signaled to him that I was leaving. I waved goodbye and mouthed the words, "I love you." He did the same, adding, "I'm so sorry, Sis!"

"It's OK," I said with a warm reassuring smile and then turned to leave.

I sank down into the comfortable seat of my car. My feet hurt, my back ached, and I was starving! I briefly thought of stopping to get something to eat, but then talked myself out of it since I was only a little more than an hour from home and eating out would take too much time.

As I pulled out of the parking lot and neared the Collegedale shopping center, the thought flashed through my mind that I should buy a book for a friend to help her deal with the loss of her daughter. I knew that there was a bookstore there, but as I was nearing the entrance, another thought came to me. It felt so good to sit down that I really didn't want to get out of the car and go through the hassle of picking out a book, standing in line to pay for it, and then walking back out to my car again. *Why do that,* I reasoned, *when I could buy a book online?* Then I said to myself, *Brenda, it is your own fault you wore three-inch heels! Get in there and buy that book!* Instantly I turned, just seconds before passing the entrance. God is so good! He gave me a parking space right next to the door! I groaned as I pulled myself out of my seat, shutting the door with a thud and clicking my remote button till I heard the beep that told me it was locked.

When I entered the building, bells tied to the inside of the front door made a loud jingle. A lady who was in the process of paying for her merchandise looked up and saw me. A surprised expression came over her face. Then she left her things on the counter and ran over to me!

"You're Brenda Walsh from *Kids Time!* Brenda Walsh from 3ABN!"

"Yes," I said, surprised and a bit embarrassed to be making such a scene.

"What are the chances that I would see you here today? I just can't believe it! Just this morning God spoke to me. I know God's voice, and He told me I was supposed to give you some money!"

Of course, this brought a big smile to my face! "That's wonderful, we can always use money!"

"Yes, but, you don't understand. I've already written the check. As soon as God told me, I went and wrote the check. In fact, it's right here in my purse! I was going to mail it today, but here you are! This is just unbelievable!" She opened her purse and reached her hand down inside. Then all at once she stopped, closed her purse, looked me right in the eye, and said, "Before I give you this check, tell me: What for and how much?"

I was a little surprised and confused, but I didn't hesitate. I told her, "Just this morning I prayed and asked God to provide the finances for a family to come and tape a program on *Kids Time.*" I then explained that this family was incredibly talented and that God had impressed me to have them on the program. "I always pray about every person that is on the show," I continued. "Since I not only host the program but produce it as well, I feel a deep sense of responsibility for everyone who participates. No one is booked unless it is a sure thing! I don't book a *maybe*. If you are booked, then I'm counting on you. Since I had been so impressed that this particular family was supposed to be on the program, I stepped out in faith and booked them even though they told me they couldn't afford the airfare. I assured them that God would provide."

I went on to explain, just that morning I had realized time was running out. So I told the Lord, *I know precious heavenly Father, that You know all things and that nothing is impossible with You, but if we don't have that money today, the cost will almost double. If it is Your will, Lord, please provide the money for this family. I am trusting this matter to You, and I pray that Your will be done.*

The lady in the store was listening intently and still clutching her purse. When I finished telling her about the need, she raised one hand in the air and proclaimed loudly, "Well praise the Lord, we know the *what for.* Now, *how much?*"

I looked at her and swallowed hard. I could barely get the words out. "I hate to tell you this, but I need a thousand dollars."

"Did you say a thousand dollars?"

I nodded my head, yes, unable to speak. Tears welled up in her eyes, and now it was her turn to swallow hard. Reaching into her purse, she pulled out a check and bent down placing her purse on the floor. Then with two hands she held out the check for me to see. The check was written for exactly one thousand dollars!

Tears ran down my cheeks. The funds had been provided in such a clear way, there could be no mistaking it was from God! I wrapped my arms around this woman and thanked her for listening to the Holy Spirit!

We stood there in the middle of that store, hugging each other and praising God. Both of us realized that something special had just happened.

"I'm so excited," the woman exclaimed. "I'm part of a miracle! I just can't believe it! God must really love me!" I felt the same way. God had taken the blinders from our eyes and revealed His plan. He had been leading both of us every step of the way!

Now I understood why God wanted me to drive all the way to Collegedale when I had a million other things to do and I knew my brother wouldn't have two minutes to spend with me. It wasn't to see my brother; it was to receive God's greater blessing. At the very moment I had been praying, God had impressed this woman to write a check for the exact amount needed. She could have mailed the check, and the airline tickets could have been purchased—but neither of us would have received God's incredible gift of *knowing* that we are a part of His plan. The thousand dollar gift was wonderful, but being used by God was priceless!

As I sat in my car, getting ready to drive home, I was overcome with emotion. My hands were shaking, and tears ran down my cheeks as I thanked Jesus. *Thank You so much for what You did here today. Lord, You knew I hadn't planned to come, but changed my mind only at the last moment. Yet, You had already impressed this lady to write a check! Then You arranged for us to be at the bookstore at the same time so I could have the funds on the very day they were needed. You are such an awesome God, and I am not worthy of Your love, grace, and mercy. Thank You, heavenly Father, for loving me, and thank You for answering my prayer. I love You, Jesus, so very much. Amen.*

What if I hadn't prayed for the money for the ticket that day during my morning devotional time with God? God still would have known about my need. He knew what day those tickets had to be purchased. He still could have impressed the lady to send the money, and when the check arrived in the mail, I would have thanked Him for the miracle—but it wouldn't have been the same. The bigger blessing is when we have that "ah ha!" moment and realize the connection between our asking and His giving. Wow! That's powerful!

It's electrifying! The mighty, holy, omniscient God of the universe heard our little prayer through the gates of heaven—and loved us enough to answer! I will never cease to be amazed at the thought!

That is why my morning devotional time is so important to me. It's hard to explain how precious this time is, but let me try. Suppose I was to arrange with Michael, my six-year-old grandson, that I'll call him every evening at seven o'clock. Then during the day, Michael and I anticipate that call. As the time draws near for our time together, we begin to think of each other, and maybe I'll even jot down some things I want to say so I won't forget. Then at seven o'clock, I settle myself in a special chair and push the automatic dial button for Michael's number. I'm thrilled when I hear his little voice say, "Hi Gramma, I love you!" It's not that we couldn't talk to each other at other times during the day. Michael knows he could call me any time. And I know that too, but our seven o'clock talk time would be special. And that's the way it is with my morning devotional time with God.

Even though I talk to God throughout the day and during the dark hours of the night, keeping a daily appointment with Him has its own special reward. My mom and dad started the practice of morning and evening devotional time when we children were small. Every morning and evening we had what we called "family worship." And the practice has stuck. If you want your relationship with Jesus to grow, there is nothing more important than keeping a daily appointment with God.

WELCOME TO MY WORSHIP ROOM

Since our daughters are grown and have moved out of the house, I have the luxury of extra bedrooms. I turned one room into a guest room and the other into my worship room. You may be wondering, "What is a worship room?" Well, for me it's a special place in my home dedicated to praising and worshiping God, a place where I can feel His presence. It's quiet and cozy and filled with my favorite things.

I picked the smallest of the bedrooms and furnished it with a comfortable overstuffed rocking chair that is right by a window. I love to sit there in the mornings with just enough light gleaming in to dance across the pages as I read. Next to my chair is a basket full of reading material. And on the other side is an end table where I lay my Bible, as well as whatever book (or books) I'm currently reading.

The time I spend in my worship room has become the favorite part of my day.

I've turned a spare bedroom into my own personal worship room. It's a special place where I can feel God's presence as I spend time in the early morning reading, worshiping, and praying.

Being alone with God is precious to me. It's something I look forward to—and something I really miss when I'm traveling and trying to create a place for worship in a motel room or at a retreat center. I know I can worship God anywhere, but my little room has become very special to me.

When I'm home, before getting dressed for the day, I put on my bathrobe and slippers, make myself a hot drink, and head for my worship room. Snuggled in my cozy rocking chair, my first words are, *Precious heavenly Father, I ask You for wisdom, understanding, and guidance. What do You want me to read today that will prepare me for whatever is ahead?*

God always impresses me with just what I need! And He'll do the same for you. It's really incredible how He reveals His perfect direction and plan for our lives if we're not too busy doing our own thing to talk to Him!

The Bible is my favorite Book to read because it's God's letter to me. I especially love to compare texts in various translations. Whenever I am unsure of a particular meaning, I read the verse first in one translation and then another. When I do this, it's amazing how clear God's Word becomes. I also like to read inspirational books by such authors as Joyce Meyer, Stormie Omartian, and Kay Rizzo—just to name a few—because when I read stories about what God is doing in the lives of others, it builds my own faith. I love the books by Ellen White because they shed so much light on the Scriptures. I keep a pen and highlighter handy to mark the things I want to remember. And, of course, I have a stack of handmade bookmarks to mark my place!

In this room I pour out my heart in prayer. I pray for friends and family, as well as asking God to bring to my mind anyone I should be remembering—and He always does! I have so many people who ask for daily prayer that I'd forget if I didn't write their names down. I also leave a space after each name or prayer request to jot down the answers God gives. I don't want to forget to praise Him and give Him the glory for the miracles that He's working for us.

My prayer journal is a great resource. It helps me remember just where the Lord and I were when I closed my worship time with Him the previous day. As I review my notes and come across the names of people I've forgotten, I say their name aloud and pray for each individual need. Sometimes, I put my finger on what I have written and claim Jesus' promise that if we ask, He will grant our petitions (see Matthew 7:7). God knows when we are merely reciting a memorized prayer or when we are passionately praying from the heart!

God loves for us to come to Him for our every need—and our greatest need is to know Jesus better and to have a closer walk with Him. My next greatest need is for God's divine guidance. Almost daily I ask Him to guide me to a promise that will set my mind at ease concerning some challenging situation.

Sometimes, I just quietly close my eyes, breathe deeply, and allow my mind to rise to heaven. I see the tree of life, the sea of glass, and the streets of gold. And, yes, I see God on His mighty throne as Isaiah paints the picture in chapter 6. There is God's throne, lifted up with two seraphim covering it. I try to imagine their six wings—two covering their faces, two covering their feet, and two ready to fly as they cry to each other, "Holy, holy, holy!" And when I am in His presence, I share what's on my mind like a little girl with her father.

Am I being too presumptuous with my imaginings? I don't think so. After all, Hebrews 4:16 tells us to "come boldly unto the throne of grace."

LISTENING TO THE HOLY SPIRIT

In addition to my morning devotional time, I talk to God throughout the day—when I'm in trouble, afraid, worried, or sad, but even more importantly, when I just want to praise Him for the awesome God that He is! I pray when I'm with my sisters, family, or friends, when I'm traveling, cooking, or doing housework. And I pray to God with strangers when I sense they need the hope and encouragement only He can bring.

I pray about everything! It's a habit—a lifestyle that I've established over the years. The apostle Paul admonishes us to be fervent in spirit, serving the Lord, rejoicing in hope, patient in tribulation, and continuing steadfastly in prayer (see Romans 12:11, 12). And that's basically how I try to live. But I'll admit, it's my morning time with God that really makes a difference. Psalm 5:3 has become the priority agenda item of my day: "In the morning will I direct [my prayer] to You."

Many times during my devotions God brings to my mind someone to pray for or something I should do for someone else. One day, I felt impressed to pray for my friend Jan. We were roommates at Georgia Cumberland Academy, a boarding school in Calhoon, Georgia, and have remained friends throughout the years. Because we both have very hectic schedules, we don't communicate as often as we'd like. On this particular day, it had been almost a year since we had spoken. I've learned not to question the Holy Spirit. If I'm impressed to pray, then I pray!

After praying for Jan I felt strongly that I should call her. I dialed the number and waited.

"Hello, Jan. Is that you?"

"Brenda, I can't believe you called me today of all days! I just can't believe it!" and then Jan burst into tears! Through her sobs I learned that she was facing a crisis at work and that there would be a meeting

The Nourollahi family. Left to right: Joseph Nourollahi, Jan Nourollahi, Nastran Anderson, Jan's daughter, holding her son, Zachary, Neil Anderson, and Jan's husband, Ken Nourollahi. Jan and I have many warm memories of our days at Georgia Cumberland Academy where we were roommates.

that very day to determine if she would keep her job. She had been falsely accused of something, and it came down to her word against her accusers. "So you see," she said, "what I'm telling you is I need a miracle!"

"Well, fortunately we serve a God of miracles," I responded. "So let's go to the Lord in prayer right now." *"Precious heavenly Father,"* I prayed, *"thank You for being the awesome God that You are and thank You for impressing me to call Jan. Lord, You know her need, and I am praying for a miracle in that meeting today. Please let each person's mind be open to truth and give each one the gift of wisdom and discernment. Please let Jan know how very much You love her and that You are with her each step of the way. I am claiming Psalm ninety-one, verse four, right now where You say, 'He shall cover you with His feathers, And under His wings you shall take refuge; His truth shall be your shield and buckler.' Lord, we are asking You to cover Jan with your feathers, and we are trusting You. Thank You in advance for what we know You are about to do!"*

Several days later I received this e-mail from Jan:

Dear Brenda, I can't believe how perfect God's timing is. You would have no way of knowing, but when you called me I was on my knees pouring my heart out to God! I know I was too distraught when we spoke to give you all the details so I thought I would share with you why I was so upset. As you know, for the past twenty years I have taught high school science, and until this incident, my integrity has never been challenged!

One of my students was injured during a lab experiment, and although she wasn't seriously hurt, her parents accused me of neglecting their child and not coming to her aid. This was absolutely not true as I tended to her right away and administered first aid. Her injury was so minor that I was totally shocked when my superintendent called me in to say that a complaint had been filed and my job was at risk.

I have always felt that teaching was my calling, and to think for even a moment that I would never teach again was more than I could bear. I was at my lowest point emotionally when I fell on my knees. It was at that very moment that you called. Just hearing your voice brought on a floodgate of tears, and when you prayed, it brought back so many memories of when we prayed together as roommates. Brenda, there was so much power in your prayer that I could feel the Holy Spirit! I know God sent you to give me the strength that I needed. Your encouragement for me to have faith in God and to trust in Him meant so much. You reminded me of God's promise that He will never leave me or forsake me.

Well, I want you to know that I am living proof that there *is* power in prayer. When I went to the meeting later that day, all charges were dropped! I couldn't believe it! There was no need even to have the meeting! You were right, God loves me, and He certainly has His hand of protection over me! I want you to know I am asking God to guide my words and my actions and to be with me every day! I want to thank you for calling me when I needed you most! I give all praise to God as I know this is a direct result of prayer. Anyway, I wanted you to know so you could have a thank-you prayer too. Thank you again, Love you much, Jan.

I was so excited after reading her e-mail that I, too, fell on my knees in praise and thanksgiving. I thanked God, not only for working a miracle in Jan's life, but also for the opportunity to be used in such an awesome way. It's absolutely thrilling to be a part of God's plan! Had I not had those quiet moments alone with Him, I might not have heard His voice speaking to me. Psalm 46:10 says, "Be still, and know that I am God." As important as it is for us to talk with God, it is equally important that we listen to Him. That's what a meaningful conversation is all about.

Some people have asked me how they can be certain that it is God's voice speaking to them. "It would just be so much easier to recognize His voice if He had caller ID!"

My answer is that Abraham didn't have caller ID, and he knew God's voice, so we can too. Here's how. The more time you spend in prayer, the more you will recognize the Holy Spirit's leading. It's like when you first meet someone and he or she calls you on the phone. You might not recognize that person's voice. But after you have become friends and have called each other countless times, you only need to hear "Hello . . . ," and there is instant recognition. So it is with God. The more time you spend with Him, the closer you will be, and you will *know* His voice.

There's one more way you can tell whether the voice in your head is God's Holy Spirit or another spirit: If the voice is telling you to lie, cheat, or go against biblical instruction, then you can rest assured it's *not* the voice you should be listening to! God is the same yesterday, today, and tomorrow, and His promises are sure. He will never lead you down the wrong path! Take the message you may be hearing and check it out with God's Word. If what you are being impressed to do will help someone, minister to someone, meet a need, or give someone a glimpse of Jesus through you, then you had better listen!

If you're still unsure whether it's God's voice that is impressing you, double the time you spend alone with Him. If you usually spend an hour, spend two—or more. Set aside a special time for God each day, because it is in those quiet moments when you'll hear His voice the loudest!

Your house may be overflowing with growing children, family, or others to whom you have offered shelter, so you may not be able to have an entire room dedicated as a worship room like mine. But you can still have a designated place for your daily devotions. Perhaps it is a comfortable chair in a cozy corner, a quiet place in your attic, or a swing on the front porch. Wherever your special place is, the most important thing is to commune daily with God and fully surrender your life to Him. Then, and only then, will you receive the full joy of knowing Jesus and the joy you will experience when you know you are following His plan for your life.

On page 91 of an old book, *A Leader of Men,* by A. G. Daniels, I found a definition of surrender that's worth passing on.

Surrender means . . . the uttermost giving up of all we have and are to the mastery of Jesus—

> *our worst,*
> *our best,*
> *our possessions,*
> *our past,*
> *our future,*
> *our life plans,*
> *our loved ones,*
> *our will,*
> *our self.*
> *That is surrender.*

When I commune with God in my worship time—and throughout my day or even in the middle of the night—my heart's desire is to humble myself and be willing to be willing.

Lord, may I never be so bold to presume I know better or to presume what I want to do is best. Rather let me find peace and fulfillment in my complete surrender to You. Amen.

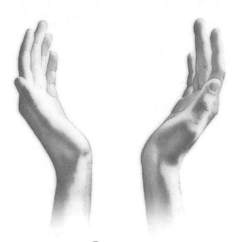

CHAPTER 7

SARAH MAKES
A WISH

For I will restore health to you
And heal you of your wounds, says the Lord.
—Jeremiah 30:17

I hit the rewind button on my answering machine to listen to the message once more. Surely I must have misunderstood. I grabbed a pen and paper and waited for the message to replay.

"This is Nancy Berry from the Idaho Make-A-Wish Foundation. I have an eight-year-old girl with a brain tumor, and we would like to make her wish come true. Her wish is to be on *Kids Time* with you. If you could please call me at your earliest convenience, I would appreciate it very much." *Beep!*

I wrote down the number and looked at my watch. I had just returned to my home in Knoxville, Tennessee, after a six-hour trip from Three Angels Broadcasting Network in West Frankfort, Illinois, where I had been taping *Kids Time*. It was Friday and too late to return the call. I would have to wait until Monday morning to find out the details.

I couldn't believe it. The Make-A-Wish Foundation was calling me! What an honor to have a child choose to be on *Kids Time*, when she could have chosen anything her heart desired! How excited I was to think 3ABN's *Kids Time* was on some child's wish list. I was well aware of this foundation and the incredible good it does. I also knew large donations allowed it to make even expensive wishes come true. I wondered who she might be. *What is the story behind this wish?* I could think of little else all weekend.

On Monday I was back taping at 3ABN in the central time zone, but Idaho is on mountain time. I had another hour to wait before the Make-A-Wish office would open. It seemed like eternity. At last I punched in the phone number.

"Is Nancy Berry there, please?"

"Yes, may I ask who's calling?

"This is Brenda Walsh from Three Angels Broadcasting Network."

"One moment please."

I waited for what seemed like forever before a voice on the other end of the phone said, "Hi, this is Nancy Berry. I'm so glad you called!"

She told me about Sarah, a precious eight-year-old girl with a malignant brain tumor who had endured many surgeries. The Idaho Make-A-Wish Foundation wanted very much to grant Sarah a wish, so Nancy had a couple of her employees visit her and learned that Sarah's greatest wish was to be on *Kids Time,* her favorite television program. Nancy admitted that she had never heard of the network or the program so she couldn't promise anything. But she was willing to try to make the arrangements.

Nancy Berry, Marcia Karakas, and Sarah at the offices of the Make-a-Wish Foundation. Marcia helped with the details to make Sarah's wish come true.

"It is so amazing that you would call now, because we are right in the middle of taping new segments for the program. If you had called two weeks later, we would have been through taping for the year! God's timing is perfect, isn't it?"

"Well, maybe not so perfect after all," Nancy responded, "because I believe Sarah is undergoing chemotherapy and won't be able to travel for three more months."

"Oh, I'm so sorry to hear that. We won't be taping three months from now. If Sarah is going to be on the show, it really needs to be in the next two weeks or we'll have to wait until next year when we're taping again."

"A year? I'm afraid Sarah won't be here in a year!" Nancy's voice trembled.

I knew in my heart there was a way God could make this happen. So I suggested, "Could you ask her doctor to see if it might be possible for her to travel during the next two weeks?"

"Yes, I'll give her mother a call right now, and I'll get back to you. Thanks so much for being willing to consider this. I sure hope it works out. Sarah was adamant that this was her wish. We offered to send her and her family to Disney World or to meet a famous singer or actor. We suggested a whole list of other things, but she turned them all down, insisting that all she wants is to be on *Kids Time*. So, yes, it is worth letting the doctor know about the scheduling challenges. With some luck, we can make this happen. Is it OK for me to give her mother your phone number? Her name is Denise Wolfe."

"Yes! Of course! I'd love to talk with her."

When I hung up the phone I began to pray, asking God to intervene on Sarah's behalf. *Lord, I believe it's Your plan that Sarah be on* Kids Time. *I don't know how You're going to work things out, but please make it happen. I also pray that You will be Sarah's Great Physician. Heal her from this terrible cancer that is destroying her brain. You have promised in Matthew chapter twenty-one, verse twenty-two, that any-*

*thing we ask of You, believing, we will receive. So I am claiming that
promise for Sarah today. Thank You for being the awesome God that You
are.*

In less than an hour my cell phone rang. It was Denise.

"I'm so excited to talk with you," she began. "I just spoke with
Nancy Berry, and she told me about the taping dates. You won't believe this, but when she called we were, at that very minute, in the
doctor's office. When I told him what the problem was, he looked at
the chemo schedule, and I couldn't have been more shocked!

" 'It would be perfect timing for her to go in two weeks,' the doctor
said, 'because we had to delay the last round of chemo.' That means
she will be in the middle of the cycle at that time. She won't start the
next round of chemo until she returns.

"Can you believe it?" Denise exclaimed. "The doctor has cleared
her to go!"

I was ecstatic and could hardly believe my ears. God is so awesome.
He cares about making a little girl's wish come true! He knew weeks
ago what would be unfolding in Sarah's life, and He had already orchestrated her medical procedures with 3ABN's taping schedule!

I told Denise that we would be taping the "Music Time" segment
with Buddy Houghtaling and the Kids Time Singers at that time and
that I was sure they would be excited to be a part of granting Sarah's
wish.

"Can you tell me more about Sarah and her illness?" I asked.

"Sure, but I hardly know where to start."

"Just start at the beginning and tell me as much as you are comfortable with. I'd love to know all about her."

Denise began to tell me about how she and her husband first
found out about the tumor. Sarah, who was only seven at the time,
was having terrible headaches. What they thought was going to be a
short trip to the emergency room turned into what Denise described
as a living nightmare that seemed to have no end. They received
the devastating news that their daughter was not suffering from

migraines, as they had thought, but had a malignant brain tumor. They were in shock! How could this be happening to their precious little Sarah?

For what seemed like endless days and sleepless nights Sarah and her family lived in the Pediatric Intensive Care Unit (PICU) of St. Luke's Regional Medical Center in Boise, Idaho. Sarah's family is a Christian family, and God's promises and prayer were their only hope. Sarah's two brothers, Levi and Tyrel, started praying along with Denise and her husband, Ivan. But they were not the only ones praying. Sarah's entire church organized prayer teams and even called a special prayer meeting to pray for Sarah. Wanting to do more, they had a huge sign made that said, "PRAY FOR SARAH," and put it up next to the road at the entrance to their church.

Not long after that, the church received a letter from Danny Dean, a "prayer warrior on wheels." Denise could hardly believe what she read:

> Dear fellow believers, I'm not a good writer, so please bear with me. I am writing to tell you a little about myself and my family and to ask about one of yours. I drive a semi-truck for a living, and I come through Cambridge, Idaho—sometimes once a month, sometimes two round trips in one week. I've seen your sign, PRAY FOR SARAH. I've made prayer requests at our church for Sarah, but we would like more information, so that we can pray more specifically for her need, rather than just a general prayer. If Sarah or her family would like a pen pal, I would be honored at least to try to fill that position. My wife and I are in our early 50s, we have ten children, nineteen grandchildren, attend Laclede Community Church, and currently live in Laclede, Idaho. Sincerely, Danny Dean.

Denise's faith grew stronger as she realized how God was using Sarah to bring others closer to Jesus. She read Jeremiah 29:11 over and over again: "For I know the thoughts that I think toward you, says the LORD, thoughts of peace and not of evil, to give you a future and a hope." Denise and her family clung to that hope!

The most incredible thing was that Sarah had an unshakeable faith in God. Even though she was only seven years old, she understood the power of prayer and had a perfect trust that her Friend, Jesus, was taking care of her and would answer her prayers.

One answered prayer in particular stands out. Sarah had been in the hospital for almost four weeks. She had been moved out of PICU and was doing well. After her first surgery she had lost the ability to speak, and the doctors didn't hold out much hope that she would ever speak again. They said there was a possibility that she would be able to communicate somewhat by making various sounds. But if by chance she were ever able to speak, it would be a very long time in coming.

Before the medical staff would give Sarah a medical release, they wanted her to be able to make some kind of sound. Their entire family, most of all Sarah, was so tired of the hospital. They all wanted to go home. Denise called her friend Wanda in Arkansas and asked her to specifically pray for Sarah's voice so they would be able to leave. That call took place at eight o'clock in the morning. Three hours later Sarah said her first word. By evening she was not only talking but singing, "Zacchaeus Was a Wee Little Man." This was nothing short of miraculous!

Not long after Sarah was released from the hospital, her doctor decided that it was time to get started on her cancer treatments. She was scheduled for six weeks of radiation followed by a year of chemotherapy. The radiation treatments required that Sarah be at the hospital every day. This created quite a hardship because the family lived two hours away, which would make a tiring trip of four hours a day! But here again, the Lord knew what they needed. A friend, Brenda Abbott, who was a student at Treasure Valley Community College, shared Sarah's story with classmates. As a result, the Student Education Association of the college and Idaho Power paid the rent and utilities for a furnished apartment close to the hospital so Sarah wouldn't have to travel so far.

It was in that apartment that Sarah was first introduced to 3ABN. The family had heard about the network, but they lived so far out in the country that they were unable to get the channel at home. Once they began watching 3ABN, the whole family loved the programming, and Sarah especially loved *Kids Time*. In fact, she loved it so much that each day, long before the program was scheduled to air, she would begin asking, "Mommy, is it almost time for *Kids Time*? How many more minutes?" *Kids Time* was a wonderful blessing to Sarah; it kept her mind off the anxiety and pain associated with her treatments. *Kids Time* was her favorite time of the day.

Just a few days into her treatments Sarah began to get sick. As the radiation continued, it became difficult for her to eat anything because she was so nauseous. Her weight began to drop, and soon this little fifty-pound girl weighed only thirty-nine pounds. Her mom began to pray that the Lord would increase the nourishment in what little food she ate, like He multiplied the amount of loaves and fishes. Again God answered her prayer, and Sarah's weight never went below thirty-nine pounds.

One day, Sarah had been having a particularly bad time. The nausea and headaches wouldn't go away, and none of the medicines seemed to make her feel any better. She was lying on the couch, resting her head on her mom's lap and watching 3ABN, when prayer requests were presented on the network. Not being able to read what was on the screen, Sarah asked, "Mama, what does it say?" Denise started reading each of the prayer requests as they flashed across the screen. After the last request was read, Sarah was quiet for a few minutes. Then she asked, "Mama, do you think they would pray for me?"

"You know, Sarah, I think they would. Let's call the prayer line and ask."

"Can I talk to them myself?"

"Sure, I think you can do that."

Denise dialed the number for the 3ABN prayer line, and when it began to ring she handed the phone to Sarah. Sarah was so weak that she needed help just to hold the phone. She began to speak. "Hello, this is Sarah. Can you please pray for me because I have a brain tumor?"

"What did you say? I couldn't understand you. Can you tell me again?"

Frustrated, Sarah handed the phone back to her mom. She still had a hard time talking because the tumor and surgery had partially paralyzed the muscles in her face and affected her ability to speak clearly. That's why she couldn't make the man at the other end of the line understand what she wanted. Denise took the phone and explained about Sarah's condition and how she had been watching the prayer requests and that it had been Sarah's idea to call.

"Please put Sarah back on the phone. I'd like to talk to her again."

Denise handed the phone back to Sarah, and a very long silence followed. Little Sarah's head was bowed and her eyes closed the whole time. When she raised her head again, she handed the phone back to her mom for her to hang up. Looking into her mother's face, Sarah said, "Mommy, now I know that I'm going to be OK; Jesus will take care of me."

A short time later Sarah had another surgery to correct some leakage in her brain. When that surgery didn't correct the problem, another surgery was done. This would be her seventh surgery! How much could one little girl take?

Denise and Ivan began to ask everyone they knew to pray for healing for Sarah, specifically that she would not have to undergo any more surgeries. It was tearing them up inside to see their little girl suffer so much. Concerned that Sarah might become discouraged if God chose not to answer their prayers in the way they wanted, Denise and Ivan decided they needed to have an important discussion with their daughter to prepare her. Ivan held her in his arms as they gently tried to explain that an answer to prayer does not always mean healing. Little did they realize that Sarah already had a pretty good idea of how God works.

"Honey, Mommy and Daddy need to talk to you about something."

"What's the matter? Is it about me?"

"No, it's about how God works in our lives. Remember how we have prayed and asked God to heal you?"

"Yes, I pray about that, too."

"Well, sometimes God doesn't always answer our prayers the way we think He should."

"Oh, Mommy, I know that! Sometimes God has a better plan."

Tears rolled down their cheeks as Ivan gave Sarah a warm hug.

"That's right, Sweetie, sometimes God does have a better plan! You are even smarter than we thought you were!"

News about Sarah spread fast and so did the number of people praying for her. That's how Sarah became known to the Idaho Make-A-Wish Foundation. One day while at home Denise received a phone call from a volunteer from the Make-A-Wish Foundation.

"Hello, is this Denise Wolfe, little Sarah's mom?"

"Yes, this is Denise."

"This is John Field. I'm with the Idaho Make-A-Wish Foundation. We've heard about Sarah and her illness, and we would like to grant Sarah a wish. Would it be OK if my co-worker, Linda Bledsoe, and I came out to your house to talk with her about it?"

"Well, sure, I guess that would be OK."

They made an appointment, and the next day they were sitting in Sarah's living room. Linda and John were so kind and personable that Sarah liked them immediately. Denise had already explained to Sarah about what Make-A-Wish does, and she was very excited. She already knew exactly what she wanted.

"So, Sarah, if you could have anything you wanted, anything at all, what would it be? What would be your greatest wish? Because we would like to make that wish come true for you."

"Oh, that's easy! I want to be on *Kids Time*. It's my favorite show, and I watch it every day. It teaches all about Jesus and how much He loves us."

"*Kids Time*? I don't believe we've heard of it, but we can certainly check it out. Is there anything else you want?

"No, I just want to be on *Kids Time*."

"Are you sure?" John and Linda couldn't believe what they were hearing. They were offering her whatever she desired, and all this little girl wanted was to be on a religious television program!

"Well, there is one more thing."

Ah, now we're getting somewhere, they thought. Linda moved forward on the couch wanting to catch every word.

"Yes, Honey, what is it? You name it, and we'll try to make it happen."

"I want my brothers to have a wish, too."

John and Linda were not prepared for such an unselfish request. They certainly had never met a little girl like Sarah who loved Jesus so much.

"Well, we have our work cut out for us. Let's go see what we can do."

When they reported to Nancy Berry at the Make-A-Wish Foundation, Nancy could hardly believe her ears. How unusual it was that a little girl would choose to be on a religious television program instead of so many other things she could have chosen. Most children would have asked to go to Disneyland or Sea World or even to meet a famous person such as a popular singer or even the president of the United States! But a religious television program? This was amazing!

Sarah and I have just met for the very first time! The joy is obvious.

Nancy's heart was so touched that she began working immediately to make this happen. She contacted 3ABN, which in turn gave her my number. That very day, Nancy Berry left a message on my answering machine. No one could have wanted to make this happen more than Nancy.

Two weeks later I met Sarah. I will never forget that moment. I had gotten to the studio early to make sure everything was ready. The press had been notified, and we were told that not only would the newspaper reporters be there to cover the story, but local television news stations would be there, as well. The 3ABN network had set up a press table in the lobby, and we had a large gift basket on the table waiting for Sarah and her family. When I saw them drive up, I ran outside to meet Denise, Levi, Tyrel, and Ivan, who was carrying Sarah. As soon as Ivan got close to me, Sarah leaped into my arms and gave me the biggest hug. "I love you, Miss Brenda!"

"Sarah, I love you, too," I said, giving her a squeeze.

I carried Sarah inside and showed her all around as her family followed. Sarah's eyes were wide with excitement as we walked into the *Kids Time* studio and she saw the set. She immediately began pointing to various places on the set telling me just what segment was taped where. "That's where the stories are from. And look, Miss Brenda, that's where you sit on the bench, right?"

"Yes, that's right. That's exactly where I sit, and here is where you will be singing with the Kids Time Singers!" She looked around at the grassy green turf on the floor and then at the brightly colored stools shaped like flowers. I could tell she was trying to process what she had seen on television with what she was seeing in the studio. Although she had a brain tumor, this was one smart little girl who obviously loved Jesus very much.

"Where are Buddy and all the Kids Time Singers?" Sarah asked.

"They'll be coming very soon. You just got here early."

"Oh," she said. Then she whispered in my ear, "Miss Brenda, I don't sing very good anymore."

"Oh, Sarah, that's OK. Jesus just wants us to make a joyful noise. Is that what you're worried about?"

"Uh huh," and she nodded her head.

"Well, Sweetie, you don't have to worry about it at all. Did you know that Jesus can make your voice sound like the angels singing?"

Her eyes lit up, and she began to laugh. "That's a good thing for me, huh?"

Sarah's face was partially paralyzed on her left side, which pulled her mouth over slightly and made it difficult for her lips to close properly. It was physically challenging for her to talk, much less sing. But I could understand every word she said!

Sarah was thrilled to meet Danny Shelton, president of 3ABN. Left to right behind Danny and Sarah: Michelle Roderick, Mollie Steenson, and me.

Sarah was so excited to see me. She had watched 3ABN so much that she considered us family. She had not let go of her grip around my neck the whole time, and I carried her everywhere. That is, until she saw Danny Shelton, the president of 3ABN, walk through the door. She couldn't jump into his arms fast enough! I had told everyone at 3ABN about Sarah, and Danny had come over to meet her personally. As he held her in his arms, her little face just beamed. She told him over and over how much she loved him and that she watched him every day. She even thanked him for telling people about Jesus. I watched his face and could tell that she had completely stolen his heart in just minutes! But what she said next had Danny so chocked up that he couldn't speak.

"Mr. Danny, I don't have a heart anymore."

Danny was confused and immediately shot me a look as if to say, "What is she talking about? I thought she had a brain tumor? Did she have a heart transplant, too?"

I shrugged my shoulders and silently mouthed to him, "I don't know what she's talking about either."

He looked down at Sarah and tenderly asked, "You don't have a heart, Honey? I'm so sorry to hear that. What happened to your heart?"

Sarah struggled to get the words out. Taking a deep breath, she said slowly, "I gave my heart to Jesus."

Everyone in the room let out an audible "Ohhh!" There have been very few times I have ever seen Danny Shelton speechless, but this was one of those times. Tears were in his eyes as he gave her a hug.

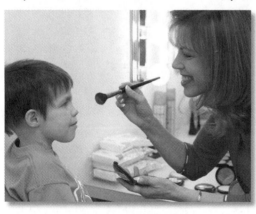

Sarah giggled as I applied her makeup. She was watching everything around her with amazement, trying to take it all in.

"I love Jesus, and I love you, too, Mr. Danny."

"I love you, too, Sarah."

It was time to get ready to tape the program, and I carried her back to the Green Room, which is where guests prepare for the program. When it was time to put on makeup, she insisted "Miss Brenda" do it for her. I applied the powder with a long soft brush, sending her into a fit of giggles. "That tickles," she said. It was wonderful seeing her so happy. Denise was taking it all in, and I could see tears of joy roll down her face as she lovingly watched her daughter.

When it came time to go out on the set, the Kids Time Singers were already warming up. They stopped singing and came over to welcome Sarah. The attention she was getting was overwhelming, and all of a sudden she became very shy. She was now in my arms again, hanging on for dear life. Her little head was buried in my neck, and I was afraid she was going to cry. I whispered in her ear, "Sarah, do you want Miss Brenda to sing with you, too?"

Her head shot right up and was nodding emphatically.

"Oh, yes, Miss Brenda. Can you please come too?"

"Sure I can, and we'll have fun singing together."

Sarah now relaxed, and the smile was back on her face. She whispered in my ear, "You had better sing extra loud so they won't hear me. I don't want to ruin your show."

I then realized just how self-conscious she was about her singing. This precious little girl understood that her disease had taken away her voice, and she was worried about how she would sound—not only to the viewers, but also to the Kids Time Singers who surrounded her. I assured her that it would be OK and that I would sing extra loud.

"Can my brothers come, too, because they can sing very loud?"

"Of course they can. We'll tell them they have to wear makeup, too."

Sarah started giggling, and her brothers were excited that they would be able to sing. They didn't even protest too much about having to wear makeup. I explained to them that the lights in the studio were so bright that if they didn't have makeup on, their faces would be shiny and look terrible on camera. Their eyes went wide with surprise when I told them that even the president of the United States

As I carried Sarah onto the set of Kids Time, her dad, Ivan, waited in the background.

Here, Sarah is singing with Buddy and the Kids Time Singers. When the song was over, Sarah looked at me, smiled brightly, and said, "You made my wish come true!"

wears makeup when he's on TV!

Buddy is a creative genius when it comes to planning the openings for each song. I'm sure most would think he has a script, but actually, he decides what they'll do right before they do it. He just prays about it, and God gives him the plan. When I explained to him about Sarah being a little shy, he quickly came up with the perfect way to start the program. He would be talking with the Kids Time Singers and then have me come walking in, carrying Sarah. As soon as we sat down with Sarah in my lap, the song would begin.

That is exactly what we did, and by the second verse Sarah forgot all about not being able to sing on tune and was really making a joyful noise unto the Lord! When the song was finished, Sarah looked up at me with her little face just beaming! "Miss Brenda, you made my wish come true!"

"Oh, Sarah, I'm so glad that you wished to be on *Kids Time*. You have made me so very happy."

When it was time for Sarah and her family to leave, we must have hugged fifty times trying to say goodbye.

"I'm going to miss you so much, Miss Brenda."

"I'm going to miss you, too, Sarah. You will always be close to my heart." I gave her a big hug, and her daddy pulled her arms from around my neck and scooped her in his arms.

"Come on Sarah, we have to go or we'll miss our plane."

We waved goodbye, and Ivan was almost to their van when Sarah started crying, reaching her arms out toward me. "Please, Daddy. One more hug; just one more hug."

"Now, Sarah, we have to go," he said firmly.

"But Daddy, I might not be here next time. I might not see Miss Brenda again."

That was just too much. I ran over to her and took her in my arms again and held her tightly as I desper-

Sarah and her mom, Denise Wolfe, sit on the set just before taping a "Sharing Time" segment.

ately fought to keep back my tears. I prayed silently for God to give me the strength to pull it together and have some words of comfort for Sarah. And then it came to me.

"Sarah," I said, stroking her back while I was talking. "Remember when you told me that you watch *Kids Time* every day?" I could feel Sarah's head nodding back and forth in the crook of my neck.

Sarah poses with a red rose and her pink hat. This picture was taken before she was diagnosed with a brain tumor.

"Well, when you watch *Kids Time*, you will see me every day. It will be like we are together. And whenever you hear me say, 'Hello boys and girls . . . ,' you will know that I am talking directly to you. So you see, we can always be together!"

A big smile came over her face. She looked into my eyes and said, "And we can always be friends?"

"For always and always, even when we get to heaven! We will have so much fun playing with the animals there, and you can have a house right next door to mine. So you see, we have so many happy times to look forward to."

That was all it took. She understood that no matter what happened she had a bright future with Jesus!

Sarah was able to tape several programs on 3ABN and even got to be on "Sharing Time," a *Kids Time* seg-

I'm standing here with Sarah's family following Sarah's baptism. Note the sign urging people to pray for Sarah. Pictured left to right: Tyrel, Denise, Ivan, me, Sarah, and Levi.

ment. There wasn't a person at 3ABN who wasn't touched by Sarah and her love for Jesus. Her faith was unshakeable, and she hugged everyone she met. Today if you visit 3ABN you will see a photo of Sarah in the lobby. It is a framed newspaper article with a huge photo of Sarah on the *Kids Time* set complete with a writeup of Sarah's wish. Several newspapers picked up the story, and it was on the local news, as well.

There have been so many people who have come to know Jesus because of Sarah's witness on *Kids Time*. People around the world saw Sarah's interview on the *3ABN Today* program and were moved at how much she loved Jesus and understood His plan of salvation for her. One such viewer, Mike Lesseg, was so touched by Sarah's story that he sat down and wrote a poem that he titled "A Sheep in Wolfe's Clothing."

Like a sheep in Wolfe's clothing, you entered my heart.
Like a lamb bleating softly, your voice rekindled a spark,
of another Lamb in another time, who loved a child like you.
Forbid them not to come unto me, he said,
for of such is the kingdom of heaven.

160

Like a sheep I've gone astray,
Lost in my own way of doing things.
Your voice was a voice I recognized
from long ago when I was a child, too.
The Wolfe shall dwell with the lamb
and a little child shall lead them.

You lead me home, Sarah, because . . .
whosoever shall not receive the kingdom of God as a little child,
he shall not enter therein.
Although I only saw you for a moment, I saw God in you.
For no random act of nature could have created you.
Even though I heard your voice just once, I saw Jesus in you.
For no accident accounts for pure love inside you.
Though I'll never meet you, Sarah Wolfe,
You made my wish come true
To see a glimpse of heaven on earth,
and there on God's timetable I'll ask Jesus to introduce me to you.

Just a few months later, Denise called me to say that Sarah was getting baptized and that the family wanted me to speak at her baptism. I wouldn't have missed it for the world. My heart rejoiced as Sarah was lowered into the water. When she rose from the water, she had the brightest, most beautiful, smile.

We don't always know why bad things happen to good people. Some people blame God when tragedy strikes. They claim that Jesus is their best Friend—until something goes wrong in their lives, and then all of a sudden it's "God's fault." I call these "fair weather friends." God doesn't cause the pain in our life. Pain is a result of sin. He does, however, allow us to experience trials in life to perfect our characters so that we can be closer to Him. If everything was easy, we would never know our need for Jesus. It is when things are the toughest that God is the closest. It is not for us to ask why, but only to trust. At her young age, Sarah understood that completely. I have never seen such blind faith as Sarah's.

Three years after Sarah was diagnosed with a malignant brain tumor, she went in for her checkup, and there was no sign of any cancer in her body! The doctor repeated the test, quite sure that a mistake had been made. But the second test only confirmed the first. Sarah experienced the promise found in James 5:15: "And the prayer of faith will save the sick, and the Lord will raise him up."

Sarah still suffers from occasional setbacks such as fevers, headaches, and seizures, but her faith remains firm. She doesn't question why, she only says, "God has a better plan." If only everyone could have the faith of this precious little girl. Now *that* would really make Sarah's wish come true!

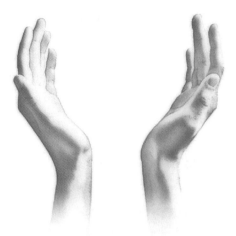

CHAPTER 8

OPENING PRISON DOORS

Then they cried out to the LORD in their trouble,
And He saved them out of their distresses.
—Psalm 107:19

Prison was the last place I ever thought God would call me to go. I had never been in a prison; the mere thought made me somewhat uneasy. Just thinking of those great, big, iron doors clanging shut behind me was enough to give me goose bumps all over!

So I read the e-mail from Kari Avery one more time. She lived in Pocatello, Idaho, and had seen the advertisements announcing that I would be speaking at the Pocatello Seventh-day Adventist Church.

> Dear Brenda, My name is Kari Avery. I have just learned that you will be coming to speak in Pocatello soon. I am involved with the women's prison ministry here in Pocatello, and the Lord has placed a burden on my heart to ask you to come to the prison to speak to the women. I read your book *Battered to Blessed,* and it was a great inspiration to me. It would be a real blessing for the women if you could give your testimony. Many are in prison because they were in abusive

relationships, and they need to hear your message of hope. Please let me know as soon as possible if you are able to come as it does take some time to get a security clearance. Many blessings to you, Kari

Denise Wolfe would be providing my transportation to Pocatello from the Boise airport, so I called and told her about the request and

asked if there would be time to go to the prison. She explained that I would be flying into Boise early in the afternoon. Denise's husband, Ivan, would fly in that morning. Denise would pick us both up at the airport and then drive the four hours to Pocatello. We would barely make it there before sundown on

Kari Avery has a passion for women's ministry and a heart for Jesus.

Friday evening. "I know you would like to minister to these ladies," she said, "but I don't see how there will be enough time."

"Well, then I guess it just isn't God's plan for me. Thanks, Denise, for trying. It was worth a shot."

I e-mailed Kari and explained that my schedule was pretty tight but if anything changed I would let her know. Before I knew it, almost two months had gone by, and I came across Kari's e-mail again. I had forgotten to delete it from my computer and while looking for something else, I saw her name. I read her e-mail and started to hit the delete key. But for some reason I pulled my finger away just before deleting it. I could not mistake the very real impression that I was supposed to go to that prison. I prayed about it and asked God to please open the door if He wanted me to go. I picked up the phone and called Denise once more. "I know my schedule is tight," I told her, "but I can't help but feel God wants me to go to that prison. What if I fly to Boise on Thursday night—could we make it then?"

"Well, I think it might work because Ivan is flying in at ten o'clock in the morning, and if we picked him up and headed straight to Pocatello, we could be there a little before three o'clock. That is, if all the flights are on time! I'll call Kari and see if that will work."

"Thanks so much, Denise. Let me know, OK?" After I hung up the phone, I said a quick prayer. *Precious heavenly Father, if You want me to go to the prison, then please open the doors to make it possible. You know I am willing and that I want to be obedient to Your will. Thank You for hearing and answering my prayer. Amen.*

In the meantime, even though Kari knew I had said it was impossible to come to the prison, she still had a burden on her heart for me to come. In faith, she began to lay it before the Lord. She even asked the ladies at the prison to pray about it. She contacted some friends from her church and asked them to pray, as well. When Denise called and told Kari that I felt impressed to come, but that the earliest I could get there was three o'clock in the afternoon, she exploded with joy! "Can you believe it?" she exclaimed. "The time for the regular visit by the women's ministry is every Friday at three o'clock in the afternoon—just exactly the time that you think Brenda might arrive. God's timetable is perfect!"

Kari instantly felt that this was a sign from God. Things seemed to be falling in place, but she also knew there were still some serious challenges to overcome to make this meeting possible.

Protocol was extremely rigid for anyone wanting to visit the prison. It would probably be easier to get into Fort Knox! Normally it took several months to obtain clearance to enter. Once, Kari had tried to get a musical group into the prison to sing. She started the process two months before they were scheduled, but it hadn't been enough time. The group was not allowed in. She also knew that Idaho required thirty days just to get a security clearance alone, and my visit was only two weeks away. State law requires that even after a potential visitor obtains a security clearance, he or she must attend a mandatory training program to learn all the rules and regulations of what is allowed and not allowed in the prison. Unless you've committed a crime, getting into the prison is not a simple process! Kari knew it would take a miracle to get me cleared, but she also believed in a God of miracles.

Kari wasted no time once again contacting the pastor and other prayer partners at her church. She urged them to "pray like crazy" because she needed a special miracle if this were going to happen. A few reluctantly agreed to pray, but they didn't really believe it was possible. Kari refused to be discouraged. She searched the Scriptures and claimed promises like Jeremiah 33:3, "Call to Me, and I will answer you." And Matthew 7:7, "Ask, and it will be given you." These promises gave her strength. She felt impressed to call Denise again.

"Hi Denise. I just wanted to call and ask you to pray. I believe in my heart that God wants Brenda to be at that prison, but I also know it will take a miracle. It takes several months to get clearance, and we have only two weeks. I'm getting ready to call the religious activities director at the prison, and I just want to ask you to pray before I do."

"Absolutely, I'll pray. But there is something else that you should know," Denise interjected. "The assistant warden at that prison is my brother-in-law. He will recognize the name Brenda Walsh because he watched Sarah when she was on the *Kids Time* program. He is not a member of our church, but he may help you out because of what Brenda did for Sarah."

"Do you have his number at the prison?" Kari knew the main phone number at the prison was a recording and that a caller had to know a person's extension to get through. And even then you had to leave a message!

"No, I'm sorry, I don't," Denise replied.

"Well, thanks for telling me about your brother-in-law. I'll pray and ask God what I should do. Thank you for your prayers as well."

Kari knelt down and presented her burden to the Lord. *"Please, Lord, I know I am asking the impossible but with You all things are possible, so I am pleading with You to give me the words to say. If I am to call the assistant warden, then somehow let me find his number. Thank You, Jesus. Amen."*

She got up from her knees and decided to look up Denise's sister's name in the phone book. She could hardly believe her eyes! There it was; plain as day. Quickly she copied down the phone number and said another prayer as she dialed. It seemed to ring forever and then she heard a child's voice at the other end.

"Hello. Is your mom or dad there?" Kari asked.

"No, they're not here right now. Can I help you?"

"Yes, this is Kari Avery, and I'm a friend of your cousin Sarah. Your Aunt Denise said that I could call. Is there a better time when I can call back to speak to your dad?"

"My dad's at work. You can call him there. Here's his number."

Kari wrote it down. After thanking the girl, she hung up the phone. Another prayer, and she felt ready to make the next call. Her hand was shaking as she dialed the number. Her face fell in disappointment when she heard the assistant warden's voice mail message. She so wanted to speak to him directly. It's intimidating to know exactly what to say on an answering machine. She explained who she was, what she wanted, and mentioned that Brenda Walsh was the television producer who had helped his niece Sarah realize her dream of being on *Kids Time.* "I know it's short notice, but if there's anything you could possibly do to speed up the clearance process for Brenda, I would really appreciate it. I feel her coming would greatly benefit the women in the prison."

She hung up the phone and was shaking all over. Kari prayed again that God would give her the words to say and then dialed the number of the prison religious activities director. She reached his voice mail as well, so she left him a message, too. Now it was up to God to work out His will. She waited and prayed and tried to keep her mind on her work. It was nine o'clock in the morning when she made the call, and when she hadn't heard anything by one o'clock that afternoon, she decided she had better call again. It was a Friday afternoon, and she assumed that the warden would be almost ready to go home for the weekend. Not wanting to wait until Monday for an answer, she called again and left a message, apologizing for bothering him, but again presenting the need.

Kari worked in a dentist's office, and her boss was wondering what she was up to making all these telephone calls. She explained what was going on, and he was very kind and reassuring. "If it is God's plan, then you'll receive permission," he assured her.

She received the long awaited call from the religious activities director at two-thirty that afternoon. If she had any doubts before about whether the meeting would take place, they were all gone now. "I've been told by the warden to do whatever it takes to make this happen for you. Get me all her information, and I'll override the regulation standards and codes for her to come. I'll need a copy of her driver's license, passport, and social security number, and I'll need those right away."

"Yes sir, thank you, sir. I . . . I . . . I don't know what to say," she stammered. "I'll get the information to you as soon as possible."

Kari was speechless. It was done! Just like that! She could hardly believe it! God had worked a miracle! A miracle! She could hardly wait to tell the pastor, but first she prayed and thanked God for His wondrous love, grace, and mercy! In fact, she called everyone she knew, rejoicing over this miraculous intervention. This was a "God thing," no doubt about it. And she wanted everyone to give God the glory.

Kari's next call was to me. I could hardly believe it when she told me about all the challenges. I had no idea what it took to get into a prison, so I had been oblivious to all that was happening to make my visit possible. When she filled me in on the details, there was not a doubt in my mind that God had been speaking to me when He had impressed me to go. As I hung up the phone, I had my own prayer of praise to God for allowing me to be used in such a special way.

That very day I mailed all the necessary documents via overnight express mail. I didn't want to take any chances. I was cleared to enter the prison in less than one week! Unbelievable!

I flew to Boise, and Denise picked me up at the airport. Sarah and her brothers were there, too. We were so excited to see each other again. We spent the night at their grandparents' house, Alvin and Coral Schnell. Alvin is a local dentist, but more importantly, he is a Christian and on fire for Jesus. He believes in evangelism, and he was the reason I was there that weekend in the first place. He had organized a rally at the Pocatello church and raised funds to get a downlink station there so people could watch 3ABN on their local cable TV. We had a great time that night reminiscing about Sarah's wish and all the fun they had on *Kids Time*.

The next day we had the car completely packed and ready to go long before it was time to pick up Denise's husband from the airport. Ivan's work takes him all over the United States as he clears trails in heavily wooded areas, and during his busy season, he can fly home only once a

Dr. Alvin and Coral Schnell with their granddaughter, Sarah. The Schnells are enthusiastic supporters of 3ABN.

month. The kids were eager to see their daddy and waited impatiently for him to arrive. We were praying that his plane wouldn't be late because we had less than half an hour buffer time in order to make our three o'clock deadline at the prison.

Praise the Lord, Ivan's plane landed on time, and his luggage was the first to come rolling down the baggage carrousel. After quick hugs for all the kids, we took off with me in the driver's seat. Ivan and I had a long running joke between us about his slow driving. I teased him many times about "driving like an old lady," and he teased me about "driving like a speed demon." Since time was of the essence, Ivan laughingly told me I should drive.

Denise's friend Brenda Abbott and her three kids, Ethan, Codi, and Michael, were driving down to Pocatello, too, and had left two hours earlier than us. I must have been driving faster than I should have because it wasn't long before we passed them on the road. I was like a horse going to the barn! I knew that if we were late for any reason, I would not be allowed into that prison.

Brenda Abbott is now a Kids Time *production assistant living near me in Knoxville, Tennessee. Here she is pictured with her three children. From left to right: Michael, Codi, Brenda, and Ethan.*

We arrived at the Pocatello Women's Correctional Facility with only ten minutes to spare. Kari was standing out front pacing and praying. Bernice Caston and Nadine Paige, who were part of the prison ministry team, were there, too, praying that God would allow me to arrive safely and on time. No wonder they were so excited to see me! After a word of prayer we each took a deep breath and walked inside. Although Denise and her family and Brenda Abbott and her family could not go into the prison, they would be lifting us up in prayer the entire time.

Bracing myself for the body search I was expecting, I walked up to the officer at the door and handed him my driver's license. He looked at it and explained that he would need to keep it while we were in the facility but would give it back when we exited the building. He then motioned for us to sign in. I had butterflies in my stomach as I signed my name. The others followed, and then we stood at the door and waited for the buzzer to sound letting us know it was time to open the door and walk through.

Bzzzzzz! The door opened, and we walked inside. We had to go through not one, not two, but three doors before we finally entered the hallway. The next thing I knew, Kari said, "Follow me," which is exactly what I did.

Kari Avery, Bernice Caston, and Nadine Paige stand in front of the Women's Correctional Center in Pocatello, Idaho.

What? No body search? No fingerprinting? No questions about what I'm bringing into the prison? What happened? Not wanting to take any chances that the guard might change his mind, I quickly followed Kari around the corner. We walked into a large room that served as the chapel. Chairs had already been set up, and the women were filing in. I was told that there could be no more women than the number of chairs. When the chairs were filled, all others would be turned away. I walked to the front of the room and prepared to speak. I watched as the last chair was filled.

I looked over the crowd and could see young girls—some of them pregnant—and others who were well past the age of retirement. *Women of all sizes, shapes, and color,* I thought to myself, *all with their own sad story.* One woman walked in with an obvious "I'm tough" attitude. She sat in the middle of the room with her arm draped across the back of the chair next to her. She had a stern, but cocky, hard look on her face, and I said a prayer especially for her right then and there. Kari, not wanting to waste a moment, quickly made the introductions then turned the meeting over to me.

"I'm so glad that I can be with you today," I began. "I wish there was time to tell you what a miracle it is that I'm able to stand before you right now, but since I have limited time, I just want to say that I am thanking Jesus for His love, grace, and mercy that has made this day possible.

"The story I am about to tell is the most difficult of all the topics that I speak about. It is my own experience with domestic violence. Many times I was beaten so severely that if it were not for my praying family, I would not be alive today. This story is too painful to tell without God's strength and guidance so before I start I want to go to the Lord in prayer.

"Dear heavenly Father, please be with me now as I give my testimony of the miracle that You performed in my life. Lord, You know how difficult this is for me, but I'm trusting You for the strength and courage that I will need. I am asking You, Lord, to fill this room today with Your Holy Spirit, and may everything I do and say bring others closer to You. I am praying especially for each woman in this room that they will know how very much You love them. Thank You in advance for what I know You are about to do."

As I began to give my testimony I watched the faces of the women before me. When I reached the part of my own experience with domestic violence, tears started to flow. I realized that these women knew firsthand what I was talking about and were reliving their own pain. As I described the blows to my body, I watched them visibly cringe in pain themselves. The tough woman's body language began to change. She no longer sat defiantly, but now slumped down in her seat with tears flowing down her cheeks. The Holy Spirit was moving so powerfully that I could actually feel God's presence.

When I finished speaking, there was not a dry eye in the room. I walked over to the piano and asked them to join me as I sang "Amazing Grace." Never in my life have I heard that song sung more beautifully or with more feeling.

Amazing grace, how sweet the sound,
that saved a wretch like me.
I once was lost, but now am found,
was blind, but now I see.

When the song was over I left them with this message: "I don't care why you're in this prison or what crime you have committed. More importantly, God doesn't care. There is no sin that God cannot forgive. He just wants you to give Him your heart. You may be a prisoner locked up in this building, but I want to tell you right now how to be free, and the answer is this simple: Just surrender your heart and life to Jesus. He loves you so very much. So much in fact, that He left heaven to come to this earth and die on a cross just so you can have eternal life. I am earnestly asking you today to allow God to set you free. It is your only hope of ever being happy on this earth. Won't you give your heart to Jesus today? He won't force His will on you. He has given you the gift of choice and is waiting for your decision. I'm pleading with you, right now, right this very minute, to choose Jesus." Then I began to pray.

"Precious heavenly Father, thank You for being with us today and for pouring out Your Holy Spirit. Thank You for each of the women in this room right now because You impressed them to come and hear Your message. Precious Lord, I am asking that You wrap each one in Your arms and draw her close to You. Allow her to fully understand how very much You love her. I am praying that You will give her the strength and courage she needs to face each day and to realize that she is not alone. You have promised in Hebrews chapter thirteen, verse five, that you will never leave us nor forsake us, and we know that You always keep Your promises. These women need to know that You are their best Friend and that they can talk to You anytime, anywhere. They don't need to pray a fancy prayer, because the most powerful prayer they can pray is only three words—Jesus, save me! There are some women in this room who are struggling right this moment because they want to choose You, but they feel they are not worthy. O Lord, let them know that You have already paid the price for their sins when You died on that cross so long ago. Please give them the courage to accept You as their personal Savior. I thank You for hearing and answering my prayer."

When I had finished praying, women were openly weeping. I walked over to the lady at the end of the first row and gave her a hug and whispered in her ear, "Jesus loves you." Then I did the same for the next woman and the next. Tears were flowing down my cheeks as I went from woman to woman, one row at a time, giving each the hug that God wanted them to have and letting each one know in a personal way that *Jesus loves her.*

When I reached the woman who had come in with such a tough attitude, she grabbed me and held me in an embrace as if she had never been hugged before. She shared with me that she was serving a life sentence for killing her husband. She had walked in on him molesting their young daughter and in the moment of shock and horror, she had shot him. Now she will spend the rest of her life locked up. "I haven't been hugged in sixteen years," she confessed. Before I moved on to the next woman, she whispered in my ear, "I want to choose Jesus."

I didn't stop until I had hugged every woman there. I had brought bookmarks with me and also business cards, and I gave one to each of the ladies. I told them that if anyone wanted to contact me, to please take one of my cards and I would be willing to pray with her at any time. A loud buzzer sounded, indicating it was time for "movement." Kari explained to me later that "movement" meant that during this time the women must move from one destination to another and *only* during this time. They could not be in the hall for any reason until "movement" was called.

Women were crowded all around me, wanting me to autograph their bookmarks and reaching for business cards. Each one wanted a moment of my time to tell me her personal story. The amazing thing was that most of the women stayed in the room, which meant they lost their opportunity for supper. One woman said, "I don't care if I eat. This is more important." I stayed until the last woman had been ministered to, and then when the buzzer sounded again, Kari indicated that we must leave.

As I heard those prison doors clang behind me that day, chills shot up my spine. Emotionally, I was completely drained, and my heart went out to each of those women. If it were not for God's amazing grace, I could have been in their same situation. Who is to say that had I stayed in my abusive relationship that I might not have snapped at some moment and killed the man who was hurting me or worse, doing something terrible to my daughter? No one knows what he or she will do when pushed to the limit. So often people are quick to judge, but is one sin really any different than another? Is one person any better than another? Not in God's eyes! Romans 3:23 says "all have sinned and fall short of the glory of God."

Everyone in that prison had been judged over and over again; not only in the court system, but also by their friends, family, and others with whom they had come in contact. What these women needed most was not judgment. It was love, God's amazing love that every one of us needs to sustain us.

Several weeks after my visit, I received my first letter from one of the inmates, asking for Bible studies for her children. While at the prison I had told the women about Kids' Club, a *Kids Time* Bible study program that sends Bible lessons to children who request them. I encouraged the women to sign up their children for the lessons and to request them for themselves, as well. This way, they could do the studies with their children and talk about them over the phone with them. They were excited to learn that when they finished all the lessons, they would each receive a Bible, absolutely free!

In this first letter, the woman also poured out her life story—the experiences that had led her to where she is today. "I've broken every one of the Ten Commandments," she wrote. She was filled with remorse and wanted assurance that Jesus really loved her.

I wrote back that very day to let her know nothing she could do would stop Jesus from loving her. I encouraged her to fully surrender her heart and life to Him.

Since then I have received countless letters from women in that prison, each telling me such painful life stories that if you heard them it would break your heart as it did mine. Oh, how it makes me homesick for heaven when I hear of such tragic destruction of lives. More than twenty women have asked for personal Bible studies at the prison, and many have given their hearts to Jesus. As of today, several have already completed their lessons and received their free Bibles.

Several months after my visit to the prison, Kari sent me an e-mail that moved me to tears. It also shed some light on prison ministry that I would have no way of knowing and made me realize even more clearly just how miraculous my visit there had been. She wrote:

Dear Brenda,

I would like to say that it has been a blessing to be a part of this wonderful miracle that God is performing at the Pocatello women's prison. Being there that day I had the privilege of seeing first hand the Holy Spirit work in a very visible way. From the moment you arrived, God was intervening on your behalf. The guards didn't stop you or ask you any questions about what you were taking into the prison. (Your bookmarks and business cards . . . not allowed!) They didn't give you any instructions or restrictions. Amazing!

As we entered the chapel, I watched the whole room soften as you prayed and began to speak. Those girls are hardened to life and to emotion. Most of the time their emotions are stone cold and controlled. You can see it in their demeanor. I witnessed everyone there melt and yield to the Holy Spirit as you spoke. Your testimony was just what they needed to hear, and I believe broken spirits were healed that day through your willingness to be a faithful servant of our Lord. I was shocked that after "movement" was called, so many people lingered to talk with you. Again, this is unheard of!

You were physically able to touch and hug each woman and share Jesus with them in a very personal way! This is definitely not allowed. Touching of any kind is not permitted! I was sure a guard would come into the room or say something over the loud speaker, but not one thing was done to prevent you from ministering to each one there! This is definitely a "God thing!"

I also have been able to observe in the months since you left just how many were touched that day and have now made a commitment to learn more about Jesus. I know hearts were changed, and the effect of your "one day" visit is still being felt.

Please pray for these women and our ministry here. Constraints on us as Bible workers are quite burdensome. We really do not get much of a chance to converse with the women. Comments are quick and to the side, and once in a while someone will open up and share during a meeting. But many times they don't want the other inmates to know what is going on with them. The Lord has given me the gift of discernment, so I am often able to understand a lot with only a few words and their look or manner. It is difficult to see consistency in the prison ministry, which is one of the things that the devil uses to discourage us most. Let me try to explain.

Things are constantly changing, as someone might be coming to your Bible study group for a while, and then you won't see them anymore, and you don't know why. Sometimes the other women will be able to tell you, but not always. The missing woman may have been sent to treatment, which could mean that she is in a different unit within the prison or that she has been sent to another prison. Many times the guards will intentionally wait to give the inmates their meds until just the time for our meeting. The women are so dependant on such high doses of medications that they will not miss "pill call." That makes them late which means they will miss the meeting because they can move in the hall to go somewhere only during "movement."

Another challenge is that many will attend meetings of different faiths throughout the week. They get so confused and discouraged. Our goal is to keep them focused on the hope that Jesus has for them. We keep our eyes on Jesus and pray that we can make a difference in their lives. If we can give them the hope that God wants them to have, then maybe they will find their way out of the darkness.

So with all this in mind, please picture this. The chapel that day was filled with a whole different mix of women than normally attend our Bible group. I wondered about it that day and even asked later if anyone knew why, but no one had an answer. I believe that God knew who should be there and directed from above. A few were there from Unit 4, which is the "lock down" unit. This is unheard of! Some were there who I never saw again, but most I eventually came in contact with during the following weeks. I believe God knew who needed to be there, yet much will remain a mystery this side of heaven.

One woman who is now baptized, expressed how the Lord worked on her heart through your testimony. Bitterness had once consumed her. She thought she had forgiven every wrong thing done to her, but after hearing you speak, she realized there was still a lot of anger within. Finally, that day, she felt release from the guilt she harbored so deeply. She is in prison for murder, although it was self-defense. This poor woman had been beaten so badly it's amazing she lived, and in the horrible nightmare of abuse, she took her husband's life. I didn't understand why she wasn't able to get a definite time to serve since it was self-defense. But her sentence is "undetermined," which means she could be there till Jesus comes!

You may remember her as the one who spoke to you after the meeting and told you how much it meant to know there was someone else in the world that could understand because her husband had been a police officer, as was your first husband. It was then I finally understood the harshness of her sentence. God loves her so much, and He wanted her to hear your story. This lady now mentors other inmates and prays with whoever needs prayer. So now, through this woman, you are still touching hearts in Pocatello.

Another lady expressed that she never really thought she could be anything different than what she was—an addict and a loser! But she said she caught a glimpse of how Jesus can change our lives. She hoped God would help her be a good person and someday be a good mother to her children. She was so inspired that God led you out of a bad situation and gave you a new life.

There were women who wanted to know more about *Kids Time* for their children. They asked if you were on the program, what it was like, and could you teach their children about Jesus? I gave out the little books you left for Bible studies on all three units I visited.

Some who read your book wanted to know, "Is Brenda for real?" "Was it really God who saved her?" "If I wrote to her, do you think she would answer me?" You see, these ladies took everything you said to heart, but they had to really think about it to decide if they could trust you and believe what you told them. The biggest challenge in teaching these precious women is helping them understand that God is real and that He can be trusted! They don't trust anybody! They have been hurt too many times. The positive thing is that many of them *did* listen to you and wanted to believe and were trying to take it all in and digest it.

I know some asked me about you because of what others had shared. They hadn't been able to attend the meeting yet wanted to learn more about you. I told them you left five of your books in the prison library and encouraged them to read it and to write to you. One lady after writing to you has been studying like crazy and devours every book I give her. The problem is that she has so many questions and I have so little time to answer them. The prison regulations will not permit me to meet with them individually. But I know God is working miracles in her heart, and it's all from the seed that you planted.

I know I have taken up a lot of your time, but I wanted to let you know how God used you—and is still using you—at Pocatello Women's Correctional Facility. May God bless you in your ministry as you continue to win souls for the kingdom. With love, Kari.

What an incredible letter. Most of the time, as we witness day after day, we won't have the privilege of seeing the fruits of our labor until we go to heaven. When small glimpses like this are revealed, it is a gift from above, and I believe God allows us to see how He is working in us to strengthen our walk with Him.

God has a plan for each of us, and, oh, how very important it is to listen to God's voice! When you have prayed passionately to God and He impresses you to do something, go for it! Don't hesitate and talk yourself out of it because it sounds to you to be unreasonable. Learn to listen to God's voice, because when you do, that is when God can use you most. And it is then He will open prison doors!

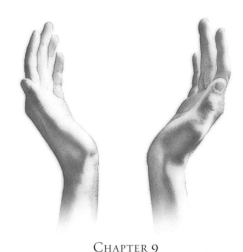

CHAPTER 9

THE LOADED SUITCASE

And all things, whatever you ask in prayer, believing, you will receive.
—*Matthew 21:22*

I pray all kinds of passionate prayers, including ones to get me out of trouble. Jesus is so good to save me from my foolish mistakes and irresponsible ways. I pray to Him about the most simple things, such as helping me find my keys or even finding my car in the parking lot in places such as the Woodfield Mall in Chicago, Illinois, one of the largest shopping malls in the world.

Yes, I lost my car in a parking lot! In fact, I spent three hours in high heels searching for it. Just when I thought I couldn't walk another step, I cried to God in desperation, *Please help me find my car!* At that very moment a parking attendant came by in his little cart and asked if he could help me. Seeing the look of despair on my face, he encouraged me to hop in. And can you believe it? In the first row the attendant randomly drove down, there was my car! God is so good!

Over the years I've prayed a lot of passionate "help me" prayers, but there is one that will always stand out in my mind. It happened in an airport. But before telling you more, let me start at the beginning so you will understand the events that led up to the story about the loaded suitcase.

I looked around the old dusty airplane hangar that was now turned into an exhibit hall. It was a hub of activity as people were setting up their booths. They had come from all over the world for this major event—the International Pathfinder Camporee! I wiped some sweat from my forehead and looked for my water bottle. It was July, hot and humid, and there was no air conditioning in this old hangar! *What was I thinking when I decided to have a booth here?* I mused to myself as I took a long, satisfying drink.

Pathfinders are very much like Boy Scouts or Girl Scouts except that there is a single club for both genders. Every five years Pathfinder clubs from all over the world come together in Oshkosh, Wisconsin, for a camporee. It's like a huge fairground with all kinds of booths where kids can do crafts and receive honor badges. Plus, this particular year there were a hundred or so vendor booths selling everything from T-shirts to tennis balls. In addition, enthusiastic youth leaders had planned challenging games, creative inspirational meetings, and all sorts of fun activities to entertain and inspire the more than thirty thousand kids who would be attending. Can you imagine? Thirty thousand young people, plus adults. That's a medium-sized town! And there I was in the middle of it all, sweating in that unbearable July heat.

I had decided to set up a *Kids Time* booth because it would give me a chance to videotape kids talking about how they share Jesus. I planned to use these videos for the "Sharing Time" segment of the *Kids Time* television program. I had an area marked off for videotaping, complete with camera, lights, interview set, and a place for kids to sit while being interviewed. There was even a section where children could sit down and rest and watch *Kids Time* programs that would run continuously throughout the day. We planned to give away *Kids Time* notepads and 3ABN lapel pins among other things. Another section of the booth was for selling *Kids Time* products, such as the *Kids Time* cookbook, *Cooking with Catie,* and the Kids Time Singers CD that had just been released.

I was especially excited because my sisters, Linda and Cinda, had agreed to help me with the booth, and our brothers were also there as staff members. Brother Jim was the youth director for the Michigan Conference, and brother Ken was a pastor. It was the first time that all five of us would be working in ministry together since we were little kids, and I was really looking forward to some bonding time! We always have so much fun being together.

"Where do you want to keep the money box?" Linda jarred me back to reality.

I glanced around. "How about here?" I said pointing to a spot behind the counter that would be impossible to see or reach from the other side. Linda quickly agreed.

With that taken care of, we took one more critical survey of the booth. "It looks good to me," Linda said. I nodded in agreement. We were ready for the grand opening. We had been working hard all day, and I was glad to be done.

"Come on," I said to Linda. "Let's get something to eat. I'm starving."

There were some definite benefits to having our brothers as part of the camporee staff. For starters, Jim gave us his golf cart that only the workers had access to, and since the fairgrounds were extensive, we were extremely grateful! I made a mental note to give him an extra big thank-you hug for this perk! Another really huge blessing was the place where we were staying.

To anyone who knows me, my next revelation will not come as a big surprise. So here goes. I am *not* a camper! Nope—not me! I don't enjoy being in the great outdoors! My sisters have long since given up begging me to go camping with them. I don't enjoy being out in the elements with the mosquitoes, bugs, wild animals, dirt, thorns, wind, rain, sun, sleet, and sometimes snow. I especially hate listening to crickets chirping all night or owls making their scary noises! And I haven't begun mentioning creepy critters like the rodents running around on the ground or bats zooming past me in the air. No, I am definitely *not* a camper!

Two very special friends, Dr. Don and Mary Ross, who not only let us use their motor home, they drove it all the way from Texas to make it available! They are so precious!

So you can imagine my enormous relief when some very dear friends, Mary and Don Ross from Texas, offered to let us stay in their beautiful motor home. They even drove it all the way to Wisconsin and set it up for us. What a luxury to have running water and electricity. Yes, I'm talking about a flushing toilet, a hot shower, and the incredible blessing of air conditioning during the horribly hot days and heat for the cold nights. Wow! God sure knows how to meet all my needs! Many times that week I thanked God for the generosity of friends.

That night, we lay in bed talking excitedly about the activities that were to occur the next day—until eventually my sisters quit answering me, and I, too, drifted off to sleep. Morning came all too soon. After a good breakfast, we headed to the booth. We got there shortly before the camporee opened; people were already lining up at the entrance. At nine o'clock sharp, the doors opened, and in rushed the kids. With so many people all talking at the same time, the noise level in that hangar must have gone off the charts!

It was easy to get swept up in the excitement as first one and then another child would come running to the booth to give "Miss Brenda" a hug! I met kids from Africa, Jamaica, Philippines, Russia, Germany, France, England, Belize, and many more countries! Even all the way from China! It was mind boggling to think of the millions of kids who watch *Kids Time* all over the world, and now I had the privilege of meeting some of them! Many had written me letters and sent photographs, but it was so much better meeting them in person.

I had fun trading pins, posing for photos, signing bookmarks, and listening to stories of how these kids shared Jesus! On average, five thousand kids stopped at the booth every day! As exciting as this was, it was also exhausting. When the booth closed, I was more than ready to head back to our motor home to put my feet up and swap stories with my sisters of the memorable events of the day.

Each night I brought home the money that we had collected in the cash box from the sales of books and CDs. Having no other place to put it, I stuffed it in the outside zippered pouch of my suitcase. I felt it would be safe there because we were able to keep the motor home locked at all times. Every night the zippered pouch became larger and larger as more cash was stuffed inside. And each time I zipped it up, I would say a prayer asking God to protect His money.

The week went by so fast that before I knew it, Sunday had arrived, and everyone was packing up and going home. My brothers came by the motor home while we were getting ready to leave and asked if I could give them a quick haircut. I have been cutting hair for years, and I know that whenever I'm going to be around family or friends that I need to pack my haircutting kit. So I was well prepared.

While I was giving Ken his haircut, a man who was pulling a big fifth wheel trailer drove past and stopped. He leaned his head out the window and asked, "Hi, aren't you the lady on *Kids Time?*" I laughed and told him that indeed I was.

"Hey, how about giving me a haircut, too?" he asked.

I looked at his long hair and scruffy beard and said, "Sure, as long as you let me cut that beard off, too!" I was only joking, but the next thing I knew, he and his wife had hopped out of their truck to wait his turn! When I had finished, he tried to pay me, but I shook my head. "No, I only cut hair to help others! I don't accept money!"

The Micheff family. Back row, from left to right: Linda Johnson, Ken Micheff, Cinda Sanner, Jim Micheff, and me. Front: James and Bernice Micheff.

He shook his head and laughed. "I can't wait to tell people that *Miss Brenda* cut my hair!"

Linda and I had a good laugh about it as we drove to her house. She lives only an hour from the campsite, so I had planned to spend the night with her and fly home the following morning. As I was getting ready for bed, Linda came in and said, "Oh Sis, by the way, I invited some people over to the house tomorrow before you leave for the airport. They wanted to hear us girls sing, and I told them you wouldn't mind. That's OK, isn't it?"

"Sure," I said. "Anytime I have a chance to sing with you, I love it!" She smiled, gave me a hug, and we said goodnight.

As I was getting dressed the next morning, the doorbell rang. Minutes later, Linda poked her head into my room. "They're here! They came early."

While Linda went to entertain them, I went into high gear, getting ready in record time! We spent the morning singing, playing the piano, and just praising Jesus! Before I knew it, Aggie Johnson, Linda's mother-in-law, came in and asked, "Brenda, what time do you need to leave for the airport?"

"Oh, not till ten o'clock. My plane leaves at noon, which means I need to be at the airport at eleven and it's only an hour away. So, yes, ten o'clock should be fine."

Aggie looked at me in disbelief! "Brenda, you do realize it is ten minutes to ten don't you?"

"What?" She had to be kidding!

"Check the clock for yourself!" She insisted. One look at her face told me all I needed to know. *Don't panic*, I tried to tell myself. I wasn't even packed! I ran to my room with Linda right behind me. She started throwing things into my suitcase.

Now to tell you the truth, this was enough to drive me crazy. I am known for being organized. Just to help you understand what I'm talking about, I'll explain. I have one of those wonderful label makers, and I have printed out labels on just about everything around my house! If you open the door of my refrigerator, you will see the shelves labeled appropriately—such as: "condiments," "leftovers," "fruits," "vegetables." Open a hallway closet, and there on the shelves are neatly stacked clear plastic boxes—again with the appropriate labels in alphabetical order. My girls tell me that if I get anymore organized, I will need some serious therapy!

When my youngest daughter, Linda Kay, was in high school, she loved to tease me whenever I went away on a business trip. When I returned she would have the contents of the entire refrigerator moved around so that nothing was in its correct place. That habit finally stopped when I started insisting that she clean the entire refrigerator and put everything back in place!

So my suitcase—normally highly organized with each shoe in a protective shoe bag and my clothing neatly folded and in its proper place—was now a jumbled mess. Things were just thrown in, jammed in, and stuffed in, so that I almost wasn't able to close the suitcase at all. Linda had to sit on it while I zipped it shut! It took both of us to carry it to the car and put it in the trunk. Then one more quick trip into the house to grab the rest of my things, a fast goodbye to Aggie and the friends with whom we had spent all morning singing, and we were off!

I decided that I should drive since I drive a lot faster than Linda. We pulled up to the airport not a minute too soon, and after giving my sis a quick hug goodbye, I raced to the ticket counter to get checked in. Without thinking, I hurriedly checked my big suitcase, grabbed my carry-on bag, computer, and purse, and headed toward security, walking so fast some might consider it running. Wouldn't you know it, it was just my luck to be picked randomly for a complete search through all my things! So clearing security took me twice as long! By the time I reached my gate, everyone else was already on board the plane and the agents were preparing to close the door! I raced down the aisle of the plane, quickly found my seat, and buckled my seat belt. I finally took a deep breath to try and relax! *Wow! That was close*, I thought! *I just hate rushing. And I hate being late! Thank You, Jesus for helping me make my flight.*

I had a wonderful time witnessing to the lady sitting next to me, and we talked the entire flight. Before I knew it, the attendant was telling us to get ready to land. Before leaving the plane, I prayed with my seatmate. Then I grabbed my belongings and went to find my connecting flight to Knoxville.

I was in the Cincinnati airport, right in front of the Auntie Anne's Pretzel Shop, pulling my roll-on suitcase behind me, when I suddenly stopped dead in my tracks. My heart started racing. I broke out into a cold sweat and felt like I couldn't breathe! *How could I have been so foolish? So irresponsible? What was I thinking?* In the rush to get to the airport on time, I had completely forgotten about the money! Yes, all that cash was in the bulging outside pocket of my suitcase; the very suitcase that I had checked before boarding the plane.

I couldn't believe it. I started to pray. *Please, dear Jesus, please protect the money. It's Your money. I'm so sorry, Lord. I was so foolish. Please forgive me. I know You can protect that money, so I am claiming Matthew chapter seven, verse seven, "Ask, and it will be given to you; seek, and you will find; knock, and it will be opened to you." Lord, I am asking, and I'm not just knocking, I'm pounding at Your door!*

Now here is where I wish I could change the story. I wish that I could tell you I was praying *believing* that God would answer my prayer, not merely *hoping* that He would answer my prayer. I wish that I had prayed with faith and trusted God that His will would be done. Because when you pray with complete confidence, knowing God is in the process of answering, there is a wonderful peace that floods your spirit. But sadly, that is not what happened. What did happen was this: My emotions were anything but peaceful. Instead I had doubt, frustration, anger at myself, guilt, a sense of failure, and the fear of loss, all swirling around inside. *And I began to cry.* Yes, I cried right there in front of all the people passing by me in the terminal, in front of all the people lined up to buy pretzels and all the other people rushing by to get to their gates. *It's not even my money. It be-*

longs to 3ABN for God's work, I sniffled. I grabbed my purse frantically searching for my cell phone and waiting impatiently for it to power up as I pushed the "on" button. Then I scrolled down the numbers in my phone for 3ABN. I had to let Danny Shelton, president of 3ABN, know what I had done!

My hands were shaking so badly I could barely push the numbers. I heard Danny's voice saying, "Hello. Hello? Is anyone there?" That did it. I burst into tears, sobbing out of control.

"Is that you, Brenda? What's the matter? What's wrong? Are you hurt?" I tried desperately to pull myself together without much success. "Take a deep breath," he ordered.

I took a minute and then between sobs I was finally able to say, "I lost God's money," and the whole story spilled out—from the race to the airport to the moment I realized what I had done. And then there was another round of tears!

"Is that all?" Danny questioned. He sounded so relieved. "Brenda, you're right. It *is* God's money, and He can take care of it. He knows you didn't leave it in the suitcase on purpose. Let me pray with you right now." And he began to pray. *"Dear Father in heaven, I just want to come to You, Lord, asking that You would be with Brenda right now. You know she didn't mean to forget about the money, so I'm asking that You protect it. Lord, it is Your money, and we want Your will to be done. We are trusting You, and if You want that money for another purpose, then that's OK. We accept Your will and Your plan. We love You so much. In Jesus' holy name, Amen."*

When Danny finished praying, I was still sniffling and wiping my eyes. My chest was still heaving with silent sobs! "Danny," I said, "do you know how much money we're talking about?"

"No," he answered, "and I don't care. It is God's money, isn't it? He knows how much there is."

"But, Danny," I insisted, "there must be thousands of dollars. In fact, there was so much cash that I could hardly get the zipper closed the last night of the camporee. We're talking about a lot of money. I don't even know the exact amount that I would need to pay back, because I hadn't stopped to count it!"

"Brenda, you said yourself that it is God's money, and He can do with it as He likes. Whatever that is, it's OK with me!"

Now a new bout of sobs erupted. I was filled with so much guilt that I couldn't bear it. "Danny, why don't you just scream at me or tell me how dumb I am or fire me or something?"With that last comment, he couldn't hold back his laughter. "I can't fire you!" he said between chuckles. "You're a volunteer, remember?"

His humor put a temporary stop to my tears as I acknowledged, "Oh yeah, I'm a volunteer!" After another encouraging admonition from Danny to put my faith and trust in Jesus, we said goodbye. *Why did he have to be so nice and understanding! I deserve so much worse!*

That reminded me of when I was a little girl and had done something wrong. Instead of the whipping that I knew I deserved, Dad would call me in and have a talk with me. I was always so brokenhearted that I had disappointed my daddy, that the talk alone was punishment enough and made me resolve to be better next time!

You would think that after praying and asking God's will to be done that I would have pulled it together and trustingly put the whole situation in God's hands. But sadly, that was not the case. Instead, I made my way to my connecting gate, found a chair where no one was sitting next to me, and sat down. I couldn't believe my ears when the gate attendant announced over the intercom that my flight would be delayed four hours! *What? How can I possibly wait four more hours to find out if someone has stolen the money?*

My mind began to imagine the worst. I knew that security was tight and that almost all bags were being hand-checked. Unless the person examining the bag was honest, he or she would surely steal the cash. And anyone who would steal, would take it all—not just some of the money.

Oh, no, here come the tears again! I reached into my carry-on bag for a tissue and my water bottle. I took a drink and tried to pull myself together. I remembered what Jesus said in Matthew 18:20: "For where two or three are gathered together in My name, I am there in the midst of them." I decided this situation was so serious, it needed more prayer. I picked up my cell phone and dialed my husband and then my parents. Next I called my sister Linda. I poured out the story to each one, and they prayed with me and promised to continue praying. I called Cinda and Kenny and left long messages on their voice mails. Next my brother Jim prayed with me. Well, that took care of the Micheff family's prayer chain.

Now it was time for friends. I opened my cell phone again and started scanning down the address book. I called first one friend and then another, pouring out a now-abbreviated version of my situation. And they, too, prayed. Seldom had anyone seen me in such a panic. Something like this might happen to others, but never to me! I'm usually so organized and responsible. Suddenly, I was very, very human—and at that moment I was very disappointed in myself!

I kept scrolling down the address book and was on the M's when I saw Aunt Myrtle's name and stopped. Aunt Myrtle has always been special to me. I could talk to her about everything, and did. Even though she had been raised a Christian, she no longer went to church. In fact, she hadn't attended church since she was a child. You would think Aunt Myrtle would be the last person I would call at a time like this! But honestly, the fact that she wasn't a practicing Christian never crossed my mind. If it had, I'm sure I would have scrolled past her name. But before I knew what I was doing, I had hit the "send" button, and seconds later I heard her sweet familiar voice on the other end of the line.

"Aunt Myrtle," I managed, and that is all I got out before I started crying again.

"What's the matter, Brenda? What *is* the matter?"

She sounded frantic so I quickly spilled out the whole sad story, ending with, "So I need you to pray and ask God to protect that money!"

My mom, Bernice Micheff, my aunt Myrtle (Coy), and me. My mom and my aunt are incredible prayer warriors.

"Well, I don't even know how to pray!" she said so quickly that I almost hadn't finished my sentence!

"Aunt Myrtle, this is serious," I said. "I'm calling you because I need you right now!"

I said it so firmly and with so much fear in my voice that she quickly replied, "OK, OK, I'll pray for you. Now just calm down!" She didn't want to upset me further.

After hanging up with Aunt Myrtle, I continued going down my list. I hadn't finished calling everyone when the agent announced the boarding of my flight. I had sat there in that waiting area for four hours calling people! I had moved only once and that was to find a chair next to the wall where there was an electrical outlet to charge my phone.

The flight from Cincinnati to Knoxville seemed longer than a trans-Atlantic flight! I thought we would never land! My heart was racing as I headed to the baggage claim area. My husband, Tim, was waiting for me as I neared the baggage carrousel, and he came over quickly and gave me a reassuring hug. We barely spoke as we waited for the luggage to start coming down the ramp. It seemed hours before the bags appeared, and I watched anxiously as first one bag and then another came by.

Then I almost froze as I pointed to my bag. Tim quickly grabbed it, setting it down in front of me. He looked into my eyes and asked, "Do you want to open it or do you want me to?"

I looked at the bag, and then back at Tim. I was shaking all over. "I'll open it," I said. "But I want to pray first." So I prayed once more that God would work a miracle and for the money to be in the suitcase. I ended with, *"But, Lord, if it is not there, I accept Your will. Amen."*

Slowly, and with trembling hands, I pulled the zipper open. I could hardly believe my eyes. Cash started falling out! Tim quickly grabbed the bills and forced them back in the pocket as I zipped it closed. I stood there and sobbed. Then Tim and I had a thank-you prayer right there in the airport! When I finished praying, I reached for my cell phone. I'm sure you can guess who I called first. Yes, Aunt Myrtle.

As soon as she heard my voice, she anxiously asked, "Is the money there? Is it all there? I've been on my knees since you called! I figured if I was going to talk to *the Man* then I better get on my knees, and my arthritis is killing me!"

"Yes, Aunt Myrtle," I almost screamed, "it's here! The money is all here! All of it!" I was laughing and crying at the same time! I decided that since it was now late at night and Danny Shelton had faith anyway, I'd wait to give him the good news in the morning.

When I called him the next day, I was shocked that he sounded so calm. He said, "Brenda, we prayed about it, and I knew God would take care of that money whether or not it was in your suitcase. If He had another plan for the cash, then that was OK with me!" I was amazed at his faith!

Why didn't I have that kind of faith? Why didn't I pray *believing*, not just *hoping*, my prayer would be answered? I know faith comes through experience, and yet I had had countless experiences where I had exercised faith. My faith should have been strong. *What had really taken place? What was God's real intention in this situation? Oh Lord what were You trying to teach me?* As I prayed, three lessons came to my mind concerning answered prayer.

Lesson #1: God sees a much bigger picture than we do. In this case, the bigger picture involves the salvation of my Aunt Myrtle. Since this experience, Aunt Myrtle has become one of my most treasured prayer partners. Whenever I'm in need of prayer or whenever I learn that someone else is in need, I call Aunt Myrtle. And she prays about it. It may be someone who is hurting or someone trapped in an abusive marriage who has asked me for prayer. Or it may be a child who has written me with a need. Or it may be any one of a host of other requests. And with all this praying for others that Aunt Myrtle is doing, she is praying herself—I sincerely believe—right into the kingdom! Isn't it interesting how God works?

If I had not doubted the power of my own prayer and hadn't urgently started calling for prayer warriors—and if there hadn't been a four-hour flight delay—I would have never gotten all the way to the M's on my cell phone's address book, and I doubt very much if I would have called Aunt Myrtle!

That's why I'm so glad that when we pray, God sees the bigger picture. His answers reflect His perspective and not just our own. That's why we should pray for God's will to be done. He doesn't always answer our prayers exactly the way we expect. However, the good news is, *He always answers!*

But does He answer the prayers of those who doubt? Read on!

Lesson #2: God honors faith of any size—even faith the size of a tiny mustard seed. I love the assurance of Matthew 17:20: "If you have faith as a grain of mustard seed, . . . nothing will be impossible." Throughout Scripture, faith is the one essential factor necessary for answered prayer, and sin is what gets in the way of answered prayer (see Psalm 66:18, 19; Proverbs 28:9; John 9:31).

But in the gulf between *faith* on the one hand and *sin* on the other, there are many questions that can be posed. For example, does not having a daily devotional time or neglecting Bible study keep us from receiving a miraculous answer to our prayers? Does the size of our faith or the number of people who are praying determine whether our prayer is answered? Why does God say that it is good if several people join together in prayer? And if we doubt, will that really prevent God from answering our prayer?

When it comes to prayer, these age-old philosophical questions beg to be answered. But there's a danger here. Don't let unanswered questions keep you from exercising faith, praying passionately, and experiencing the joy of having God answer your prayers. Our role in the love relationship with God is not to *understand* Him. Our role is to *trust* Him and *passionately communicate* with Him.

As you grapple with questions concerning answered or unanswered prayer, here's a perspective you may want to consider: A spiritual battle is going on over the ownership of the earth and every one of the people who have ever been born here. Satan is saying, "They're mine. I won them fair and square in the Garden of Eden when Adam and Eve doubted what God said and believed me!" Jesus is saying, "They're Mine. I created them—each one special—and I paid for their redemption. I bought them back by My love and My blood."

Now imagine the angelic beings that are fighting for their respective leaders. When Satan rebelled and was cast out of heaven, he took one-third of God's angels with him. These beings so totally changed their characters to conform to their evil leader that they have become known as demons!

But the good news is that two-thirds of the angels remained loyal to God. So in every spiritual controversy, in every spiritual battle you fight, whether it's over an addictive habit, negative emotions, or impulsive behavior, the odds are always stacked on God's side. For every one of Satan's demons who is trying to pull you down, there are at least two of God's angels who are trying to lift you up!

Now what does all this have to do with the power of our faith-based prayers or the number of people who join together in prayer? Just this: Satan is loudly claiming ownership and control of the earth. And if you look around at the crime, gambling, illicit relationships, murder, abuse, pornography, and violence in the world today, it seems as if he's been successful. But when we pray, it gives God permission to crash through whatever barriers Satan has tried to impose and meet the needs of His children.

Imagine now the battle scene. One of God's children—let's say it's me, Brenda Walsh! I'm desperate about the safety of the money in my suitcase. I've made a foolish mistake, and because of it I may be out thousands of dollars. I've been irresponsible with someone else's money. But at the moment, I can't do anything about it. My hands are tied.

This is exactly the hopeless condition in which Satan likes to find God's children. Immediately, negative emotions rush in to harass my mind and body. I'm angry at myself; I feel I've failed the trust of others; I'm embarrassed that I've made such a stupid mistake; and I'm scared I won't be able to pay back what I've lost. Satan is doing a number on me—he's good at that. The demons of anger, failure, embarrassment, and fear are having a heyday! They're in control, even though God's angels of love, peace, contentment, and forgiveness are standing by. The battle has begun. What I choose to do next will determine the victor.

Thankfully, I have learned through my love relationship with Jesus that when I can't help myself, I have God and all His mighty angels on my side. So I send up an SOS. In desperation, I realize I can't do anything about my dilemma. The loaded suitcase is somewhere in the airport transportation system over which I have no control. So I call on God to protect the money.

You might say it's a selfish prayer. "Lord, save *me* and the money!" But that doesn't matter to God. If it's a sincere prayer, the moment it hits heaven's prayer bank, God's forces are rallied. Immediately, good angels are standing next to that suitcase blocking it from the view of anyone whom Satan's demons might try to persuade to investigate what's in that bulging pocket.

In fact, God might have answered my prayer before I even prayed it, because He knew that suitcase needed protection. God can do anything. He doesn't need prayer permission to intervene in human affairs (see Isaiah 65:24). *But,* we have to remember that there is a universe of beings watching this great controversy between Christ and

Satan, between God's good angels and Satan's demons, that is being fought here on earth.

If God would always exert His power over evil to protect His earth children without them ever asking, the accusation could be made against Him that He isn't fighting fair. Satan made this very accusation once concerning God blessing Job, so it's likely he has continued making it throughout earth's history. And he's probably doing so over you and me!

But when we pray, it gives God permission to ignore those evil accusations while at the same time it empowers God's angels to fight the demons on our behalf. The more people who pray—and the more passionately they pray—the more justification God has to intervene on behalf of His children and do His will on earth in spite of Satan and his demons and their accusations.

Plus, the more people who pray, the more people there will be who are going to be blessed, have their faith strengthened, and give God the glory when He does break through with a mighty miracle. It's a win-win situation!

Lesson #3: God is more interested in our faith than He is in whether we occasionally doubt. Many Christians chastise themselves when bad things happen to them because they erroneously think that God would have answered their prayers the way they wanted Him to if they had only had more faith. A father wouldn't have died; cancer would have been healed; the divorce wouldn't have happened; they wouldn't have been fired; the stolen car would have been returned—and on and on.

"Since God didn't answer my prayer," they reason, "it must have been because I didn't have enough faith or didn't pray hard enough or I didn't call enough prayer chains to get enough people to pray." Once a person begins reasoning like that, he or she takes on the burden of responsibility for the bad things that happen in life. "It's my fault that God didn't answer." And the next step is *guilt!*

This kind of thinking is very dangerous. It's the kind of thinking that Satan takes great delight in, because it takes him off the hook and puts us on it! The truth is, bad things are the result of sin—and Satan is the originator of sin. God does not demand perfect faith before working miracles in our lives. He doesn't play games with us, blessing us with miracles if we have enough faith, but denying our requests if we don't.

All of us at one time or another have entertained doubt. Most of us, when it comes to prayer and having our prayers answered, have identified with the father in the Bible who honestly admitted, "Lord, I believe; help my unbelief!" (Mark 9:23, 24). Do you remember the story? I love the way pastor Smuts van Rooyen tells it:

A man came to Jesus one day, cursed with such honesty that he was engaged in a titanic struggle with faith. He was desperate. His boy was possessed with demons trying to kill him. Somewhere he had heard that Jesus could heal the child, but he did not really believe it. Yet more than anything else in the world he wanted his boy well again. And so he went to Christ.

Can you imagine the journey there? His friends walk with him and fill his ears with strong admonitions. "Say nothing of your unbelief. This is your only chance. It's for your kid. Don't reveal too much about your own convictions, and remember that a little pretending can go a long way."

Then he is face to face with Jesus, who confirms his worst fears by saying, "If you can believe, all things are possible." Oh, no. What now? Can he repress this cursed doubt and save his child? Can he just this once affirm what his mind denies? But he will not. He exercises his terrible honesty and cries out, "Lord, I believe; help my unbelief!"

The response of Jesus to such intellectual anguish is profoundly moving. All discussion about faith stops. Jesus is satisfied. The child is promptly healed. What does this demonstrate? It shows that double-mindedness does not shut us out of God's concern. It shows that God does not demand that we give up our intellectual honesty as the price of His love. . . .

What does this teach us about doubt? Live by what you believe and not by what you question. Unbelief is not home; nobody can live happily in it. What you accept, no matter how small, is a hundred times more important than what you reject. Chronic cynicism is a devastating disease. Refuse to cry, "Lord I don't believe." For the benefit of your own soul, shout the honest, entire truth, "Lord, I believe; help my unbelief!" (*Fit Forever: One a Day Devotionals for Body, Mind and Spirit,* edited by Kay Kuzma, page 253).

Every time I look at my suitcase, I'm reminded of how God answered my prayer *and* the prayer I didn't pray! I knew God could protect the money. I even knew in my heart that my prayer alone would be enough for God to assign, if necessary, His whole angel force to my case. But in my overwhelming agony over the potential loss of the money, my faith needed strengthening by having my friends and family praying with me. Isn't it amazing how God allowed me to momentarily entertain a smidgen of doubt, or as I prefer to say, "weak faith," in order to compel me to call everyone I knew? If I hadn't done that, and if God hadn't delayed the plane, others—including my Aunt Myrtle—would not have been blessed by the miracle that God was in the process of performing. What I experienced was the fulfillment of Romans 8:26, "Likewise the Spirit also helps in our weaknesses. For we do not know what we should pray for as we ought, but the Spirit Himself makes intercession for us with groanings which cannot be uttered." Or you might say, "groanings that cannot be expressed in words." I'm so glad God always sees the greater picture.

Chapter 10

Prayed Up and Ready to Go

For the Lord Himself will descend from heaven with a shout, with the voice of an
archangel, and with the trumpet of God. And the dead in Christ will rise first.
Then we who are alive and remain shall be caught up together with them in the clouds
to meet the Lord in the air. And thus we shall always be with the Lord.
Therefore comfort one another with these words.
—1 Thessalonians 4:16–18

People often ask me, "Where did you get such a passion for prayer?" For me, it was when I fully realized my great need for God. It is through our darkest hours that we come to know how vital our relationship with Jesus really is. That is why we shouldn't view trials and tribulations as curses, but rather as blessings. It is through our struggles that we truly realize our desperate need for a Savior! It is then that we are filled with a burning desire to be close to God. I'm talking about the kind of longing in our hearts where we are aching to hear His voice. The more time we spend on our knees, the more we desire oneness with Him.

I have had many mentors who pray passionately, starting with my parents, brothers, and sisters, but I would be remiss if I didn't tell you about my grandma, Helen Micheff, the greatest prayer warrior our family has ever had. I've thought long and hard about where to begin her story, and I've decided that the best example of Grandma's passion for prayer and the peace that it brought to her shows up most clearly in the last few hours of her life.

It was Friday afternoon. I was driving from my home in Knoxville to Nashville, where I was scheduled to speak for the Kentucky-Tennessee Women's Ministries Retreat. As I was traveling through the outskirts of Nashville, my cell phone rang. It was my sister Linda, and I could tell she had been crying.

My precious grandma, Helen Micheff. I loved her with all my heart, and I miss her every day. (I painted the picture in the background especially for her—while she watched me paint and told me what she wanted me to include.)

"It's Grandma. She's in the hospital. They've run tests, and they say she won't make it."

My entire body began to shake. This couldn't be happening. I wasn't ready to say goodbye to my precious grandma. I loved her too much to bear the thought of losing her.

"It could be hours, days—maybe two weeks, but not more," Linda informed me.

I had known this moment would come some day. Grandma Micheff was ninety-four years old and was suffering so terribly from arthritis in her knees that they swelled three times their normal size. She could barely get around with a walker. The doctor said that the only thing that made it possible for her to move at all was her strong will to walk, regardless of the pain! Most people in her condition would have been bedridden years ago. The arthritis had ravaged her neck, back, arms, hands, and feet, as well. In addition to a multitude of other medical problems, Grandma also had a very weak heart.

But the one thing Grandma had going for her was her mind. She was as mentally alert as anyone and could remember details of events that happened decades earlier. As she grew older, suffering from dementia or Alzheimer's absolutely terrified her. I remember her praying, *"Dear God, please don't let me lose my mind. Please keep me sane until I die."*

But she didn't just pray about it. She did everything possible to prevent dementia. Years earlier, she'd learned that memorization was one of the best things a person could do to keep the mind healthy. Memorization stimulates the brain and keeps it alert and functioning. So that's exactly what Grandma did. She memorized whole chapters of the Bible, especially the Psalms, which were her favorite portions of Scripture.

Blinking back my tears, I struggled to concentrate on the road ahead. Grandma lived in West Frankfort, Illinois, just a few miles from 3ABN.

My mom and Grandma taped a special Mother's Day program on 3ABN several years ago. People still tell me they remember seeing my grandma on that program and that they were blessed by it. Left to right: Mom, Grandma, and Dad.

I had to be with her. *Isn't God's timing incredible,* I mused. *The trip from my home to West Frankfort is a six-hour drive, and here I am already halfway there! It will take the other relatives much longer—maybe a day—to reach her side!*

I quickly made a few calls to arrange for someone to cover my speaking appointment at the women's retreat and then pressed down on the gas pedal, heading straight for southern Illinois.

The three-hour drive from Nashville seemed more like thirty hours. Memories of the good times I'd spent with Grandma Micheff washed through my mind, bringing with them new bouts of tears. I remembered hearing her stories about my great-grandmother and how she—Grandma Helen—grew up in Hungary with her sister Susie and brothers John and Bill. Her parents—my great-grandparents—had left their children behind to move to the United States. With the outbreak of World War I, their plans to send for their children became impossible.

After the war, Grandma's parents sent enough money for their two sons to come to the United States. However, the Hungarian government would not issue visas for males of mil-

Susie and Helen Czeke. This photo was taken soon after the girls arrived in America via Ellis Island. Helen would later marry Steve Micheff, and they would become my grandparents.

itary age. Because of this, twelve-year-old Helen—my grandma—and her older sister, Susie, came to America in place of the boys. Instead of the warm reception the young girls expected, their parents were angry! A short time later, the sisters were sent to Chicago to work for the Marshall family, co-owners of the Marshall Field's department store.

An excellent cook, Grandma cooked and cleaned for the family. And as kind as they were to her, she always remembered "her place." Despite her long hours of labor, she never saw any of the money she earned. All of her wages went to her parents. When she turned sixteen, her parents brought her to their home in southern Illinois to be married to a young man from Bulgaria, Steve Micheff. A naturalized citizen of the United States, Steve had a good job working in the coal mines, and he owned a car. Owning an automobile convinced Grandma's parents that this twenty-five-year-old was rich, which in their eyes made him a good match for their daughter. Two days later they married.

Fortunately for Grandma Helen, Steve proved to be honest and hard working, but definitely not rich—nor was he twenty-five. Grandpa

Grandma was an excellent cook, and she taught my mom to cook. She could make homemade noodles and roll them into a perfectly round circle. She gave me the board and homemade rolling pin shown in the picture. They will always be special to me and remind me of the times I spent in Grandma's kitchen.

Steve didn't write too well, so he asked his new wife to write to the government in Bulgaria for his birth certificate. While Grandma had no formal education, she had taught herself to read and write from the only textbook she could afford—the Bible.

After several months the birth certificate finally arrived. To his absolute shock and horror, my grandfather discovered he wasn't twenty-five, but thirty-five—ten years older than he thought he was! At twelve, he'd been forced to leave home and find work. He never saw his family again. With a large number of children in the family, his parents couldn't support him. Having to work long hours as a young child, day after day, he eventually lost track of his age. Grandma admitted they'd never shared a romantic kind of love, but they had a loving respect for each other that grew through the years. Now, Grandpa Steve was long gone, and my precious grandma was dying.

I arrived at the hospital in record time and hurried down the hall to her room, a room she shared with another lady. When Grandma saw me walk into the room, she gasped in surprise. I ran to her and threw my arms around her. Tears ran down her cheeks as she stroked my hair and kept saying, "Oh, Brenda, I should have known you'd come; I should have known you'd come."

Tenderly, I kissed her cheek. "Grandma, no one could have kept me away!" When I asked her to tell me exactly what the doctors said about her condition, her demeanor changed. She sat up straighter and had the biggest smile on her face. Startled, I felt confused. *Is there good news? Is she going to live after all?*

"I'm so excited, Hon, because the doctors say I'm not going to make it. And guess what, it could be a few hours, maybe even tonight. The doctor doesn't know for sure, but it will be soon. And guess what? I won't mind that sleep in the grave—because I won't know anything! It will be just like I'm having a nice restful sleep. And the next voice I hear will be the voice of Jesus on that great resurrection day! We'll all be together again, and I'll have a new body. No more arthritis or pain! I can hardly wait!"

What? Am I hearing things? My grandmother had just learned she was dying, and she acted as though she was getting ready for a party!

Grandma looked into my eyes and saw the bewilderment. In her thick Hungarian accent, she told me what had happened.

"At home this morning I had a sudden, most excruciating pain. It hurt so badly that I screamed loud enough that Uncle George heard me from the yard where he was working. Well, he rushed me to the hospital. The doctors did a bunch of tests and discovered that my intestines had ruptured. So anything I eat or drink

Left to right: Michael James, my daughter, Becky, and Grandma Micheff. Becky loved spending time with Grandma and would brush her hair for hours or rub her back, making sure she was comfortable. Becky is an RN and definitely chose the right profession! I think Grandma was her favorite patient. Of course, it might have had something to do with getting lots of Grandma's undivided attention!

just drains into my abdomen." She went on to say that the doctor told her he would operate if she so desired, but with her heart condition, he didn't think she'd make it through the surgery.

"Well, I told him 'No' in no uncertain terms. I wanted time to say goodbye to my family and friends and to get ready to meet my Maker!" Her face beamed with joy. She was ecstatic. I couldn't find a trace of self-pity, anger, or sorrow in her demeanor. "Now, Brenda, let's start calling people because I have some goodbyes to say."

"Grandma, remember how you always said you wanted to die at home? I'm a nurse; I can administer your pain medications. We could get an ambulance to take you home if that's what you want."

She thought for several seconds. "You know, Hon, you're right about that. I always thought I wanted to die at home. But it wasn't until this moment that I realized that it really doesn't matter. I think I would just as soon stay right here." She patted the bed with her hand and giggled. "Besides I have a nice little call button here. When I push it, someone comes running."

This was from a woman who'd worked hard her entire life meeting other people's needs. We both giggled.

"OK, now we have to hurry. I might not have much time. Let's call Becky and Linda Kay and, of course, Tim."

Since Grandma was hard of hearing, we used my cell phone because it had a volume control that made it easier for her to hear. One by one, she talked with all her family, even her grandchildren and great-grandchildren who lived far away. We called a list of her friends. I listened as she excitedly told each of them that she was dying and that the next voice she'd hear would be the voice of Jesus. "You make sure you are right with Jesus because I want to see you on the great resurrection morning," she would tell them.

When all the calls had been placed, I watched Grandma Helen's gnarled hands straighten imaginary wrinkles from the bed sheets covering her frail body. She looked pleased with herself. "Well, now that I've said my goodbyes, I'm ready to go. What time is it?"

I told her, but a few minutes later, she asked the time again. Once more I told her. Frequently she asked that same question, disappointed each time that she hadn't "departed" yet. Whenever a nurse or hospital worker entered her room, she reminded them that they needed to give their hearts to God. "Jesus is coming soon, and you need to be ready. You can't serve two masters; you must choose either God or Satan. I want you to know that Jesus loves you, and I would like to see you when Jesus comes back for us."

As excited as a school girl, she preached to anyone who would listen. This was a side of my grandmother I had never seen before.

A nurse entered the room armed with medication. She prepared to add it to Grandma's IV. Remembering my own bad hospital experience when I was almost killed by two doses of a drug accidentally being added to my IV, I asked, "What are you giving her?"

The woman gave me a benign smile. "It's something to help her heart beat stronger and keep the infection down."

I frowned. I didn't like the sound of that. "I don't want you to give it to her. I want to see her doctor. When will he be in?"

Flustered, the nurse stepped back. "He won't be in again today, ma'am."

"Please go call him. Tell him that Helen Micheff's granddaughter is here. Tell him I am a registered nurse and that I'm requesting to see him tonight. Until I speak with him, Helen is refusing all medications."

My youngest daughter, Linda Kay, and Grandma. Linda Kay liked to listen for hours as Grandma told her stories of growing up in Hungary. She has many precious memories of times spent right on this sofa with her grandma and of the words of wisdom her grandma gave her—everything from finding the right man to being a "good wife."

"Yes, ma'am. I'll tell him." With that she collected the unused medication and hurried from the room.

Thirty minutes later the doctor stormed in. He looked irritated. I wasn't a stranger; I had met him many times during previous office visits.

"Good evening, Doctor, I'm sure you remember me—Brenda Walsh, Helen's granddaughter. Can you tell me why you are giving my grandmother medication for her heart and also antibiotics?"

After casting me a measured gaze, he explained the desired effect of each medicine.

"I'm confused, Doctor. Is my grandmother dying?"

He nodded.

"Is there a chance she will live?"

He shook his head. "Your grandmother's heart would not be able to stand the surgery needed to repair the hole in her intestine. I don't know how long she has. It could be today, tomorrow, or even a week, but probably not much longer. The longer she lives, the more painful her death will be because of the peritonitis in her abdomen." He took a deep breath and continued the dismal recital of what was to come. "Her abdomen will swell and increase in size as if it were a balloon ready to pop. There will come a point when no amount of pain medication will be able to keep her comfortable." He looked genuinely sad. "I'm sorry."

I knitted my brow in confusion. "Then why would you give her medication to prolong her life even a moment?"

"What do you expect me to do?" A hint of confusion could be heard in his voice.

I retorted with a quick answer. "What I expect is for you to help her die. I want all medicine discontinued immediately, except for pain medicine. I want Hospice called, and I want her to be kept as comfortable as possible. I want her moved to a private room today. And I want a morphine drip that I can use to monitor her pain. I am a registered nurse, and I will be with her until the end." I barely paused long enough to breathe. "If there is any of this you can't live with, tell me now, and I'll find another doctor who will allow her to go in peace with as much dignity and as pain-free as possible. That's what I expect!"

All five foot two inches of me stared straight into his eyes. This was my grandmother's life. And while I'd never be able to fight for myself with such vigor, I would fight to the death for someone I loved.

By now all the irritation had drained from his face. I could see that he genuinely cared for my grandma. He spoke in a gentler voice, "I've been your grandmother's physician for over forty years. I don't want her to suffer either. I agree with what you have suggested. And I'll do it immediately. In medicine, we are so used to preserving life that I guess we sometimes forget we're doing a disservice by not allowing a person to die naturally." A sad, tired smile filled his face. "Thank you for reminding me of that. If I can help you in any way, please tell the nurses to call me right away." With that he turned and left.

Now, my grandmother was of the old school. For her, a doctor was one to be obeyed and never questioned. But as I turned to face her, I saw a twinkle of pride in her eyes. "Thank you for taking such good care of me."

I gave her a gentle hug. "Oh, Grandma, I love you so much. I just want this last bit of time you have, however long, to be the best it can be, and I don't want you to suffer."

"I know, Hon, and I appreciate it. I really do! And I'm so glad you're here."

"Grandma, I'm not going to leave you. I will be here when you take your last breath!" I hugged her again, lingering a little to capture the moment forever in my mind.

Before the hour passed, Grandma was moved to a bigger and more comfortable private room across the hall. I pulled a reclining chair up to the side of her bed so I could be closer to her. After the hospital staff got her into bed, I fluffed her pillow and gave her a wet washcloth to moisten her dry mouth. Constantly thirsty, she couldn't even have ice chips due to the hole in her intestines. That would only increase her pain.

I watched when the nurse arrived and connected her to the morphine drip. Now I could push the button every ten minutes as needed to ease her pain. Once I was certain there was nothing more I could do, I sat down beside her. She took my hand in hers.

"Hon, I want you to promise me something."

"What Grandma? I would promise you anything."

"I want you to promise me that you won't cry for me when I'm gone. I want you to be happy for me that I am no longer suffering and in pain. I want you to know that my heart is right with the good Lord and that when I wake up from a long sleep, the next voice I'll hear will be the voice of Jesus. Can you be happy for me? Can you do that for me, Hon?"

Oh, great! The tears I'd stifled since I entered the hospital spilled out and ran down my cheeks. I quickly turned my face from her so she couldn't see.

"Brenda!" Her voice changed. "Would you get me a waffle? I'm so hungry!"

She knew she couldn't have any food! Thinking my grandmother was losing it, I whirled about to face her.

Seeing the panic on my face, she burst out laughing. "Gotcha! You know I can't have anything to eat. You thought I'd lost my mind, didn't you?"

Grandma loved my husband, Tim, very much. They had a special bond. When she called him to say goodbye, Tim couldn't hold back the tears. This photo was taken at Grandma's house one day on our way to church. Grandma and her Bible were never separated. Left to right: me, Grandma, and Tim.

"Grandma, don't do that again!" Her laugher was contagious, and I laughed in spite of myself.

"Just remember to always keep a good sense of humor! It will help you a lot in life." Grandma had given me so much wisdom throughout my life, and now, facing death, she was still teaching me.

When I married Tim she had told me, "Remember, marriage is not fifty-fifty.

Sometimes it's seventy-thirty or even ninety-ten. But the woman always has to give the most. You must never expect life to be fair. It never is. If you're always willing to give more, you will be happy." The women's lib movement would be up in arms to hear Grandma's advice to me, but over the years, I'd discovered that what she had to say held a lot of truth.

Beyond the hospital window, the sun drew closer and closer to the horizon. How different this Sabbath would be from the one I'd set out to enjoy several hours ago when I thought I was driving to the women's retreat.

"Would you read the Bible to me, Hon?"

As I read, she mouthed the words along with me. We stopped for a while and sang a song. And then I would begin reading again. At one point, a nurse asked if we'd mind if she cracked the door open a little so the patient across the hall could listen.

Grandma smiled with delight. "Keep it wide open if you'd like."

From then on we sang a little louder: " 'Tis So Sweet to Trust in Jesus"; "The Old Rugged Cross"; and "In the Sweet By and By." I will forever hold in my mind those precious memories of the last hours I spent with my grandma.

"Wouldn't it be wonderful if the good Lord would take me on the Sabbath day? I do hope I get to go on Sabbath." Excitement filled her voice. "It could even be tonight."

A little later I settled her down for the night. I turned the lights down low and encouraged her to try to sleep.

"Sleep? Why? I'm too excited to sleep. I want to talk some more." So we reminisced about the summers I spent at her house—how I'd stayed by her side when the older children went swimming or played outside. I confessed to her, "The truth be told, it wasn't fear as much as I really enjoyed all the special attention I received when I didn't have to share you with everyone else."

She reached over and squeezed my hand. "And you'll be the one by my side till the end."

"Oh yes. I'll be here."

"There is one thing I would like you to do before you report my death to the nurse on duty."

"What's that, Grandma?"

"Check me over really good to make sure I'm really gone. Also, can you stay with me until the *funeral man* comes? I wouldn't want to be just lying here dead and some poor soul come wandering in and get scared to death seeing a dead old lady lying here." She giggled a little.

"Yes, Grandma, I won't leave until the *funeral man* comes for you."

"Good! Then there's just one more thing I need to tell you. It is really important to me to end my life like a prayer. I want the last words on my lips to be, 'In the name of the Father, the Son, and the Holy Ghost, Amen.'" I remembered how my grandmother always ended her prayers like that.

Grandma loved her grandchildren with an unconditional love, and she had a way of making each of us feel special. She spoiled us, always ready to cook us a meal or tell us a story. She had the softest hands and the biggest heart!

"OK, Grandma, I'll remember."

She talked for some time about how much she loved her children and her grandchildren. And while there had been a lot of pain and heartache in her life, the love of her family made it all worthwhile. We continued talking for more than an hour, laughing and reliving old memories.

She told me about the time when my father was young and the children's division had a part in the church program. "The teacher asked your father what he'd do if another boy poked him in the nose."

"Why, I'd poke him right back!" he replied.

Horrified, the teacher quickly asked, "Is that what Jesus would do?"

"And your father retorted, 'You didn't ask me what Jesus would do. You asked me what *I* would do!' " Grandma admitted, "I was so embarrassed I cried all the way home."

As I sat there in the darkened room, I realized that my grandmother had been the prayer warrior for our whole family. She'd prayed me through the formation of *Kids Time*. I would call her and tell her whatever I was currently praying for, and she'd pray for it, too. Whenever there was a direct answer to prayer, I would call her immediately so we could rejoice together. During the last years of her life, she was nearly blind and confined to a couch in one room of her house. She spent her time studying a large print Bible through a magnifying glass and praying. When she saw the first *Kids Time* program, she was as excited as I was. We praised God together. In the years to come, I knew what I'd miss most. It would be Grandma's prayers.

That night I decided I would not let myself sleep. I wanted to be awake to push the button for the morphine drip. The IV pump had now been increased to release a dose every eight minutes, but only if I manually pushed the button. I didn't want Grandma to be in pain for even one minute longer than necessary. If I let her pain level increase, it would be harder to make her comfortable again.

I was lost in my personal reverie when Grandma smiled at me and squeezed my hand. "OK, we've talked enough. I'm all done talking, and I'm ready to go."

I leaned over her bed. She took me in her arms. I lay there for a few minutes, neither of us wanting to speak. I gave her a gentle squeeze. "Grandma, I love you with all my heart."

She returned my squeeze and stroked my hair. "I love you too, Hon."

I sat back down in the chair and watched her raise both hands toward heaven. In a clear voice, she called, "In the name of the Father, the Son, and the Holy Ghost, Amen." With that she dropped her hands and closed her eyes. After five minutes she opened one eye.

"Am I still here?"

"Yes, Grandma, you're still here."

"Oh . . ." She sounded disappointed. She extended her hand toward mine. "Here, take my hand. Every few minutes I'll give it a squeeze. After a while, if I don't squeeze your hand, check me to see if I'm dead."

"OK, that sounds like a good plan." I couldn't help but smile to myself. Three or four times she again raised her hands and repeated aloud, "In the name of the Father, the Son, and the Holy Ghost, Amen," and then drifted off to sleep.

As I watched her sleep, I remembered the time she taught me how to roll out egg noodles into a perfect circle and how to make so many other recipes. She taught me the importance of being kind and generous, of never being too proud to serve others. She taught me how to make brown gravy and cook meat to please my new husband, even though I'd been a vegetarian all my life. She taught me how to have a happy marriage, and now she was teaching me how to die. What an incredible lady!

Oh, Lord, I prayed, *please don't let her suffer. I love her so much, and I know that You love her even more. Please don't let her die in pain.*

I held her hand throughout the night, sometimes praying, sometimes reminiscing. Whenever I got sleepy, I walked around the room and then sat back down and took her hand again. The next morning when she opened her eyes, she looked so disappointed.

"Brenda, is that you?"

"Yes, Grandma, it's me."

"Does that mean I'm still here?"

"Yes, you're still here."

"Oh, I so wanted to go last night." She heaved a sigh of disappointment. "I guess the good Lord will take me when He's ready." With that, she perked up. "Let's enjoy the Sabbath together."

After bathing her and making her comfortable, I again read the Bible to her. I read from John and Matthew, but always ended up with the Psalms. We sang more songs. As I started another hymn, she patted my hand. "Wait, Hon, why don't you open the door so someone else can receive a blessing, too."

I obeyed. We sang until my voice was almost gone. I stopped every now and then to moisten her lips with a wet washcloth. As the hospital staff entered her room on their rounds, she praised Jesus to them. I hadn't seen that spark in her eye in years. Everyone knew she was getting ready to die, but no one would have believed it by the way she acted.

One concerned nurse pulled me into the hallway. "Does your grandmother realize she is dying?"

Seeing the confusion on her face made me laugh. "Yes, Grandma is mentally alert and aware that she's dying." I explained about how much she loved Jesus and looked forward to soon hearing Jesus' voice and how she wanted everyone to be ready to meet Him, too.

The nurse shook her head. "I wish all my patients could die like this."

Throughout the day, Grandma grew tired, and I encouraged her to rest. Every time she'd start to close her eyes, she would raise her hands toward heaven again and say, "In the name of the Father, and the Son, and the Holy Ghost, Amen."

Uncle George stopped by to see her. She urged him to "get right with God." "I want to see you in heaven, Son. Please give your heart to Jesus."

When he left, we had a special prayer for him. She asked me to keep praying for him after she was gone. Mom and Dad arrived by noon the next day. We spent the afternoon visiting, talking, and praying. We sang hymn after hymn. The song Grandma wanted to sing most was "Leaning on the Everlasting Arms." I could see her feet moving to the music beneath the sheet. My parents seemed surprised to find her so excited and happy.

Dad was Grandma's youngest child, and she loved him deeply. They would talk often on the phone, sharing Bible promises and thoughts about the Lord. Dad and Mom called Grandma every Friday evening to welcome the Sabbath—and ended their conversation with a heartfelt, passionate prayer.

That evening, my cousins came by to see her. My cousin Nancy brought Grandma's favorite flower, a beautiful white rose. Of course she urged them to "get right with God." At the end of the evening, we gathered around her bed, and Daddy prayed the most beautiful prayer. Then they each gave her a hug and left. I stayed just like I promised.

After making her as comfortable as possible, I prayed for her again and told her how much I loved her. Closing her eyes, she lifted both arms into the air and in a clear voice repeated, "In the name of the Father, the Son, and the Holy Ghost, Amen." A few minutes later she did it again, but this time she spoke in Hungarian. Those were the last words her lips uttered—just as she'd wanted.

Once more she lowered her arms. A few minutes passed. Without opening her eyes or saying a word, she reached over and felt for my hand. I held it while she drifted off to sleep. The increased medication was making her sleepy.

The next day, my mother and father stayed with me as we listened to Grandma's labored breathing. She had not awakened and was in a deep sleep. Uncle George sat in the room for a short while before returning home. We had requested no visitors. I didn't want anyone walking in and seeing Grandma like this. I was determined to protect her dignity. Toward evening my parents left to get some sleep. My mother tried to talk me into leaving, as well, or to let her sit with Grandma for a while. I refused. I'd given my word. Besides, I was beyond sleepy. My body was numb from lack of rest. From the chair, I watched the rise and fall of Grandma's chest. At 10:55 P.M. I heard a distinct difference in the sound and rate of her breathing. As a nurse, I knew the end was near.

Suddenly I saw a movement out of the corner of my eye. I turned my head in time to see the lovely white rose my cousin Nancy had brought that afternoon slowly droop over in the vase, its face to the floor. I quickly turned back to look at my grandmother and saw her exhale her last breath.

She had died just as I had prayed she would. Not once did she wince in pain! Not once did she cry out in agony! That in itself was a direct answer to my prayer. I sat on the edge of the bed and laid my head on her chest, choking back my tears. I desperately wanted to keep my promise not to cry. Sitting up, I repeated her last words, "In the name of the Father, the Son, and the Holy Ghost, Amen."

I called the nurse and then the funeral home. I waited a most painful three hours for the "funeral man" as Grandma had called him, to arrive. Watching someone you love breathe their last breath is difficult enough, but watching someone you love grow cold, stiff, and their color turn blue, was almost unbearable.

I helped the mortician prepare her body. As he wheeled her from the room, my knees felt weak. I sat down on the edge of the bed and prayed for strength. After collecting her personal items, I started to leave. I took one last gaze about the

Dad preached at Grandma's funeral. I kept my promise not to cry, but when my sisters and I sang the final song, "I Want to See My Savior Most of All," I could no longer hold back the tears. Left to right: Linda Johnson, Dad (James Micheff), Mom (Bernice Micheff), me, and Cinda Sanner.

room. My eyes rested on the rose. Picking up the rose, I walked from the room, turning off the light behind me.

As I climbed into my car to leave, I realized I had nowhere to go. It was three o'clock in the morning. Mom and Dad were sleeping at my 3ABN apartment where there was only one bed. Having no other options, I drove to my room and knocked gently. Mom opened the door, and I fell into her arms.

"It's over; she's gone." I choked back the sobs that I knew would come if I said one more word. I was so grateful for the comfort of my mother's arms. My heart ached, and I silently prayed for strength. *Oh why had I promised Grandma no tears!*

I hadn't slept in four days, and my whole body was numb with grief. Mom gave me one of the blankets from the bed, and I collapsed on the floor, emotionally and physically exhausted.

God gave me the strength not to cry at Grandma's funeral. Dad preached, and my sisters and I sang. I played the organ exactly as she'd instructed me to. I didn't cry until we began singing, "I Want to See My Savior First of All" at the grave-site. When I began crying, my sisters did, as well. I felt badly for breaking my promise to my grandmother until I realized that I wasn't crying for her; I was crying for me!

She'd been such an important part of my life and had shaped me into the person I'd become. I haven't a doubt that I will see my grandma when Jesus comes. Until then, I will cherish the lessons she taught me. Yet of all the valuable lessons I've learned from her, perhaps the most important lessons of all were the ones she taught me on her deathbed! And what I will miss the most is my grandma's precious prayers!

In the name of the Father, the Son, and the Holy Ghost, Amen.

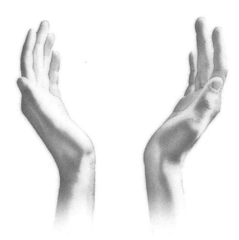

CHAPTER 11

FLYING FIRST CLASS FOR THE LORD

"You are My witnesses," says the Lord,

"And My servant whom I have chosen."

—*Isaiah 43:10*

I was packing for a trip to Belize, Central America, where Rosinell Craig, the Women's Ministries leader, had asked me to share my personal story of abuse. She said that domestic violence was a major problem in her country and that the women there needed to hear my message of hope. I was humbled and amazed at how God continues to use the darkest times of my life not only to bring healing to hurting people but also to draw others closer to Jesus.

"Let's see, I have my clothes, shoes, blow dryer, and—oh, yes, I don't want to forget my bookmarks." I hurried to my office to grab a couple hundred bookmarks and then tucked them into the suitcase. I called to my husband, Tim. "Honey, I'm ready to leave for the airport!"

Thirty minutes later I was sitting at the gate in Knoxville's airport waiting to board Continental's flight to Houston, Texas, where I would change planes for Belize City. I began looking around at the other passengers. *People are so interesting,* I thought. Some were dozing in their chairs; others were talking on cell phones so loudly that everyone else could hear; and still others were quietly sipping coffee and reading. One mother was trying to distract a crying child who had obviously been awakened too early. *I wonder which of you God wants me to witness to today?* I said to myself.

Every time I fly I ask God to seat me next to someone with whom I can share Jesus. Today was no exception. I closed my eyes and began talking to my heavenly Father. *Dear God, You know all the people who are flying with me today. You know their hearts. Lord, please seat me next to someone I can witness to; someone who needs to hear how much You love them.* I continued to pray for others on my prayer list and for the women in Belize who would attend the retreat. Before I knew it, we were boarding the plane.

As I slid into the wide soft leather seat I had been assigned, I whispered another prayer, *"Thank You, Jesus, for letting me fly first class."* It had been a long time since I had flown first class. This kind of privilege just didn't fit into a full-time volunteer's budget! I was in this wide seat only because the person responsible for purchasing my ticket had waited too long and the only seats available were in first class!

When everyone was boarded and the flight attendant had closed the door and instructed us to fasten our seat belts, I was disappointed. The seat next to me was empty. *Oh well, Lord, You know what You're doing. Is there someone on my connecting flight that You want me to witness to? Is someone hurting that needs to hear Your plan of salvation? If so, please anoint my lips and let me be a vessel You can use. Amen.*

In Houston, I changed planes. As I made my way down the aisle, I quickly found my seat, 2B, and sat down. Again, the seat next to me was empty. I began to plead for the Holy Spirit to fill that seat! I didn't have to wait long before a lady carrying an oversized purse said, "Excuse me, I believe I'm in the seat by the window."

As we both settled in, I asked, "Have you been to Belize before or is this your first visit?"

"No, I've been there many times," she answered. "My husband and I vacationed there several years ago, and we fell in love with the country. In fact, I'm meeting him there. We're buying a house and retiring. The cost of living is so much better in Belize than in the United States. You just can't beat the weather, and the people are so warm and friendly. How about you? Is this your first visit? Oh, by the way, my name is Beth."

After introducing myself, I commented, "I'm in Belize only for a few days."

Before I could say anything else, Beth interrupted, "Why in the world would you come to Belize for only a couple of days! What are you doing? Are you traveling on business?"

Wow! Thank You, Jesus! I breathed in silent prayer. *You sure opened this door in a hurry!* I quickly explained that I was going to Belize to give my testimony, based on my book, to a group of women. I had a copy of the book with me, so I pulled it out of my carry-on bag and handed it to her. "It's called *Battered to Blessed*," I said, "because I was abused in my first marriage." Before I knew it, I had told her my whole story. As I finished, I commented, "There are so many hurting people around the world. I understand that Belize has its share of domestic abuse, as well. I am praying that God will use me this weekend to be a blessing in someone's life! Maybe hearing my story will give someone hope because Jesus wants to save her, too!"

I continued, "God is so full of grace and mercy. He delivered me from that abusive relationship and made me whole! I thank Him for each day that He gives me, because so many times I was left for dead and never should have survived. It doesn't matter what we are going through; God is with us every step of the way. All we need to do is pray and ask Him to come into our lives!"

"It's amazing," Beth responded, "that you can talk about God so freely. I have to tell you, I don't think I have ever heard anyone speak about God in such a personal way. You make it sound so natural, so easy, like you know Him personally!"

I had to smile as I saw the bewildered look on her face. "I *do* know Him personally; He's my best Friend. I can talk to Him about anything and everything. And I know He hears me. The real purpose of prayer isn't just to ask for things, but to get to know Jesus! And when you talk to Him, you've got to listen. When I was in the midst of my worst moments of abuse, I was praying and pleading, begging God to save me. But I wasn't listening. I would figure out how I thought God should answer my prayer, and then ask Him to make it happen. Then I'd wonder why it didn't. I wasn't listening to His voice directing me. It is never God's plan that we should be hurt, physically or emotionally. God wants to give us the desires of our heart. But we must first learn to listen to His voice."

Beth sat there for a moment, silently taking in what I had just said. She looked deeply troubled, and I could sense the emotion building up inside her.

She looked directly at me and said, "I have to tell you that I think it was God's plan for me to sit next to you today. I have a wonderful husband now, but it wasn't always that way, and I still struggle with feelings of resentment from years of rejection. I don't know you at all, but I don't detect any bitterness in you. How is that possible? How did you move past the pain?"

"Oh, that's simple." I replied. "I can sum it up in one word: *forgiveness!* If you refuse to forgive, you will live with that pain for the rest of your life, and it will totally destroy any chance of happiness for you on this earth *and* in heaven. God tells us in the Bible that if we do not forgive others, He will not be able to forgive us.

"Beth, you have a choice to make. You can choose to live a miserable life dwelling in the past and harboring bitterness and resentment, or you can choose to forgive and give that burden to Jesus! If you choose to forgive, that burden will be lifted from your shoulders, and you will experience the real joy that Jesus has to offer!"

Tears rolled down Beth's cheeks, and she reached for her purse to retrieve a tissue. "You make it sound so easy, but how can you forgive someone who has done such horrible things to you?"

I reached over and took her hand. "Jesus can give you that forgiveness. All you have to do is ask Him. You may not be able to love him with your human love, but you can love him with *God's love.*"

"How will I know if I've really forgiven him or not?" she asked.

"Oh, you'll know all right. You will experience incredible peace and joy. When you have truly forgiven, there's no bitterness or resentment. God will replace that anger and hate with His love! You will even find yourself asking God to bless whoever has wronged you with the same blessings that you'd ask for yourself. God is so full of grace and mercy, and that's what Jesus wants us to have!"

We continued talking. She asked questions, and I answered first one and then another. I could see that she was searching for something that was missing in her life. There was no doubt in my mind that God had placed me in that first-class seat beside Beth for a reason.

The flight attendant's voice came over the loud speaker, "Please place all tray tables and seats in their upright position and prepare for landing."

What? It can't be time to land already! The two-hour flight had gone by so quickly, and there was so much more that I wanted to share with Beth.

"I'd like to give you a book to read," I said. "It is a book that will answer some of your questions, and more importantly, it will help you see just how much Jesus loves you."

I pulled the book from my carry-on bag and placed one of my business cards inside. "It is called *Passion of the Christ*, and I believe it will be a blessing to you." I handed her the book.

She looked at it and held it almost reverently. "Thank you so much, but not just for the book. I can't thank you enough for what you did for me today. You certainly have given me much to think about."

Before leaving the plane, I leaned over and asked if I could pray with her.

"Yes, I'd like that very much."

I took her hand in mine and began to pray. *"Dear Father in heaven, thank You so much for allowing Beth and me to sit together today and for giving us the opportunity to talk about You. Please come into Beth's life, Lord, and give her the forgiveness in her heart that she is seeking. Lord, replace the bitterness and hurt with Your love. May she have so much joy and love in her heart that her marriage will be happier than she could have ever imagined and she will know it is because of You! I am also asking, Lord, that somehow You will let Beth know how much You really love her and that she will have a desire to be closer to You! Thank You for being the awesome God that You are. Amen."*

When we finished praying I gave her a hug. She was crying now, oblivious to the people around us that were already getting off the plane.

"I want you to know that I will be praying for you," I told Beth. "And if we never meet again on this earth, let's plan to be neighbors in heaven."

"I'd like that very much," she said. And with that we went our separate ways. All the way to the baggage carrousel I was praising God for answering my prayer and giving me the opportunity to witness for Him.

GOD'S BIRTHDAY GIFT

Tomasa Smith picked me up at the airport and dropped me off at my hotel. She told me she would give me a couple of hours to check in and get settled before she picked me up for the evening meeting. As I walked toward the registration desk, I glanced toward a door that was opening and watched as three girls and a woman carrying a child walked out from the restaurant. One of the girls had some helium-filled balloons in her hand, and the others were carrying gift bags.

Suddenly the girl carrying the balloons looked at me and shrieked! "Miss Brenda! I can't believe it's you! Mom, look, it's Miss Brenda!"

The girl ran toward me, and I dropped my suitcase and carry-on bags just seconds before she wrapped her arms around me. She was jumping up and down and still screaming my name. Then turning to look at her mom, she exclaimed, "Oh, Mom, thank you so much; this is the best birthday present ever!"

Quickly putting two and two together, I hugged her and wished her happy birthday. I looked toward her mom who mouthed the words "Thank you" to me. We moved over to the lobby, where we sat down in the lounge chairs and visited for about thirty minutes. The little girl's name was Tanisha, and she told me about how she watched *Kids Time* every day and how much she loved the program.

Tanisha's favorite singer on Kids Time *is Joshua Lance. He's very special to "Miss Brenda," too!*

She went into great detail, talking about her favorite singers and sharing her dream to someday meet Joshua, who sang on the "Praise Time" segment. She also loved "Cooking Time" with Catie Sanner and "Nature Time" with Ranger Jim. Tanisha rattled on and on, stopping now and then to give me another spontaneous hug. Her two friends were just as excited; each wanted special attention. They took turns sitting next to me, and I gave them some of my special bookmarks. I didn't leave until photos were taken and I had signed everything they wanted me to sign!

As I turned to go, Tanisha ran after me for one more hug. "Miss Brenda," she exclaimed, "I will never forget this birthday! You are the best present ever! I love you, Miss Brenda."

One more hug, and they were gone. I learned that 3ABN is a very popular station on cable TV throughout the country. Tanisha lived fifty miles away and had just come into the city to celebrate her birthday at the hotel restaurant.

Wow! I thought as I entered my room. *God knew that I would be walking into this hotel lobby the very second that Tanisha and her mom and friends would be leaving!* I marveled at God's perfect timing and also at the huge responsibility that He had entrusted to me. *Thank You, Jesus, for allowing me the privilege of witnessing to these children.*

MINISTERING IN BELIZE

A record number of women attended the weekend retreat. Instead of one thousand women the leaders were hoping for, almost two thousand came! It was wonderful to meet so many precious people eager for a spiritual feast! Several buses even came from Guatemala bringing a large number of Spanish-speaking women to the retreat. This meant that someone would need to translate.

As I listened to the translator during the preliminaries, it became quite apparent to me that she was having difficulty. Many times she would stop to clarify a word or thought with the speaker.

I began to pray, *God, please send someone to translate for me!* I looked around anxiously, *Lord, surely there must be someone here who knows both Spanish and English fluently.*

As I heard my name announced and began walking toward the platform, I was still praying, *Lord, I know You have everything under control. I am placing my faith and trust in You.* Just as I reached for the microphone, Rosinell Craig came forward and took it from my hand.

"Is Julie Archibold here?" she asked. A woman in a pale lavender suit raised her hand. "Julie, would you mind translating for Brenda, please?"

Seconds later, a beautiful, tall, poised, eloquent woman walked toward the platform. But the most striking thing about her was her face—I could see Jesus shining through her!

As I began to speak, Julie translated every word perfectly! She was so quick that I paused only briefly to give her time to interpret. She matched every expression in the tone of my voice, even making the identical hand gestures that I was making! As I continued speaking, it flowed so perfectly that I almost forgot that translation was necessary! I couldn't believe it! God answered my prayer far beyond my wildest dreams!

When the program was over I spoke to first one lady and then another as they shared their own personal experiences of domestic violence. Some were crying too hard to talk, so I would just hold them in my arms and say a prayer quietly in their ear. Others handed me letters that they had written prior to coming to the meeting, wanting me to read them later. Each of the women asked for prayer. I will never forget one lady with a blackened eye, bruised face, and lips so swollen that she could hardly talk.

She wanted to tell me that after hearing my testimony she now had the courage to leave her abusive

Julie Archibold and me. God sent Julie in answer to my prayer. She has not only become a wonderful prayer warrior, but also a dear and treasured friend.

situation. Her husband had not wanted her to attend this event, and because she had insisted on going, he beat her very severely. Still, she was determined to come, and while her husband was sleeping, she left in the wee hours of the morning, walking a long distance since she had no money for bus fare. One after another, the women shared their burdens and thanked me for being willing to tell my story. By the end of the day I was exhausted, but praising Jesus for the opportunity to witness for Him. I had prayed that God would use me in a special way, and He certainly did! I marveled at His goodness!

Rosinell Craig, Women's Ministries Director for the Belize Conference, organized a tour of orphanages in the area. Left to right: Sandra Augustus, Julie Archibold, me, Lisa Flores, Rosinell Craig, Tomassa Smith, and Michelle Smith. Incidentally, Sandra is an excellent cook; my mouth still waters for her delicious eggplant ratatouille.

The next day, Rosinell, Tomasa, Julie, and a few others took me to visit a few orphanages. It nearly broke my heart when one little boy wrapped his small arms around my legs and pleaded, "Please, Miss Brenda, will you be my mommy? I promise I'll be good, and I can work hard, too!" I desperately wanted to pick up that little boy and tell him that I would love to be his mommy! But I knew that God had entrusted a world of children to me through *Kids Time* and that it would be impossible to focus on just one.

"Jesus loves you so much, and I do, too," I said, giving him a big hug. Before I could say anything more, other children were pushing toward me, eager for their hugs, too. I left with tears in my eyes and a

Visiting at one of the orphanages. The children wanted me to know that Kids Time *is their favorite TV show!*

heavy heart, knowing how needy the children were and knowing that I could offer only a hug. I prayed silently as we drove away that Jesus would come soon to put an end to all the suffering and sadness in this world!

The morning I was to fly home, Dr. Ranju took me to one more orphanage. She told me it was on our way to the airport, but it seemed to me like a major detour. All of the kids there watched *Kids Time*, and she knew how much it would mean to them to be able to meet "Miss Brenda."

Dr. Ranju is a medical doctor who could easily be making a fortune practicing medicine elsewhere. But God called her to Belize City, where she tirelessly tends to the medical needs of His children, the

Women's ministries leaders in Central America. From left to right: Coty de Calderón (Women's Ministries Director, Guatemala), Sandra Augustus, me, Dr. Nesamony Prakasam (better known as Dr. Ranju), and Caroline Scott (wife of the president of the Belize Conference of Seventh-day Adventists).

orphans, widows, and those unable to pay. Yet God has blessed her in ways that surpass any monetary compensation! She depends on donations from those more fortunate, and she shared with me how God always supplies her needs. I agreed that *total dependence* on God is what brings us close to Him!

My return flight

Before I knew it, I was back at the airport. I breezed through security and ran to my gate, barely making my flight. I settled into my first-class seat, struggling a little to get my carry-on bag to fit under the seat in front of me. I started to fasten my seat belt and then decided to wait to see if someone would sit next to me.

These sure are nice, comfortable seats, I thought to myself as I ran my hand across the soft leather. *I could sure get used to this.* Then I smiled to myself as I realized that this experience probably would never happen again! For now, I'd just settle back and enjoy the blessing of flying first class for the Lord.

I watched as the passengers passed by on their way to the coach cabin. I wondered if anyone was going to sit next to me and began to pray that God would have someone special fill that seat! The flow of people stopped, and I was just beginning to think that no one else was coming, when a man showed up wearing a khaki shirt with some fishing lures sticking out of his pocket. He paused and said, "Excuse me, Ma'am, I believe that is my seat by the window."

I quickly got up, let him in, and then took my seat again. We both fastened our seat belts as the flight attendant stood up to give the usual instructions. Since I fly frequently, I barely paid attention, but that wasn't the only reason for my inattentiveness. I was praying that God would give me an opportunity to witness to this man. I didn't have to wait long for an answer.

"Hi," he said, "my name is Charles."

"It's nice to meet you, Charles. My name is Brenda. Have you been down here fishing?" *Duh,* I thought to myself as I realized how silly that sounded. *He's obviously been fishing. Why else would a man have fishing lures in his pocket? What a foolish thing to say!*

Charles chuckled a little and replied, "Yes, I was here *trying* to fish, but it sure was a lousy trip. I didn't catch a thing. What were you doing here? Vacation?"

"No, not a vacation. I was here to speak at a Christian women's retreat." I went on to tell him about the incredible weekend. I shared with him how I had written a book about my personal experience with domestic violence and how women had confided to me about the abuse they had suffered.

"Do you see this bag?" I pointed to my carry-on tucked under the seat in front of me. "That bag is full of letters from women who wanted to tell me their stories and also letters from their children. There were so many people and not enough time to talk to each of them that many brought letters and thrust them into my hands, wanting me to pray for them."

"Wow. That is really something. I'm not what you'd call a church-going man myself, although I know I should." Then out of the blue, he asked, "What church do you go to, anyway?"

"I'm a Seventh-day Adventist."

"I've heard about that church; they're pretty strict, huh? You don't dance, drink, smoke, or basically do anything fun. How am I doing so far?"

Now it was my turn to laugh. "I can tell you this, that there is no greater joy than serving Jesus! And I don't have a 'left out' feeling, if that's what you mean."

He grinned and asked, "What do Seventh-day Adventists believe?"

I could hardly believe my ears. God had given me an incredible opportunity to share! This is what I had been hoping for! I mentioned some of our basic doctrines, starting with believing in Jesus Christ as our personal Savior and how He came to this earth to give His life so that we could have eternal life. I talked about God's amazing love that enabled Him to leave heaven and take on the life of humanity subject to all the trials, temptations, and sins of this world. "He didn't have to do that! Jesus died on the cross because He loves each one of us so much!"

Over the next hour we went all the way to Calvary and back, as I described God's plan of salvation. Charles listened intently, taking in everything I said. Occasionally he would nod his head in agreement or ask a question, but for the most part, he just listened. That is, until he made one simple comment. "Well, I may not be a church-going man, but I've always known I don't have to worry because my sweet mother is in heaven looking out for me."

"No, she's not," I answered.

Charles looked up, and for the first time since he had sat down, he looked upset with me. He adjusted himself in his seat, sitting up a little straighter.

"Now, listen here," he pointed his finger at me, "my mother was a saint! I'm talking about a wonderful woman. And I'm telling you right now my mother is in heaven!"

"No, she's not." I said again, this time with a little more firmness in my voice.

But before I could explain, Charles interrupted, looking angry. "Now listen here! I've agreed with everything you have said so far. But when you're talking about my mother, who never missed a Sunday in church, then, then . . ." he cleared his throat, unable to continue.

"Charles, I'm sure your mother was a wonderful Christian woman, but she is not in heaven." I put my hand up to allow time to explain. I leaned over to retrieve my Bible from my carry-on bag. "Let me show you what God says about what happens when a person dies."

I read first one text and then another about how the dead know nothing, but are as a person who is asleep, waiting for Jesus to come. I read Psalm 146:4, "His spirit departs, he returns to his earth; In that very day his plans perish." I continued reading: Psalm 6:5; Psalm 115:17; Job 7:9, 10; Ecclesiastes 9:5–10; Ecclesiastes 12:7; and Matthew 27:52, which reads, "and the graves opened; and many bodies of the saints who had fallen asleep were raised."

I looked at Charles and softly said, "So you see, I'm not the one saying that your mom is not in heaven. That is what the Bible says. There are so many more texts to support this truth. You believe in the Bible, don't you?"

He nodded his head. I could see him relax in his chair, taking in this shocking revelation.

"Why am I hearing this for the first time? It's so clear after hearing you read it directly from the Bible. Why does most of the world believe that a person goes to heaven when he dies?"

"Charles, this is why it is so important to study the Bible. Don't ever take what a pastor preaches or a friend says or even what I say, for that matter, as the gospel truth. Study the Bible yourself, and don't forget to pray first because God *will* send His Holy Spirit to enlighten you and impress upon your heart the message He has for you."

The flight attendant interrupted, asking for our beverage glasses, since we were getting ready to land in a few minutes. I handed her my glass and asked, "But isn't this a two-hour flight? We can't be ready to land just yet."

The flight attendant smiled, "It is a two-hour flight, but the two of you have been so absorbed in your conversation, that I'm sure it feels more like ten minutes!" Charles and I both laughed.

Now I began to pray fervently. *Lord, I know Charles is open to truth and that he needs to hear more. But we are running out of time. Please impress upon me what he needs to hear the most in the few minutes that we have left. What is it that You want me to share? Please, Jesus, give me the words You want me to say. Please use me, Lord, right now to win Charles's heart for Your kingdom. Amen.*

Before I had even finished praying, the voice of the captain came over the loud speaker. "Ladies and Gentlemen, this is your captain speaking." Everyone stopped their conversations and began listening intently. "It seems there is a freak storm that has come up over Houston, and all three airports are closed. We're going to hang out in the air here for a while and see if the storm passes. So just sit back and relax. This should just be a short delay."

I could hardly believe my ears! The same God who held back the hands of time for Joshua in biblical times, was doing it again right now! God's amazing power nearly took my breath away. *Thank You, Lord, for answering my prayer.*

Charles looked over at me, "Well, maybe I'll get a chance to ask you a few more questions."

I smiled and said, "I can't help but think that God's hand was in this delay."

He nodded and said, "I wouldn't be a bit surprised."

For the next hour, I answered question after question, always letting the Bible give the answers. I keep a compact Bible study guide in the back of my Bible so that I can always give a Bible study on any topic at any time. My father had taught me not to miss even one opportunity to witness for Jesus. I have many memories as a child being in the car with Daddy when we stopped for gas. That stop could easily become a two-hour "fill up" because Daddy would be giving a Bible study to the man next to him at the pump. I grew up knowing how important it is to share Jesus everywhere I go.

I could tell that Charles was deeply affected by the Bible truth he was hearing. His questions were thoughtful and earnest. An hour went by quickly, and the captain's voice came over the loud speaker once again. "Well folks, it seems this storm is in no hurry to move on so we are going to land temporarily in Corpus Christi to keep from using up our fuel. We'll stay on the ground until we get the all clear from Houston. Unfortunately, we will not be able to let you off the plane when we land since Corpus Christi does not have a Customs and Immigration Department to handle incoming international flights. So just sit tight in your seats and wait for the all clear."

I was overjoyed! Then suddenly I realized I was probably the *only* passenger on the plane that felt that way, so it would be a good idea to hide my excitement! God is so good! *Thank You so much for giving me more time to witness*, I prayed.

Our Bible study continued as we sat on the runway. During our discussion the flight attendant would interrupt occasionally handing us soft drinks and snacks. I had just finished telling in detail about the work that God had me doing now and how far-reaching the benefits were, when I looked down at my carry-on bag and noticed some letters that were sticking out. Without thinking, I reached for a handful of letters and handed some to Charles. "Here, do you want to help me read some of these?"

Without giving him time to respond, I heaped a big pile of letters onto his lap. We sat in silence, reading first one letter than another.

"Brenda, listen to this one," his hands were shaking as he began to read.

Dear Miss Brenda, I couldn't be at the retreat today so I asked my daughter to bring my letter to you. I wanted to come so badly to hear you speak, but when I told my husband that I was going to go, he forbade me. I told him that I was going no matter what, and well, this made him very angry. Miss Brenda, he beat me so badly, I cannot walk. It is too painful even to move from the floor where he has left me. I need you to please pray for me that my husband will stop beating me and my children. Please pray for me; I need help. I am begging you to help me. I keep praying to God, but He does not hear me. I know that He listens to you. Please, please help me. Elmina.

Tears welled up in my eyes. I looked over at Charles and could see that I wasn't the only one touched by this desperate woman's letter. "Isn't it sad, Charles, that there are so many hurting people in this world? This just breaks my heart! And the saddest thing is, she doesn't even realize that God hears her when she prays. The prayers that God loves most are the simple, earnest pleas from a sincere heart! You don't have to use eloquent words or be highly educated. Just a simple cry for help will do. 'Jesus, save me' is the most powerful prayer when spoken to our Lord and Savior, yet it consists of only three words! Isn't that amazing? There is so much pain in this world. Can you see why I have such a passion to witness for Jesus? I'm so homesick for heaven, I want Jesus to come soon!

"Just think, when we get to heaven there will be no more sin, suffering, pain, or death, but each day will be more glorious than the day before!" I reached for a tissue from my purse and wiped my eyes.

"Would you mind if we said a quick prayer for Elmina?" I asked.

"Uh, sure, I guess that would be OK."

"Dear heavenly Father, thank You for the awesome God that You are. We know that You see, hear, and know everything. And, Lord, You know where Elmina is right now. You know the aches and physical pain she is experiencing, and also the ache in her heart. Please come into her life today. We're asking that You send Your Holy Spirit to give her the peace and comfort that she needs, and she will not have a shadow of doubt that You love her and are with her. Please let her feel Your presence. And precious

Lord, we are asking that You wrap her in Your arms of love because there is no better place for her to be! Thank You for hearing and answering our prayer. May Your will be done in her life. We pray all these things in Your precious holy name. Amen."

Charles looked a bit uncomfortable. "Well, that was a first. I don't think I have ever had prayer on a plane before. Matter of fact, I know I haven't. I can't even remember the last time I prayed in a church!" He chuckled nervously.

"You can pray anytime, anywhere, and God will hear you," I explained. "How can you expect God to be your best Friend if you never talk to Him? God loves to hear from His children, and not just when we are in trouble!"

For the next couple hours we continued to read letters. Sometimes we would read them aloud. Others we read silently. I gently tore open another envelope lying in my lap. "Here, listen to this letter," I said.

Dear Miss Brenda, I am thirteen years old, and I love *Kids Time.* I watch it every day. It is my favorite show. I especially like it when you read the letters. Could you read my letter sometime? I drew a flower on the envelope so you would know which one is mine. I want to give my heart to Jesus, but I don't know how. My mom says that there is no God since my dad got killed and left us. I want to go to church, but my mom won't let me. Miss Brenda, will you please pray that my mom will let me go to church? I believe you when you say that God loves me. Thank you for Kids Time. I love you, Jasmine.

P.S. Could you please send me an activity book to my grandma's house. (She said it's okay and lets me watch *Kids Time* at her house.)

"Wow! That one sure gets to me," Charles commented. "I guess I've been just as guilty blaming God for the bad things that have happened in my life, including when my mother died. Brenda, I want you to know that I am not the same man that walked onto this plane. I don't think it was any accident that you sat next to me!"

He continued, "I am the president of an oil company, and I've been pretty blessed in my life. I've made a lot of money and can go or do anything that I set my mind to. Someone else runs the company for me now, and I spend my days pretty selfishly, although, I didn't think that way prior to this flight."

He looked over at me and smiled. "I was fishing down in Belize for the past week, and tomorrow I'm heading out to go duck hunting with some of my buddies. I fly around the world going from one sport to the next, and I never really thought about how meaningless my life is. If I died today, I don't think there is one person that I could point to and say I made a difference in their life."

He pointed to the stack of letters on my lap and said, "I look at how God is using you to help so many people around the world, and I can't help but think what a rich lady you are. You might be a volunteer, and you told me you haven't been paid in eight years, but you are far more wealthy than I am!"

The captain interrupted with, "Ladies and gentlemen, we just received the all clear from Houston. I apologize for any inconvenience this delay may have caused. Flight attendants, prepare for take off."

We spent the next few minutes talking about our families and plans for the next day, as I replaced all the letters into my carry-on bag. It wasn't long before we had landed in Houston and had taxied to the gate. As soon as the seat belt sign went off, people immediately stood up and started retrieving their personal items from the overhead racks. You would think after spending seven hours on the plane we would be jumping out of our seats to exit the aircraft. But not Charles or me.

"Charles, would you mind if I sent you some books so you could learn more about God's truth? I'd also like to send you my book, *Battered to Blessed*. But I don't want to send it if you won't read it."

"Brenda, I don't think you heard me when I said I was not the same man that walked onto this plane. Yes, please send any book you want, and I promise I'll read it. Besides, I know that you'll pray about it first." He gave me a smile. "You are the praying-est lady I've ever met!"

I laughed and said, "Well, that's not a bad thing to be called now, is it?

"No, I guess not."

"Would you mind if I prayed with you right now?"

"Sure, I'd like that," he said. I reached over and took Charles's hand and began to pray. *"Dear heavenly Father, thank You so much for this flight and for the time that You have given us to talk about You. Lord, I know it was no accident that we are sitting here today, and I want to thank You for choosing our seats. I ask that You would be with Charles in a very special way and that You will give him no peace or rest until he fully surrenders his heart to You! Please let him fully realize how much You love him and want to save him! Give him the desire to learn more about You, and as he reads the books that I will send, please give him understanding and an open heart for truth. I pray that someday soon, when You come in those clouds of glory, that Charles will be there along with his entire family and we can be neighbors in heaven! Oh, what a reunion that will be! In Jesus' precious name, Amen."*

When I finished praying, tears were rolling down Charles's cheeks—and mine too. Neither of us cared that the first-class section had already exited the plane and now streams of coach passengers were rushing past us to finally leave the aircraft!

I reached down into my bag and fumbled around until I found what I was looking for. I handed a Micheff Sisters CD to Charles. "This is one of my CDs I told you about. I'd like to give it to you as a special gift. The name of this CD is *Leaning on Jesus*, and that is something that I'd like to encourage you to do every day. I pray that it will be a blessing to you and that every time you listen to it, you'll think about how much Jesus loves you."

"Well, at least let me pay you for it," he began to pull his wallet from his pocket.

"And let you steal my blessing? Not a chance!" I smiled as I gathered my belongings and leaned over to give him a hug. "I want to make an appointment with you right now, for us to meet in heaven at Jesus' feet!"

As I walked toward the baggage carrousel, I wasn't a bit tired. I marveled at the miracle that God had just performed. What should have been a two-hour flight had turned into a seven-hour Bible study! I couldn't have had a more captive listener. Charles couldn't have moved out of his seat even if he had wanted to! I smiled to myself. *Lord, You sure know what You're doing! I now understand why You had me flying first class!* I would have never met Charles in the coach section. It's amazing how God orchestrates circumstances to accomplish His purpose in our lives if we are willing. *Lord,* I prayed, *I'll fly first class for You anytime!*

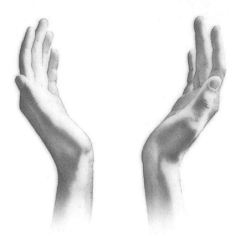

CHAPTER 12

WHEN YOU REALLY NEED A MIRACLE

The things which are impossible with men are possible with God.
—Luke 18:27

Over the years there have been countless discussions and debates about miracles. Most Christians are firm believers in miracles while non-Christians aren't quite so sure. Some admit there are certain events or happenings that can't be explained, but are not willing to give God the credit. To deny the possibility of miracles is to discredit the Bible, and that is what many atheists have been doing for centuries.

So, just what is a miracle? The dictionary gives this definition: "An extraordinary event manifesting divine intervention in human affairs." Wow! Amazing isn't it, that even a nonreligious book such as a dictionary gives God the credit?

Someone once said that miracles are when God makes something spectacular happen and yet chooses to remain anonymous. But I see it quite differently. Miracles are when God reveals Himself! It is often when we are in our darkest hour and crying out to Him, acknowledging Him as our Lord and Savior, that we experience His divine intervention.

Miracles are supernatural happenings, but it's important to remember that God is not the only One who can perform miracles. It is also in Satan's power to do so whenever it suits his evil purposes. That's why it is so important that we not be deceived and that we stay closely connected with our heavenly Father for His divine direction. In Matthew 10:16 Jesus tells us, "Therefore be wise as serpents and harmless as doves."

Jesus performed many spectacular miracles while He was on this earth. They are recorded in the Bible to be passed on from generation to generation so that we will realize His power and the incredible love He has for all of us. I'm specifically thinking of such miracles as when He walked on the water, when He fed five thousand people with a few loaves of bread and some fish, when He resurrected Lazarus, and so many others.

God is a God of miracles—not only in Bible times, but throughout all ages. And He continues to work miracles today. Sometimes His miracles are very subtle and quiet, sweeping in like a gentle breeze. Other times, they are more obvious and evident. It doesn't matter how much money or education you have, the color of your skin, how accomplished you are, or anything else—miracles can happen to anyone!

WE NEED A MIRACLE!

I have known Dona Klein for years and admire her incredible talent for playing the organ. Her hands glide effortlessly across the keys, and the music she produces is spiritually uplifting. It is as if her fingers instantly respond to what her heart is singing! She could easily

My precious prayer partner, Dona Klein. Dona is, by far, my favorite organist. She has recorded many CDs—all dedicated to the glory of God.

Left to right: Kenneth Cox, me, Dona and Gordon Klein. This photo was taken in front of the 3ABN booth at camp meeting. I had just finished taping an hour-long "LIVE" Kids Time special program, and Dona was praying for me the whole time!

make a fortune playing in secular places, but she chose when she was young to dedicate her musical talent to God. Twenty-one years ago, Dona and her husband, Gordon, teamed up with Kenneth Cox Ministries, and since then they have traveled around the world helping Ken with evangelistic outreach.

Gordon is the associate director of the ministry, and Dona plays the organ and takes care of the administrative duties. I'm not sure they even know how many series of meetings they have participated in; they don't stop to count. They just keep on doing what God wants them to do.

Dona and I became friends when Pastor Ken Cox became a 3ABN evangelist. I will never forget the first 3ABN camp meeting almost ten years ago, when Dona was scheduled to play the organ. She waited patiently for her turn to practice while I continued rehearsing for my *Kids Time* special. As soon as I was finished, I immediately went over to welcome her to 3ABN.

"Hi Dona, my name is Brenda Walsh, and I'm so excited you're here! I have loved your organ music for as long as I can remember!"

"Well, thank you, but all the glory goes to God."

She was so open, warm, and friendly, it seemed as though I had known her all my life. I asked her if she'd mind if I stayed and listened to her practice.

"Oh Sweetie, if listening to my organ playing will bring you a blessing, then please stay and listen."

I loved her from that moment on. Not only is she super-talented, but she has a sweet Christlike character! She is a humble Christian who loves Jesus—that was evident just from being around her. Our friendship grew over the years, and she has become a most treasured prayer partner.

So when Dona called to share with me her own petition that she was laying before the Lord, I knew she would need every prayer partner she could find. Gordon had just been diagnosed with a malignant brain tumor.

"Oh, Dona, no! Are the doctors sure? Did you get a second opinion?"

"Yes, they're sure. He's scheduled for surgery next week. I just called to see if you would pray for him. He's going to need lots of prayer."

"Yes, of course I'll pray for him, and I'll pray for you too! This has to be terribly difficult for both of you. How is Gordon taking this?"

"Brenda, Gordon has placed his life in God's hands, and he has such peace. He's not discouraged or despondent at all."

"That is so amazing! Only someone who is walking with Jesus can have that kind of peace. I know God will be with you every step of the way. He has promised that He will never give us more than we can handle, and He always keeps His promises!"

"Yes, I believe that, too," Dona agreed. "Can I share with you what I read this morning for my worship? It encouraged me so much! Let me get the book; it's right here by the sofa. 'When in faith we take hold of His strength, He will change, wonderfully change, the most hopeless, discouraging outlook. He will do this for the glory of His name.' So, when things look the bleakest, we need to go forward."

"Wow! That's powerful, isn't it?" I responded. "Where did you find that?"

"It's from page two hundred and sixty in *Prophets and Kings*. Ellen White is one of my favorite authors."

"I love her books too. And what she says is so true, because nothing is hopeless when God is leading in your life. I don't think it was any accident you read that this morning, Dona. I believe God impressed you to read that passage to give you the courage and faith you and Gordon will need to press on."

"I know. Isn't God's amazing! Whatever happens, I know He will take care of us."

We talked for quite a while about how the tumor had been discovered. I was spellbound as Dona shared their story.

In December, she and Gordon were getting ready to leave for Guam, where they would be holding a series of meetings for the entire island. During all the hustle and bustle of preparations, Gordon accidentally bumped his head on a low shelf; he nearly lost consciousness. After a few minutes, however, he began feeling better, so he thought everything was OK.

About two weeks later, he began experiencing periods of numbness on his right side, lasting only twenty to thirty seconds. Remembering the bump on his head, he felt sure the numbness was related to his head injury, so he didn't go to the doctor. Several days later, when the numbness didn't go away, Dona got worried.

"Gordon, you have to go to the doctor. I'm worried about you. This is just not normal. You have to find out what's wrong!"

"All right, Honey, if you really think I should go."

Dona made the appointment and prayed as she sat beside Gordon in the waiting room. They were both relieved when the doctor told them that everything was fine. The MRI showed a "shadow" on the brain, but the doctor felt it was probably due to bleeding from the bump on the head and nothing to worry about. Gordon was given the green light to go to Guam.

"I feel that the devil was working overtime trying to stop our evangelistic crusade," Dona told me. "The day that we arrived, a typhoon was on its way, threatening to completely shut down the island on opening night. But God intervened, and the meetings were held as scheduled. Then came a volcano with all its ash and smoke, and even a six-point-six earthquake hit, but God did not let anything stop the meetings!"

"Dona, the enemy was attacking you from every angle!" I said, amazed at what I was hearing.

"That's for sure! And if that wasn't enough, many of our team members became ill. Gordon continued having numbness on his right side, and even Pastor Cox got sick. Some of the local leaders told us maybe we should just give up and go home. Our team got together for prayer and guidance and felt more strongly than ever that God wanted us in Guam. We were determined to stay even if that meant *dying on the battlefield.* We were not going to give in to the devil. After making that decision, we felt such a peace that we knew we were right where the Lord wanted us to be."

"Well, Dona, God has promised that He will never leave us or forsake us, and He certainly demonstrated that, didn't He?"

"Oh, Brenda, He surely did. More than two hundred and fifty people were baptized at the end of our meetings, and we rejoiced at God's goodness! When we left for home, we had no idea that we were soon going to be hit by the most difficult days we had ever experienced."

Dona continued telling me what happened next. The first sign of trouble started when she and Gordon went to pick up their motor home. Gordon sat in the driver's seat, just staring at everything. She asked, "Honey, are you OK? What's wrong?"

"I don't remember how to drive. I don't know what I am supposed to do."

Obviously, something was terribly wrong. They immediately began to pray, pleading with God to help them. Dona had no idea how to drive such a big motor home and didn't know anyone they could call. They sat there and prayed for another thirty minutes until Gordon's memory returned. All the way home, Dona guided him, telling him where to turn, and when to change lanes or apply the brakes. She had no idea what was wrong, but she knew it wasn't good, whatever it was. When they arrived home, Gordon began dragging his right foot when he walked, and his speech became slurred.

Dona immediately called the doctor. She was worried Gordon was having a stroke. After another MRI, the doctor delivered the devastating news. Gordon had a malignant brain tumor—and not just any brain tumor. He had a glioblastoma multiforme stage four, the worst kind of brain tumor you could have! The doctor gave him only two or three months to live.

"Dona, God is still on the throne; it's not over until He says it's over!" I said emphatically.

"Yes, I believe that too. We are putting all our faith and trust in Him, and we are ready to accept whatever His will is for our lives."

Before saying goodbye, Dona and I prayed together on the phone. *"Dear precious heavenly Father, You are such an awesome God—the God of the universe who can do all things! We know that nothing is impossible for You, and that is why we are approaching Your throne room right now. Lord, You know the diagnosis that Gordon has received, and I'm asking for You to place Your healing hand upon him. Please be his Great Physician, and if it is Your will, please perform a miracle in his life. Yes, Lord, I am praying for a miracle to save him. You know how much he loves You and how he has every desire for You to use him in a mighty way! Please be especially close to my friend, Dona, too. Wrap her in Your arms and keep her close to You. Comfort her and let her know how much You love her and Gordon. Precious Jesus, let her see that You are leading in their lives, even in the midst of this, their darkest hour. I know You love Gordon even more than she does, and we are trusting him in Your care. We love You, Jesus. In Your name I pray. Amen."*

As I hung up the phone, I couldn't help but think how life can be turned upside down in a split second! A single diagnosis changes everything! One moment all is fine, and the next you can be facing a death sentence. I knew Dona and Gordon would have many dark days ahead, and right then I decided to make them a priority on my prayer list. So many people ask me to pray for them that I can't possibly name each one daily in prayer. But Gordon and Dona needed daily, *passionate prayer* to sustain them. I prayed another prayer, asking God to bring them to my mind throughout my day, every day. *Lord, please help me to know what to pray for. I don't want anything that is against Your will, and I know that they don't want that either! I don't understand how or why this has happened to them, but You do, and I am trusting in Your love, grace, and mercy. Please make me the kind of friend they need most—one who will encourage and uplift, always reminding them how much You love them. Please bring Gordon and Dona to my mind every day. I don't want to get so busy with life that I forget to lift them up to You in prayer. Oh, Jesus, You are such an awesome God, and I praise You for Your goodness! Amen.*

I got up from my knees and activated the Micheff family prayer chain, asking each person to make Gordon and Dona a matter of daily prayer. Then I called 3ABN and asked for Gordon and Dona to be added to the 3ABN prayer list. Next, I called every prayer warrior I knew to "pray for Gordon and Dona." I always included Dona in my prayer request because when something bad happens to a loved one, it doesn't just affect that person. It affects the whole family and anyone who loves him or her.

After the surgery, I called Dona and learned that Dr. Walter Johnson, of Loma Linda University Medical Center, had successfully removed an "egg-sized tumor," from Gordon's brain.

"Brenda, it doesn't look good," Dona said. "The doctors say that without chemotherapy, Gordon has only two or three months to live. With the therapy, he might have twelve to fourteen months at the most."

"Is he going to take the chemo?"

"No, he's not. We have both prayed about this, as I'm sure you can imagine, and neither of us feels that he should take the chemo. We are going to leave it in God's hands."

Again, I prayed with Dona on the phone, asking God to heal Gordon if it was His will. Two months later, the doctors discovered two more tumors at the base of his brain. Both tumors were inoperable.

Radiation and chemotherapy were the only options. Gordon and Dona were disappointed, but not discouraged. After much prayer and meditation, Gordon agreed to the treatment. Those truly were their darkest days.

But God is closest to us in our darkest hour. Gordon and Dona clung to God's promises, claiming first one and then another. They read the biblical instruction in James 5:13–15: "Is anyone among you suffering? Let him pray. Is anyone cheerful? Let him sing psalms. Is anyone among you sick? Let him call for the elders of the church, and let them pray over him, anointing him with oil in the name of the Lord. And the prayer of faith will save the sick, and the Lord will raise him up."

Both Dona and Gordon felt it was important to have an anointing service for Gordon. So while attending the General Conference Session in St. Louis, Missouri, Gordon was anointed by Pastor Kenneth Cox, Pastor Don Schneider, and their good friends, Jimmy and Pam Rhodes. Their faith and courage became even stronger along with their belief that God was in charge and that everything would be all right, no matter what happened.

During a particularly hard week, Dona poured out her heart to God. She put her finger on Psalm 103:1–3 and prayed the prayer in that text:

> *Bless the LORD, O my soul;*
> *And all that is within me, bless His holy name!*
> *Bless the LORD, O my soul,*
> *And forget not all His benefits:*
> *Who forgives all your iniquities,*
> *Who heals all your diseases.*

That night she had a dream. It was so vivid, so real, that when she awoke, she had no doubt in her mind that God had spoken to her. In her dream, a voice said, "The tumors are shrinking." She couldn't wait to tell Gordon; they rejoiced together, believing that this was one more message from God.

During this time, Dona would often lay out a fleece before the Lord, just as Gideon did in the Bible. She and Gordon experienced so many answered prayers that it gave them strength to keep going forward. They prayed daily for God to give them direction and guidance and faith to sustain them. Dona spent many hours on her knees in quiet solitude on the floor of her closet. Through it all, God was answering their prayers.

Dona claimed promises in the Scriptures daily. On days when she was tempted to doubt, she would lay her hand on the Bible and pray James 1:6, 7: "But let him ask in faith, with no doubting, for he who doubts is like a wave of the sea driven and tossed by the wind. For let not that man suppose that he will receive anything from the Lord." Wow! That was enough to destroy any shred of doubt!

When the doctor gave them some particularly bad news, Dona read Psalm 37:3–7:

> *Trust in the Lord, and do good;*
> *Dwell in the land, and feed on His faithfulness.*
> *Delight yourself also in the Lord,*
> *And He shall give you the desires of your heart.*
>
> *Commit your way to the Lord,*
> *Trust also in Him,*
> *And He shall bring it to pass.*
> *He shall bring forth your righteousness as the light,*
> *And your justice as the noonday.*
>
> *Rest in the Lord, and wait patiently for Him;*
> *Do not fret because of him who prospers in his way,*
> *Because of the man who brings wicked schemes to pass.*

She would read these texts to Gordon, and their faith strengthened. They reminded themselves that it didn't matter what the doctors said. Only what God said really mattered!

I know from experience that when you work full time in ministry, there isn't a lot of money for personal use. And Dona and Gordon's bank account reflected a lifetime of working for the Lord! When the doctor suggested an expensive medication to combat the side effects of nausea, they knew they couldn't afford it and that their insurance wouldn't cover it. Several days later, a large supply of this very medication showed up in the mail! Another faith-building answer to prayer!

Gordon determined that whatever time he had left on this earth, he wanted each moment to be dedicated to serving Jesus. That is why as soon as his radiation was finished, he traveled across country for the next set of meetings, bringing his supply of chemotherapy pills with him! He and Dona only missed two weeks of meetings during his entire illness, and that was due to radiation treatments. After traveling several months, they returned home for Gordon's checkup. The doctor asked to see the test results from the past few months.

"What are you talking about?" Gordon asked the doctor.

"I want to see the paperwork showing the results of your blood work each month."

"I didn't know I was supposed to have any tests, so I never had any blood work done!"

"What? No blood work?" The doctor could not believe it! He explained that there are serious side effects from the chemotherapy and that it is critical that blood work be monitored throughout the treatment. When Gordon's blood work came back later that day, he tested absolutely perfect! Another testament of how God was caring for him!

He and Dona returned to the evangelistic meetings, knowing God was leading, and kept on working! Many prayers were answered during this time, and never once did they feel abandoned by God.

When Gordon's chemotherapy pills ran out, he called his doctor for more medication. But the doctor refused to give him any more pills without a follow-up exam. Gordon called another doctor, and his answer was the same. He and Dona were right in the middle of an evangelistic series, and Gordon didn't feel that it was God's plan for him to leave his responsibilities at the meetings. He knew how much everybody depended on him. And after all, they were doing the Lord's work!

Feeling their faith was being put to the test, Gordon and Dona took their burden to the Lord, and when they arose from their knees, they felt a peace and assurance that God would take care of Gordon's health—with or without the medication. A few days later, a year's supply of chemotherapy medication arrived in the mail. To this day, they have no idea who sent it. It was just another of God's amazing miracles!

During these months on the road, Gordon had several MRIs to monitor his progress, all of them in different locations, depending on which state they were holding meetings in. While in Chicago, Gordon went to see a doctor who, after reviewing Gordon's medical records, ordered another test. The news wasn't good. "I am so sorry to tell you this, but you need to go home and get your affairs in order. You don't have long to live."

I happened to call Dona just after they had received this devastating news. I often called just to pray with her and offer encouragement. Gordon answered the phone and filled me in on what the doctor had said.

"So you see, Brenda, what I'm telling you is that *I need a miracle.*"

"Well, our God is a God of miracles, so that's exactly what we'll pray for."

"There is a specialist at Duke University in Raleigh, North Carolina, who specializes in the kind of tumor I have. Dona and I are getting ready to go there to see if there is anything he can do to help me."

"When is your appointment?"

"It's at two o'clock on Monday afternoon."

"Well, I will be in the air at that moment, flying to Hawaii, but I want you to know I will leave my watch set on eastern standard time so that when I'm on the airplane, I will be praying for you at the exact time of your appointment."

"Oh Brenda, I appreciate that so much, and I want to thank you for all the prayers you have been praying for me these past few months. It is the prayers of all our family and friends that have sustained us. We definitely feel God watching over us. I'm not discouraged. Whatever God has planned for my life is OK with me."

Daily, I continued to lift up Gordon and Dona in prayer. That Monday afternoon, I made sure that I was praying for Gordon and Dona at the exact time of his appointment. You can imagine my joy when I received a very special phone call the next day.

Kay Kuzma and her husband, Jan, were in Hawaii visiting family. I had flown there so we could work together on our book *Between Hell and High Water*. We were sitting in a condo with a view of the Pacific Ocean, enjoying the warm breeze blowing in from the deck. We each had our laptops and were busy writing away when my cell phone rang.

"Brenda, this is Dona. I just had to call and tell you that God has worked a miracle! Gordon's tumor is gone!"

"Gone? What do you mean gone?"

"I mean there are no more tumors! It's a miracle! I'm telling you—a miracle!"

Dona could hardly talk she was so overcome with emotion.

"We went to Duke University and . . ."

Dona and Gordon Klein. They are praising God for answered prayer!

"I know, I know," I interrupted. "I want you to know I was praying at the exact moment of Gordon's examination."

"Yes, Gordon told me he talked to you. Well, we had taken all of his medical exams and past MRI results, and after reviewing them, Dr. Henry Friedman ordered another MRI. When the results were back, he called us into his office."

Dona then relayed the moments that followed. I sat spellbound listening to every word!

"Gordon," Dr. Friedman said, "I don't see any tumors!"

Gordon sat up straight in his chair, confused about what he was hearing. "What do you mean, you don't see any tumors?"

"I mean that I can't find any tumors anywhere!"

Now it was Dona's turn to sit up. She moved to the edge of her chair. "Are you sure?"

Dr. Friedman could see they needed convincing. "Follow me. I want to show you something."

Gordon and Dona followed the doctor to the next room. There on the screen was the MRI from the previous week in Chicago, and right next to it was the one that had been done just a few hours ago.

Dr. Friedman pointed first to the earlier MRI. "See, this is where the tumor was." Then pointing to the new one, he added, "And this is where it isn't!"

Dona and Gordon looked at the MRIs and then at each other. Dona began to cry, and Gordon took her in his arms.

"Honey, it's a miracle! We prayed for a miracle, and God gave us a miracle!" Gordon was crying and laughing at the same time!

"Oh, Brenda," Dona's voice trembled on the phone, "we are still in shock! We are just praising God and rejoicing in His grace and mercy! I just had to call and let you know! We had fully surrendered to God's plan, and if He had chosen to answer our prayer in a different way, we would have willingly accepted His desire for our lives. But we are so excited that He chose to work a miracle! I know God still has work for Gordon to do! I can't help but think of the Bible promise in Psalm thirty, verses one and two, that I have claimed over and over again these past few months.

"I will extol You, O Lord, for You have lifted me up,
And have not let my foes rejoice over me.
O Lord my God, I cried out to You,
And You have healed me."

Dona continued, "God has honored our prayers. He has healed Gordon, and I'm just thanking and praising Jesus! God is so good!"

I had my own special thank-you prayer; I couldn't wait to tell all my prayer warriors about how God answered our prayers for Gordon! God is a God of miracles—yesterday, today, and tomorrow!

It's important, of course, to remember that not all prayers are answered in the way we want them to be. God knows the bigger picture, and if we could know the end from the beginning, we would not want any other way than God's way. I am reminded of the three Hebrews—Shadrach, Meshach, and Abednego—whose only desire was to do God's will. When these three Jewish men came up against the worst trial of their lives, they held on by their faith in God.

They had a choice: either give up their love for their God or be thrown in the fiery furnace. Their response is recorded in Daniel 3:17, 18: " 'If that is the case, our God whom we serve is able to deliver us from the burning fiery furnace, and He will deliver us from your hand, O king. But if not, let it be known to you, O king, that we do not serve your gods, nor will we worship the gold image which you have set up.' "

God honored their faith by walking in the fire with them and setting them free. Just like the three Hebrews, Dona and Gordon chose to put their trust in their heavenly Father and accepted His will to live or die. Psalm 37:39 says, "But the salvation of the righteous is from the LORD; He is their strength in the time of trouble." We should remember that God's plan is always the best plan.

When you believe in God, you gain an awareness of Him. You see everything in a new light. He shows His great power through the trials and tribulations of life, through science and nature. Not every miracle supersedes laws of science or is as dramatic as the miracle God performed for Gordon. Some miracles defy all the laws of nature, having no logical explanation except divine intervention. Such is the following story.

FROM THE FURNACE TO THE FREEZER

Gena Reynolds carried in the last bag of groceries from the car and carefully set it on the kitchen counter. It was a hot, humid July day, and she had just finished buying her groceries for the week. Shopping could be exhausting with two young children. She preferred to shop when her husband, Greg, was home and could watch the kids.

"Mommy, did you buy me some Gummy Bears?" Makayla asked. She was excitedly looking through the grocery bags.

"No, I didn't. You know I don't buy Gummy Bears. Do you remember why?"

"Yes, because there's too much sugar in them." Seven-year-old Makayla looked so disappointed.

"And do you remember what Miss Jackie, your dentist, said?"

"Yes, she said the sugar bugs will attack my teeth and that sticky stuff is not good."

"That's right, you *do* remember! Look, Honey, I bought some juicy oranges and apples. And I know you love grapes," Gena said, holding them in the air. "Don't these look yummy?"

Makayla's eyes danced with delight. Gena took a moment to wash a handful of red grapes and handed them to her daughter. "Come on, you can help Mommy put the groceries away. You are such a big help to me." Makayla smiled, shoved a couple of grapes in her mouth, and started poking through the sacks.

Two-year-old Mitchell came toddling in and wanted to "help" too. He proceeded to dump a bag of groceries on the floor, spilling the contents everywhere.

"Greg," Gena called to her husband, "can you come get Mitchell? He really wants to play cars with Daddy right now."

Greg laughed, "Oh he does, does he? Or does Mommy want Daddy to play cars?"

"OK, I'm busted, but can you distract him long enough for Makayla and I to get the food put away?"

"Sure, no problem. I'm just giving you a hard time. Come on, Mitchell, want to play with Daddy?" Mitchell dropped a box of crackers and ran to follow Greg into the other room.

Placing the last bag of frozen vegetables in the freezer, Gena checked to make sure the freezer door was shut tight. Later that evening, while fixing supper, when she went to get some blueberries from the freezer, she noticed that the bag felt rather soft, as if it weren't completely frozen.

Oh no, what's wrong with my freezer? I know I didn't leave the door open because I went back and checked it twice. She then examined the rest of the food. Sure enough, nothing was as frozen as it should have been. Next, she inspected the electrical outlet. Yes, it was plugged in. She checked to make sure there wasn't a tripped breaker in the circuit. No, that seemed to be OK, too. Everything seemed to be fine—except that the refrigerator/freezer wasn't working as it should. Then she noticed that the little red light at the bottom of the refrigerator was off. It wasn't getting electricity. Now what was she going to do?

She had just used all her grocery money to purchase a week's supply of food for her family. Much of it was stored in the freezer. In fact, the freezer was full. She just couldn't afford to lose any of this food! If she could get the freezer fixed before the temperature dropped further, then the food could be saved. She wasn't worried about the food in the refrigerator. A little ice in an ice chest could save that. It was the freezer that concerned her. *It's already too late to call a repairman,* Gena thought. *I'll have to call in the morning.*

The next morning, Gena called the repairman. After checking the freezer, he told her he would need to order a part in order to fix it. "Today's Friday, and I don't work weekends. I'll order your part today, and hopefully it will be in on Monday. That's the best I can do!"

"But I can't wait until Monday. I'll lose all my frozen food."

"Well, Ma'am, I can't do anything about that. Maybe if you don't open the door, the food will keep."

Gena felt sick to her stomach just thinking about all the money that would be wasted without refrigeration. They needed the food. She had no money to replace all the frozen items. *What am I going to do?*

She thought of all her friends who might have a freezer where she could store her food, but no one came to mind. Then she remembered a furnace! Yes, *a furnace!*

She remembered that her mom was reading a book just the week before, in which there was a story about a family that had no money in the middle of winter for fuel to heat their home. The father had placed his hand on the furnace and prayed, asking God to provide heat for their home. While he was still on his knees, the furnace came on and *stayed on for two weeks* until the family had enough money to pay the fuel bill! Gena couldn't get that story out of her head; the more she thought about it, the more convinced she became. *If God can start that furnace, He can surely start my freezer! What I need is a miracle!*

Just then, Makayla came into the kitchen and saw the concerned look on her mom's face. "Mommy, what's wrong? Are you sad?"

"No, Honey, I'm not sad. I'm just worried about all the food in our freezer, because the refrigerator has stopped working, and now our food will spoil. I'm going to ask Jesus to help us. Do you want to pray with me?"

Makayla nodded her head. "Yes. Let's pray about it. Jesus can fix anything."

So Gena and Makayla knelt down in front of their refrigerator and held hands. Gena began to pray. *"Dear Jesus, as You know, something is wrong with our freezer, and if we can't get it fixed, then all our food will spoil.*

You know I don't have the money to replace all the groceries so I'm asking You to please fix our freezer if it is Your will. Lord, I know You performed a miracle and started a furnace once, and I believe that You can work a miracle today and fix my freezer. Amen."

Makayla and Gena Reynolds keel down to pray, "Please, God, fix our freezer!"

When Gena and Makayla got up from their knees, Gena had a sense of peace—the kind of peace that comes from knowing God will take care of things.

Sure enough, just a few minutes after they finished praying, Makayla shouted, "Mommy, Mommy, look! The light is on! It's red!"

Gena ran to look and couldn't believe her eyes! Sure enough, the refrigerator's red light was on, and she could hear the low humming of the freezer's motor! Back on her knees, Gena prayed, *"Thank You, Jesus! Thank You for answering our prayer! You are a God of miracles! Thank You for saving our food! Amen."*

On Monday, the repairman came, but he had ordered the wrong part. He told Gena it would take another week to order the right part. Again, Gena prayed that God would keep her freezer running. The next week, the same thing happened. This continued every week for six weeks. By now Gena was getting very frustrated with the repairman, but God kept her refrigerator/freezer working.

Having lost faith in the repairman, but not in God, Gena called another appliance repair service. The morning the new repairman was to arrive, her refrigerator quit running. The new repairman came and fixed it on the spot; it needed only a twenty-five dollar heat sensor!

During the whole six weeks that God kept the freezer working, not one morsel of food was lost!

When Gena told me this story, I was moved at how God answered her prayers. If she had called the second repairman first, she would never have realized the miracle God wanted her to experience. He loves her so much that He kept her freezer running—not just for a week or two, but for six weeks! That's incredible!

I was also thrilled to know how God was using the furnace story to strengthen the faith of others. Because you see, the man in the story that Gena's mom had read—the man who prayed for the furnace—was my own father, and the book she had read was my book, *Battered to Blessed!*

Now Gena and her family have their own miracle story to tell!

WHERE DO YOU LOOK WHEN YOU REALLY NEED A MIRACLE?

There are so many texts in the Bible in which God promises that if we ask, we shall receive. For example, Matthew 21:22 says, "And all things, whatever you ask in prayer, believing, you will receive." Here are three more of my favorite prayer-promise texts:

- "Ask, and it will be given to you; seek, and you will find; knock, and it will be opened to you" (Matthew 7:7).
- "You do not have because you do not ask" (James 4:2).
- "Be anxious for nothing, but in everything by prayer and supplication, with thanksgiving, let your requests be made known to God" (Philippians 4:6).

Do these promises really mean that whenever we want something, anything at all, we just have to ask—and we will get it? My six-year-old grandson is struggling with his perception of what God is all about. He loves to pray, and quite often he will call me up and ask me to pray for him on the phone. One of those phone calls came just a week before I was to fly to Boston to see him.

"Hello Gramma, are you there?"

"Yes, Michael, I'm here. I'm really getting excited to see you soon. Just six more sleeps!" (He measures time by how many nights he goes to bed.)

"I know, Gramma! That's why I'm calling. Things are really getting stressed out around here, and Mommy says she doesn't know how she's

My precious grandson, Michael James Coffin, who loves to pray about everything. He is an incredible joy in my life—and definitely "Grandma's boy."

going to get everything done before you get here. I'm talking stress, Gramma, and it's a big problem. And Jason's not helping! He keeps dumping his toys out all over the place, and I have to pick them up. It's just not fair. He's driving me crazy. Gramma, will you pray for me right now?"

"Why, sure Michael. Let's ask Jesus to help." I prayed and asked God to be with Michael and his mommy and to help them to get everything done they needed to do. I also asked Jesus to give all of them patience and love toward each other.

Michael called me the next day, bubbling with excitement. "Gramma, I've got some really big news. Jesus answered my prayer! We got all the work done. Yup, we are all ready for you to come, and Mommy and I even made cookies for you!"

"Michael, that is so awesome. I'm so happy you know Jesus is the One who answered your prayer."

"Oh, Gramma, sure I do. I'm pretty smart about these things, you know."

I could tell he had truly experienced what it felt like for God to answer prayer. But not all of Michael's prayers are the same.

I flew to Boston for his sixth birthday and took him to Toys "R"

Us to make out his birthday list. We walked up first one aisle and then another. He squealed with delight as he pointed out certain items that needed to be on his list. When we reached the department with all the motorized vehicles, Michael could not contain himself. He ran to the four-wheeler, jumped on, and began making realistic engine sounds and going, "beep, beep," pretending he was blowing the horn.

Without warning, he jumped off the four-wheeler and ran over to me, grabbing my hands. Bouncing up and down in front of me, he pleaded urgently, "Please, Gramma, please will you pray for me! I need Jesus to get me that four-wheeler for my birthday present! Hurry, Gramma, we have to pray quick because it's the last one!"

No matter what I said, I just couldn't seem to make him understand that Jesus doesn't give us all the things we want or ask for. Instead, He always thinks about what is best for us.

"But, Gramma, you said that God would give us anything we asked Him for. I heard you, Gramma. You read it from the Bible. Remember? And God doesn't lie."

I tried many different ways to explain to him how God "works," but I'm not sure I was successful. Unfortunately, Michael isn't alone in his childish theology. Many of us have the "gimme syndrome." "Gimme this and gimme that." We need to understand that prayer is not just asking for things, although that is a part of it. Far more importantly, prayer is getting to know Jesus better!

God knows what is best for us, and He answers our prayers accordingly. Sometimes He chooses to work a miracle as He did when He healed Gordon. He knows the end from the beginning and what is best for each individual. At other times, God uses miracles to strengthen our faith, such as when He caused Gena's freezer to keep on working.

God doesn't answer our prayers by giving us everything we want, but more importantly, He gives us everything we need. He is thinking of our eternal life with Him. He gives us gifts so that we can have that abundant life. He is looking at the eternal goal; we tend to look only at our earthly goals. We must learn to trust Him and give Him permission to make decisions in our lives.

When we pray for something—if our motive is to get to know Jesus better—then He can safely answer. If in His almighty knowledge, God knows that a miracle will enhance our relationship with Him, then it happens. If a miracle can touch lives and awaken people to a heartfelt desire to know God better, then He uses His power to perform a miracle.

For a few, finding lost keys or having a refrigerator that keeps working might ignite that desire to know God better. For others, it might be a supernatural healing. Only God knows. God doesn't answer our prayers capriciously. He doesn't spin the "Wheel of Fortune" and determine whether or not it's time for someone to get a miracle. No! Every response He makes to our petitions is for our own good—*and* for Him to more intimately reveal the multiple facets of His character to His children. When those two things are in place, then miracles happen.

I remember reading somewhere a quotation that went something like this: "Prayer is a privilege that is always ours; but the *power* of prayer is always *His!*" I believe a miracle is the greatest manifestation of divine power that is available to us today. God invites you to ask. That's your privilege. Take Him at His word. Pray passionately! I'm so glad we serve an all-knowing, all-powerful God of miracles.

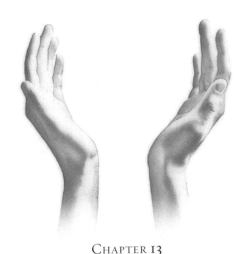

CHAPTER 13

FINDING THE BIBLE LADY

Man shall not live by bread alone;
but man lives by every word that proceeds from the mouth of the Lord.
—Deuteronomy 8:3

The words of Scripture are a vital component of passionate prayer. Moses said that our very life is sustained by God's Word. Jesus agreed (see Matthew 4:4). The Bible guides us to truth (John 16:13). It teaches us what we should do (Psalm 32:8). It corrects us (2 Timothy 3:16). It gives us wisdom (Proverbs 2:2). It inspires us with hope (Romans 15:4). It shows us how good God is (Psalm 34:8). It keeps us from sin (Psalm 119:11).

It's no wonder we're admonished to search the Scriptures daily (Acts 17:11), to hide God's Word in our hearts (Psalm 119:11), and to do what the Bible tells us to do (James 1:22). And when it comes to prayer, if we pray the promises of God's Word, it becomes quick, powerful, and sharper than any two-edged sword (Hebrews 4:12).

When I began my passionate prayer journey, the Bible became my constant companion. I've always enjoyed reading Scripture—especially the poetry of the Psalms and the wisdom of Proverbs. In the New Testament, Philippians and James are my favorite books. Once

I developed a passionate relationship with Jesus, I became hungry to know what He wanted to say to me each day through His Word. So, now I find myself searching for special texts that speak specifically to my need. If Jesus tells me He will do something for me—or for someone I know—I hold on to that text as if I were holding on to a life preserver—that's what we call *faith*. I claim that promise as my own and live with the unshakable expectation that God will fulfill it. I don't know when, but I know He will. When you begin living this close to Jesus, you'll want to have His Word at your fingertips at all times.

That's how Sherry Helveston of Biloxi, Mississippi, felt. *She loved her Bible.* Then on Monday, August 29, 2005, Hurricane Katrina's fury devastated the Mississippi Gulf Coast, destroying the home of Sherry and her husband, Lloyd, and everything they owned—including Sherry's Bible.

Grateful to be alive, but left with only the clothes on their backs, Sherry and Lloyd visited a relief center to see if they could find some clothes that might fit. How thankful they were that people from all over the country had sent clothing and other items to meet the needs of those who now had nothing. They looked around at all the boxes. Nothing was labeled. Where should they begin?

Sherry immediately noticed a pair of cowboy boots sticking out of the top of one box. She thought they might fit Lloyd. She handed him the boots and then started rummaging through the rest of the box. At the bottom she felt a book. She looked more closely. It was a Bible.

"Lloyd, look what I found," she exclaimed. "It's a Bible. I've been asking God for a Bible. This must be His gift to me. And look, it has giant print so I can read it without my glasses." Then she noticed a folded piece of paper in the pages of the Book. She opened the paper and read the words, "A Note from Sherri."

A note from Sherri? She thought. *That's my name, even though the spelling is different. Strange, isn't it, that a Sherri wrote the note and another Sherry—spelled with a y—found it. This can't be a coincidence.*

This Bible is meant for me. Then Sherry read the message Sherri had written:

> To whomever finds this Bible: I feel so helpless to help you. You are so very far away. Please accept our meager offerings and please accept this Bible. It was my grandmother's. She is 101, suffering from Alzheimer's and probably would have been one of the first to die if East Tennesseans had suffered this disaster. Please find comfort in the Word of God. Although you may be angry with Him, remember He loves you. You have friends in East Tennessee. Please tell us what you need. We will do whatever we possibly can do to help. The congregation of Union Cumberland Presbyterians are praying for you. Feel the power of our prayers and have faith. Godspeed, Sherri.

About a week after Sherry found the Bible in the box, I met her and Lloyd when I was interviewing Hurricane Katrina survivors for the book *Between Hell and High Water* that Kay Kuzma and I were writing. We were so impressed with Sherry's love for her Bible and the story of how Sherri (with an "i") had given a Bible and Sherry (with an "y") had found it, that we chose to include the story in our book. We were convinced, just as Sherry was, that this was more than a coincidence. We believed that God was working out His divine plan for Sherry Helveston's life. What we didn't know was that God's plan was far bigger than we could imagine.

"We've got to find the lady who gave this Bible," Kay said. "I have a feeling she might be in Knoxville." Since Kay was in Mexico at the time, the search fell upon my shoulders. I prayed and made dozens of calls. I even found the Union Cumberland Presbyterian Church that was mentioned in the note, but the secretary assured me there were no Sherris with an "i" in that church. She explained, "We had a drop box in our church parking lot, and people from all over the city contributed. There would be no way of tracing the identity of the Sherri who gave away her grandmother's Bible." When I asked to speak to the pastor, she told me he would not be able to offer any more information.

I was disappointed, but I didn't give up. I knew there had to be a way of locating the person we were now calling the "Bible Lady." Internet searches came up empty. I even tried to interest the local newspaper and television stations into doing a public interest story, hoping Sherri would come forward. Every avenue I tried, failed.

Finally, time ran out. We had to abandon the search and send our manuscript to the publisher without finding the "Bible Lady."

Then, *one year later*, November 30, 2006, I was sitting at my desk when the phone rang. It was Ann Goodge, the administrator of Little Creek Sanitarium that is literally right next door to where I live in Knoxville.

Sherri Childress with two very special people in her life—daughter, Riley, and grandmother, "Mama Layman."

"Brenda, the strangest thing happened today. I received a call from the granddaughter of one of my patients. She told me she had donated her grandmother's Bible to the Hurricane Katrina victims and that a friend of the Gulf Coast resident who found the Bible had just contacted her. She exclaimed, 'They have even put the story in a book called *Between Hell and High Water*.'

"That title sounded familiar, so I asked her, 'Who wrote the book?'

"Her reply? 'Kay Kuzma and Brenda Walsh.'

"I exclaimed, 'I know them both; they're friends of mine. In fact, Brenda lives so close to me I could throw a stone and hit her house. Would you like her phone number?'

" 'Yes! Yes,' Sherri exclaimed. 'That would be great. I can't believe this! I've been wanting to talk with them and hear the whole story.' "

Ann told me that the granddaughter was very excited, but she couldn't have been more excited than I was. I was ecstatic. I was screaming, crying, and laughing all at the same time. I couldn't believe it. Ann finished by saying, "The granddaughter's name, by the way, is Sherri Childress."

Sherri Childress with Channel 10 anchor, John Becker, during Sherri's television interview.

Immediately, I dialed Kay. What an incredible moment it was for us! Now we were both praising God and shouting for joy. Imagine my excitement when just a few days later I was finally able to meet Sherri—with an *i*. Channel 10 News had set up an interview at the Little Creek Sanitarium with Sherri and her grandmother, Mama Layman, to do a feature story. I was so excited, I arrived about thirty minutes early; Sherri had done

the same. When I walked around the corner, she jumped from her chair, and we ran to each other and hugged and cried. I was overjoyed to finally come face to face with the "Bible Lady." It was an incredible moment I will forever treasure.

I know God's timing is always perfect. There had to be some reason God waited over a year before the "Bible Lady" turned up. In the next few days, as I pieced together the story, I realized God wanted to include many more in the blessing of being a part of the search and the miracle of

I finally had the privilege of meeting Sherri (with an "i") who generously gave away her grandmother's Bible.

finding Sherri. Because of the media coverage this story was receiving, it would be an amazing testimony to millions of just how meaningful God's Word can be in the life of a person—especially in times of trouble and loss. Everyone would be touched to learn how the unselfish act of one person blessed another so deeply. But I'm getting ahead of my story.

When I had talked to Sherry Helveston a year before, she expressed an intense desire to find the granddaughter who had given away the Bible. Even though my efforts failed, it didn't discourage Sherry. She told the story and showed her Bible to everyone she met. Over the next year, more than a hundred people must have gotten involved in trying to find Sherri—the donor of the Bible. But it was the efforts of Barbara Miller, along with Anne Hawkins and John Acuff, that actually found her. Barbara and Anne were part of a volunteer group of Presbyterians helping rebuild the Helvestons' home during the fall of 2006. As they worked together, Sherry shared the story and showed Barbara her precious Bible.

Immediately the burden of finding Sherri was laid on Barbara's heart. "I'm going to find her, with God's help, if it is the last thing I do," she declared. Sherry Helveston had heard this before. She appreciated Barbara's enthusiasm, but Sherry had been disappointed so often that she wasn't sure anyone would be successful.

Barbara, however, meant what she said. She loves God with all her heart, and her confidence was based on her belief that "with God all things are possible," as the Bible says in Matthew 19:26. Anne Hawkins was equally confident. Finding the "Bible Lady" became their mission, and they were relentless in the search. They shared the challenge with friends like John Acuff, who promised to help. And they all prayed earnestly that God would lead them.

On November 22, 2006, Barbara called the Union Cumberland Presbyterian Church in Knoxville and was told—as I had been told a year before—that there was no one named Sherri in that church. Barbara then e-mailed every pastor of every Presbyterian church in east

Tennessee, pleading with them to ask from their pulpits if anyone knew of a woman named Sherri, who spelled her name with an *i* and who had given her grandmother's Bible to the Katrina survivors.

At the same time, Anne Hawkins called one of the television stations in Knoxville, asking for help in finding Sherri. She talked with John Becker, the news anchor for Channel 10; he seemed interested and said he would see what he could do.

The next day, John Acuff, who was spending the Thanksgiving holidays with his mom in Knoxville, felt impressed to search Union Cumberland Presbyterian Church's Web site. Just maybe he would find someone else he could contact since Barbara had not been successful. On the Web site he found the phone number for the church membership clerk, Nettie Mae Sherrod. He called her home on November 24. When her husband, Fred, answered, John told him the story and asked if he could help. Fred was excited about the possibility of finding the "Bible Lady," and he was sure his pastor would be, as well.

On Sunday, November 26, at the Union Cumberland Presbyterian Church in Knoxville, Pastor Leonard Turner made an announcement before his sermon: "Something really special has happened concerning our shipment to Hurricane Katrina victims. Since I don't have all the details I'm going to ask Brother Fred to come up and share it with you."

Fred went to the pulpit and said, "Yes, it's true that something very special has happened with our eighteen wheeler load that we sent down to Mississippi. Somebody sent a Bible . . ." Sherri Childress, sitting in the congregation, thought, *I bet lots of people sent Bibles.*

But then she heard Fred say, "We're looking for a woman named Sherri who spells her name with an *i*. This woman gave away her grandmother's Bible." Now when Sherri heard this, she was mortified and sunk lower in her pew. She was ashamed for anyone to know she had given away her own grandmother's precious Bible. Members of a close-knit Southern family would have never donated a *family* Bible. They would have purchased a new one—but would not have given away the Bible that had belonged to their 101-year-old grandmother!

By this time, Sherri's twin sister, Linda, who was sitting next to her, lifted her hand above Sherri's head and started wildly pointing toward Sherri, saying, "It's her! It's her!"

Fred then looked directly at Sherri and said, "Do you know there are hundreds of people all over the country looking for you? The lady who found your Bible suffered terrible loss. Everything she owned was destroyed, even her beloved Bible. When she was at the depths of despair, searching through boxes in a parking lot relief center, hoping to find something she and her husband could wear, she found your grandmother's Bible. That Bible has been her lifeline. She was so grateful to have a giant-print Bible. She felt that it was a gift from God.

"When she read your note and saw that you cared so much about the plight of the Katrina survivors and that you were willing to give them your own grandmother's Bible, it meant more to her than you could possibly know. Then, when she noticed that the two of you shared the same name, except for different spellings, she *knew* that God had sent that Bible just for her. She clung to it for dear life. When her situation seemed hopeless, that Bible gave her hope."

As Fred finished the story, the congregation broke into a thunderous applause. Many of them—including the church secretary—did not know Sherri because she was a relatively new member of their church. Now they all knew her, and how proud they were to be a part of this unfolding miracle.

By this time, Sherri was crying. The pastor started his sermon, but Sherri didn't hear a word. She was in shock. She thought back to her struggle about whether or not to give up that Bible. When she first felt impressed to donate it, she resisted. She didn't want to. She even called her sister, Linda. "I think God wants me to give away Mama Layman's Bible. What do you think I should do?"

Linda said, "If you're impressed to donate it, then you should give it."

Sherri was shocked. She had thought her sister would be against the idea and would tell her in no uncertain terms that Mama Layman's Bible was a keepsake. Now what should she do? But the longer she procrastinated, the stronger the impression became that God wanted her to give the Bible.

Her grandma was affectionately called "Mama Layman" by all her grandchildren because even in her eighties she didn't feel she was old enough to be labeled "Grandma." She had been so special to Sherri all her life. Now she was 101 years of age and in a nursing home. She suffered from Alzheimer's. Sherri considered the Bible the most precious gift her grandmother had left her. "Please, God," she prayed, "don't make me give it away."

But the impression to do so continued, and finally she surrendered to the Holy Spirit and decided to put the Bible in the box of things she was sending to the Gulf—but not before writing a letter to the person who would find the Bible. She wanted that person to know just how special this Bible was and how much she would be praying for all the Katrina victims.

After packing up her box, Sherri took it to the church. Somehow, when things were being loaded onto the truck, her box got pushed behind the soda machine in the back lobby. Just as the truck was starting to drive away, Dave Ingram, a member of the church, noticed Sherri's box. Quickly grabbing it in his arms, he bolted out the door, yelling to get the driver's attention. He had to run the full length of the parking lot, holding on to the box with one arm and waving frantically with the other until the truck driver finally noticed him and stopped. They opened the back of the truck and added Sherri's box. Even two minutes later, and it would have been too late!

Even after the truck left, Sherri still did not have peace about her decision. All the following year, she agonized about giving away her grandmother's Bible. *What kind of person would do such a thing?* she asked herself. She would see news reports about all the boxes of supplies destined for hurricane victims, rotting in parking lots because there were not enough volunteers to help distribute the items—and she would cry thinking of her grandmother's Bible, possibly rotting away in some dump. She chastised herself over and over again. She shuddered to think what her precious Mama Layman would say if she were in her right mind.

Then, when Sherri found out that day in church how God had used her grandma's Bible to bring hope to just the right woman, she was overwhelmed to think God had His hand on this Bible and that she was, indeed, a part of His bigger plan. She was overwhelmed to realize the power and love of God, and she thanked Him for not giving up on her when she had been such a reluctant giver.

After the church service, Fred gave Sherri the phone number of Barbara Miller. Sherri's hands were shaking when she made the call. "This is Sherri Childress," she told Barbara. "I spell my name with an *i*, and I believe you're looking for me." She couldn't say any more because Barbara was screaming.

"I promised Sherry I'd find you no matter what it took," Barbara exclaimed. "I can't believe I'm actually speaking to you." Barbara then told Sherri all about the woman who had found the Bible and how much it meant to her. But when Sherri asked for Sherry Helveston's phone number, Barbara wouldn't give it to her. She said, "I want to get you two together, but I need to make some phone calls first." Sherri pleaded, but Barbara wouldn't give in. Barbara was thinking how wonderful it would be if she could get some media publicity and catch Sherry's reaction on video tape when the "Bible Lady's" identity was revealed to her.

Meanwhile, Sherri was so excited she couldn't sleep all night; the next day she couldn't concentrate at work. That night Sherri called Barbara again and begged for Sherry's number. Since Barbara wasn't able to line up media coverage, she relented and gave it to her.

Sherri's hands were trembling with excitement as she dialed the number. Impatiently she waited for someone to answer. Finally Lloyd Helveston picked up the receiver.

"May I speak to Sherry please?" Sherri asked.

When Sherry answered, the "Bible Lady" simply said, "My name is Sherri Childress. I'm from east Tennessee, and I spell my name with an *i*."

Now it was Sherry Helveston's turn to start screaming and crying for happiness. "I've been looking for you for over a year! In fact, there are people all over the country looking for you. I have your grandmother's Bible, but it's not hers anymore. It's mine."

By this time the "Bible Lady" was crying too. "Yes, it is; yes, it is; the Bible *is* yours."

A few weeks later, Sherry Helveston had the shock of her life! Television anchor John Becker from WBIR, Knoxville's NBC affiliate, secretly arranged for Sherri Childress to surprise Sherry Helveston at her home in Biloxi, Mississippi. John and a cameraman began an interview with Sherry inside her home. She showed him her Bible and briefly told how she had found it. Then John suggested they go outside to get some pictures. At that moment, Sherri Childress stepped out from behind the old FEMA trailer, but before she could

From left to right: Sherry Helveston, John Becker, and Sherri Childress. Thanks to WBIR, Knoxville, Tennessee's NBC affiliate, television anchor, John Becker, made it possible for Sherry to finally meet Sherri, "The Bible Lady."

say, "Hi, I'm Sherri with an *i*," it was instant recognition! Both women screamed as they flew into each other's arms and sobbed for joy. Later Sherri Childress exclaimed, "Sherry Helveston is the most precious lady. Her spirit just envelops you. I am so blessed that God sent me this woman. She'll always be part of my life. It's so incredibly powerful to realize what God did to put us together." The bonding was instantaneous!

If I had found Sherri Childress the year before, this story would not have had the impact that it had later and that it continues to have. There would have been no media coverage, and thousands of viewers would have missed the blessing of knowing how valuable God's Word is to those who are seeking His direction and care. Isn't God good?

JUST HOW PRECIOUS IS GOD'S WORD TO YOU?

Every time I think back to how much Sherry Helveston treasured her Bible, I realize once more just how privileged we are to have access to God's Word. God speaks to us through the Holy Spirit directly affecting our minds—especially as we pray—and through the Holy Spirit impressing us as we prayerfully read God's words in the Bible. We develop a relationship with Jesus through both the Bible and the Holy Spirit. Here's how the apostle John puts it: "In the beginning was the Word, and the Word was with God, and the Word was God. He was in the beginning with God. All things were made through Him, and without Him nothing was made that was made. In Him was life, and the life was the light of men. And the light shines in the darkness, and the darkness did not comprehend it" (John 1:1–5). There is no doubt in anyone's mind that the "Word" that John is talking about is Jesus.

I don't claim to fully comprehend how Inspiration works; I just know that my Bible is not merely a book like any other book. It's so much more than words on a page. It's God's Word, and John says that, likewise, Jesus is also God's Word.

Yet so many of us take the Bible for granted. Even though year after year the Bible remains at the top of the best-seller list, do we read it as passionately as we would read the latest *New York Times* bestseller? Most of us in the Western world have at least one Bible. In fact, we probably have more than one. But is your Bible precious to you? Do you look upon it as God's Word, and hunger after the delightful "soul" food that is there for you? Each day, are you eager to read what the God of the universe has written for you? When you are struggling with a decision, do you go to God's Word seeking guidance; when the Holy Spirit speaks to you through the Bible, do you see this as God's prophetic Word to you? Do you hold on to this Word of the Lord as His promise to you? Do you pray God's Word? Do you claim His promises and expect Him to answer? If you do, you know the peace that can come to you even before you've experienced His answer. It's a mind-boggling experience which we can have when we connect with God through His Word—the Bible—because that's how we connect with Jesus.

Speaking of connecting with Jesus, not long ago I received an e-mail that compared the way we treat our cell phones to the way we treat our Bibles. You might want to consider whether you are as attached to your Bible as you are to your cell phone. Here is the e-mail:

The Bible vs. the Cell Phone

I wonder what would happen if we treated our Bible like we treat our cell phone?

What if we carried it around in our purses or pocket?

What if we turned back to retrieve it when we forget it?

What if we flipped through it several times a day?

What if we used it to receive messages?

What if we treated it like we couldn't live without it?

What if we gave it to our kids as a gift?

What if we used it as we travel?

What if we used it in case of emergency?

What if we upgraded it to include 24/7 tech service from the Holy Spirit?

Oh, and one more thing. Unlike our cell phone, we don't ever have to worry about our Bible being disconnected—because Jesus already paid the bill.

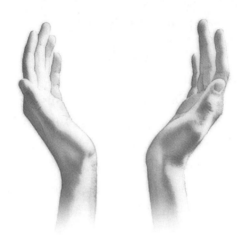

CHAPTER 14

CLAIMING POWER-PACKED PROMISES

I will perform that good thing which I have promised.
—Jeremiah 33:14

For so many years I've been claiming Bible promises as I pray that I do it almost without thinking. Certain verses have special meaning to me, and I quote them so often that they were burned into my memory long ago. I'm constantly increasing my list of promise texts as I continue to find new ones that speak to specific prayer needs. I believe the power of my prayers is increased by using God's Word.

Adoniram Judson (1788–1850), the well-known nineteenth-century Baptist missionary to Burma, once said, "The future is as bright as the promises of God." I've thought a lot about that, and it's true. As long as we can hold on to something that God has promised, we can be optimistic about what's ahead. Why? Because we know God has good things planned for us (see Jeremiah 29:11) and that He will not allow anything to come to us that we won't be able to bear (see 1 Corinthians 10:13).

The following are some of my favorite power-packed promise texts. They are general promises that I can claim no matter what my need may be. They are the kind of texts that you don't want to get up in the morning without!

- "Then you will call upon Me and go and pray to Me, and I will listen to you" (Jeremiah 29:12).
- "He will be very gracious to you at the sound of your cry; When He hears it, He will answer you" (Isaiah 30:19).
- "Now this is the confidence that we have in Him, that if we ask anything according to His will, He hears us. And if we know that He hears us, whatever we ask, we know that we have the petitions that we have asked of Him" (1 John 5:14, 15).
- "It shall come to pass that before they call, I will answer; and while they are still speaking, I will hear" (Isaiah 65:24).
- "Then you shall call, and the Lord will answer; You shall cry, and He will say, 'Here I am' " (Isaiah 58:9).
- "He shall call upon Me, and I will answer him; I will be with him in trouble; I will deliver him and honor him" (Psalm 91:15).
- "The righteous cry out, and the LORD hears, and delivers them out of all their troubles" (Psalm 34:17).

Using one or more of these texts, I might pray something like this: *"Dear heavenly Father, You have said that if we ask anything according to Your will, You will listen and You will answer. And in Psalm 91:15 You have promised to be with me when I'm in trouble and that You will deliver me . . ."* After beginning my prayer like this, I let the Lord know exactly the kind of trouble I'm in and ask that His will be done. It's amazing what this kind of praying does to my peace of mind! I claim Bible promises every day for very specific things—such as when I'm afraid or concerned about someone.

Perhaps things are hectic at work, and you need direction. Maybe there are financial worries or even more importantly, someone you love doesn't know Jesus. Whatever the need, there is a Bible promise for every life situation you could possibly face. There is nothing too great or too small for God to handle.

I had a friend who confided she didn't pray about her "silly little problems" because she didn't want to burden God with them. Can you imagine? I wouldn't want to go one minute carrying my own burdens! God is so much stronger and wiser than I am; He knows just what I need. He wants us to come to Him in prayer. That's why He has given us so many beautiful promises to claim—to reassure us how very much He loves us and that He is always there for us!

I have approached God's throne room countless times with what my friend deems "silly little problems." And God always hears and answers my prayers. Here's an example of a situation that may seem trite to some, but was a real concern for me.

TRAPPED IN AN UNLOCKED ROOM

As I put the key into the ignition of a brand-new rental car, I paused and bowed my head. *Precious Lord, I'm asking You to be with me this weekend. Please give me the words that You want me to say and above all else, use me in a powerful way to bring others closer to You. I thank You for the privilege of serving You. As You know, Lord, I am not worthy. I ask for an outpouring of Your Holy Spirit upon the entire camp meeting so that when people leave they will have a burning desire to know You better. And one more thing, Lord. Help me to get to the campground safely. Guide my way so I won't get lost and put Your hand of protection over me. Thank You, Jesus. In Your name I pray, Amen.*

I started the car and eased out of the parking lot, remembering to give a bookmark to the man at the gate. Driving west on Airport Boulevard toward Gardner Road, I wondered silently how I had ever survived without the Internet and the ability to print out driving directions to almost anywhere. Before I knew it, an hour had passed and I was turning left onto Caswell Beach Road. As I neared the campground, I took in the beauty. No wonder the camp meeting was held right on the ocean. I stopped at the entrance and told the man at the gate where I was going. He waved me through. But before I drove on, I handed him a bookmark. "This is beautiful," he exclaimed. "How much do I owe you?"

"Absolutely nothing. It's a gift—just a reminder to let you know that Jesus loves you. Have a good night."

"Thanks," he said, waving the bookmark.

"You're welcome." I rolled up my window and drove slowly. By now, the evening meeting was almost over. *I'd better just go find my room and get settled,* I decided. The lodge was similar to a motel where you park near your door. After carrying my luggage inside, I began to unpack, hanging my suit jacket and skirt in the closet and setting out my toiletries in the bathroom. I was just about to get undressed and crawl into bed, when I noticed another door in the room. I assumed it was a door to the adjoining room, but I decided I should check to make sure it was locked. To my surprise, it opened easily; behind it was a small kitchenette.

What a nice idea! There was some fruit on the table, and I nibbled on some grapes. This was a welcome treat since I hadn't had time to stop and eat. Looking around, I saw yet another door and assumed it probably led to the next room. I listened carefully, but I couldn't hear anyone. The people staying in that room were probably still at the meeting. It was already 9:30 P.M. and I decided that the preacher must still be giving his message. That reminded me of the many times my dad had preached way past quitting time. I chuckled as I remembered the time when Dad asked me, "Do you know what it means when a preacher says, 'Now in closing'?" I shook my head. He smiled and replied, "Absolutely nothing." We both had a good laugh.

I left the kitchenette and returned to my room, closing the door behind me and turning the lock to secure it. But the lock refused to budge. I turned the knob again—and again—without success. No amount of pushing, pulling, or turning made any difference. The lock on the door was broken. *Now what am I going to do? Perhaps I could push a chair up under the doorknob and secure the door that way.* But there wasn't a chair in my room. *Maybe a kitchen chair would work.* But the back of the kitchen chairs were too thick to fit under the doorknob. *Now what?*

I sat down on the edge of the bed and pondered my dilemma. I couldn't sleep in a room that had no lock. People in the next room would have access to my room. It would be fine if a woman were next door. But what if it were a man—or even a couple?

Dad had counseled me since I was a little girl about the importance of avoiding the appearance of evil. I remembered my daddy getting calls at all hours of the night from church members needing him to visit them regarding some personal crisis. Dad never went on a house call without Mom—even if it was only to study the Bible. He said it just wouldn't look right if a woman happened to be home alone. "Bibby," he warned me, "don't ever put yourself in a compromising situation."

Well, one thing was for sure—even though I was exhausted, I couldn't go to bed until I knew who my neighbors were. Not knowing what else to do, I got down on my knees on the cold wooden floor and prayed. *Precious heavenly Father, You know the predicament that I am in right now, and I don't know what to do. It wouldn't be wise to sleep in a room that can't be locked, and I don't know where else to go. I know that there won't be anyone who can fix the lock tonight, but if my neighbors could just be women, then everything would work out. I know that is asking a lot, but You can do anything. And I know You wouldn't want me to stay in a place where my reputation could be compromised. Lord, I am trusting this matter to You. In Psalm chapter ninety-one, You have promised to protect me. You have said in verse eleven that you will send Your angels to keep me safe. In Isaiah chapter forty-one, verse ten You have told me that I don't need to fear, for You are always with me. Thank You for answering my prayer. Amen.*

I got up from my knees feeling better. I didn't know how God would answer, but I knew He would. I called my husband, Tim, and explained the situation, asking him to pray with me, too. When I finished, the clock by the bed told me it was 10:15 P.M. I started to gather some blankets to sleep in the car when I heard voices next door.

I knocked gently. A few seconds later, the door opened, and a woman with the most beautiful smile said, "Brenda, it's so nice to meet you. I'm Debbie Rapp." She had barely gotten the words out when I heard the sound of another feminine voice. Two women! *Thank You, Jesus, for answering my prayer.*

Before Debbie could say another word, I threw my arms around her and exclaimed, "Oh Debbie, it is so wonderful to meet you." Then I explained why I was so excited to have two women next to me.

By that time Debbie's friend, Ann Walton, joined us. I ran over and gave her a hug too. Before I could say anything else, Debbie filled her in. We all had a good laugh over the agony of the broken lock and my fear of having men next door. We ended up talking for almost an hour. I fell asleep that night still thanking God for His goodness and mercy—and His protection.

Debbie Rapp, Women's Ministries Director for the Carolina Conference. Debbie has a passion for sharing Jesus. What I love most about Debbie is her generous heart that is overflowing with God's love. I'm looking forward to being neighbors with her in heaven! She is a blessing in my life.

God opened the windows of heaven and poured out such a blessing that weekend! After I gave my testimony, several women who were in abusive marriages asked for prayer. One young woman showed me bruises all over her arms, legs, and stomach where she had been hit by her jealous boyfriend. We prayed

Vinnie Springer is one of the ladies I met at the Oak Island camp meeting. The joy of Jesus just shines through Vinnie, and I count it a privilege to call her my friend.

together, and God used me to help her understand that it was never God's plan for anyone to be beaten or abused. She later e-mailed me that she had broken up with him and that she wanted to give her heart to Jesus.

Many women shared personal experiences of physical and emotional abuse. Some wanted counseling, and I assured them that I was not a counselor, but that I could lead them to Jesus, the best Counselor of all.

While driving back to the airport, I reflected on the weekend's blessings and thanked God for protecting me as He promised to do.

I've used God's promises of protection many times in prayer as I did when I was trapped in that unlocked room, and I always feel an immediate sense of peace when I do. But there are many more power-packed promise verses. Let me just share a few specific ones that you will find worth memorizing. Here are some of God's power-packed promises:

GUIDANCE
- "He will be our guide even to death" (Psalm 48:14).
- "In all your ways acknowledge Him, and He shall direct your paths" (Proverbs 3:6).

HEALTH NEEDS
- "No good thing will He withhold from those who walk uprightly" (Psalm 84:11).
- "Bread will be given him, his water will be sure" (Isaiah 33:16).

PHYSICAL NEEDS

- "But those who wait on the LORD
  Shall renew their strength;
  They shall mount up with wings like eagles,
  They shall run and not be weary,
  They shall walk and not faint" (Isaiah 40:31).
- "Come to Me, all you who labor and are heavy laden, and I will give you rest" (Matthew 11:28).

TEMPTATION

- "But thanks be to God, who gives us the victory through our Lord Jesus Christ" (1 Corinthians 15:57).
- "The Lord knows how to deliver the godly out of temptations" (2 Peter 2:9).

DISCOURAGEMENT

- "And we know that all things work together for good to those who love God" (Romans 8:28).
- "The steps of a good man are ordered by the LORD,
  And He delights in his way.
  Though he fall, he shall not be utterly cast down;
  For the LORD upholds him with His hand" (Psalm 37:23, 24).

LONELINESS

- "I will not leave you nor forsake you" (Joshua 1:5).
- "I am with you always, even to the end of the age" (Matthew 28:20).

A BROKEN HEART

- "Weeping may endure for a night, but joy comes in the morning" (Psalm 30:5).
- "He heals the broken-hearted and binds up their wounds" (Psalm 147:3).

DOUBT

- "What He had promised He was also able to perform" (Romans 4:21).
- "The Lord is not slack concerning His promise, . . . but is longsuffering toward us, not willing that any should perish but that all should come to repentance" (2 Peter 3:9).

PARENTING

- "For I will contend with him who contends with you, and I will save your children" (Isaiah 49:25).
- "All your children shall be taught by the LORD, and great shall be the peace of your children" (Isaiah 54:13).

If you find it difficult to memorize texts, such as those above, try making up a little tune to go along with the text. Each time you repeat the text, be sure to say where it's found. In that way, even if you can't think of the exact words of the promise text, you can find it in your Bible, place your finger on the text, and praise the Lord that He's in the process of answering that particular promise that He has made to you!

Use my list as a basis for your own list. Then each time you find a wonderful promise, claim it immediately, share it with someone else, and write it down. The more you use these promises, the more they will become part of you, and the more confident you will be that your prayers will be answered. The result is more passionate prayer!

MIRACLE AT MCDONALD'S

Because I pray daily that God will use me to be a blessing to others, I began searching for a promise text that I could claim as I made this request. God led me to Galatians 6:3, 4. In the *New Living Translation* this text reads, "If you think you are too important to help someone in need, you are only fooling yourself. You are really a nobody. Be sure you do what you should, for then you will enjoy the personal satisfaction of having done your work well." Wow! I like that. What better promise, what better reward, could I receive for reaching out to help others than to have the personal satisfaction of having done my best for Jesus!

But on the day I met Charity, my prayer wasn't the fulfillment of Galatians 6:3, 4; it was the fulfillment of Luke 19:10. Here's the story.

It was a beautiful day for my sister Linda and me to drive to 3ABN to prepare for the taping of our cooking program. Sister Cinda needed to stay home one more day to celebrate a family birthday, so she would be coming later. We packed the car, and just before pulling out of the driveway, we bowed our heads for prayer. *"Precious heavenly Father, please protect us as we drive and let us be a blessing to someone today. Lord,"* I pleaded, *"give us a soul to witness to. In Luke chapter nineteen, verse ten we're told that You came to seek and to save people who were lost. That's why I'm praying that You will use us to lead a soul to You. Let our paths cross with someone who needs to know how much You love them."*

When I got through praying, Linda chuckled. "Well, the Lord sure has His work cut out for Him today, since we're driving six hours nonstop to 3ABN and then going directly to our apartment."

"Oh, God can still answer our prayer," I assured Linda.

"I know He can," she agreed.

Not even ten minutes after leaving my driveway, I was suddenly thirsty. "There's McDonald's," I commented to Linda. "Before getting on Pelissippi Highway, I'm going to stop and get something to drink." I was going to go to the drive-through window, but because it was lunch time there was a long line. "I'll just run inside; it will probably be faster." I pulled into a parking place, and Linda, not wanting anything to drink herself, decided to wait in the car.

There were a lot of people in line inside the building, as well— mostly men who looked like construction workers. One girl was at the counter trying to pay for her order. Everyone in line was fidgeting and waiting impatiently. The girl was searching through all her pockets, finding a quarter in one pocket and a nickel in another. "Can you wait just a minute?" she said to the clerk. "I think I might have some more money in my truck." Without waiting for an answer, she turned and ran out the door.

Only one register was open, so no one else could order until she returned. Now everyone was moaning and groaning because they had to wait. I could hear some people swearing. They all seemed quite agitated about the delay.

I stepped out of the line and asked the clerk, "Excuse me, Ma'am. How much does she owe?"

"Six dollars and forty-two cents," she replied.

"I'd like to pay that for her," I said as I handed over a ten-dollar bill.

You could hear an audible, "Ohhh," go up from the people waiting in line. One man joked, "You want to pay for my meal, too?" Now everyone was watching me.

"Are you sure you want to do that?" the clerk asked.

"Yes."

By the time the girl came back, the line had moved so fast that it was almost my turn to order. I watched as she came running up to the counter with a few more quarters. She still didn't have enough money and was ready to return a few items when the clerk handed her the bag of food. "You're all set," she told her.

"What do you mean?"

"That lady over there paid for you," the clerk explained, pointing to me.

"You did?" The girl was shocked. "I can't ask you to do that. Give me your name and address, and I'll send you the money."

"No, no," I assured her. "That would steal my blessing. In fact, I have something else for you." I pulled out a bookmark. But it wasn't one of the usual bookmarks I hand out with Bible texts. It was a *Kids Time* bookmark with the words, "It's Kids Time to Share Jesus." I explained that I hosted and produced a children's program on 3ABN.

"You can watch it in the Knoxville area on Channel 14." All the people around were listening.

"What is 3ABN?" a burly man sitting across the room asked as he wiped ketchup off his chin with the back of his hand.

"It's the second largest religious network in the world," I explained, "and there is so much wonderful Bible truth presented. My sisters and I tape cooking shows as well as the kids' program. In fact, that's where we're headed right now."

The girl was still in shock. She just couldn't believe that someone would pay for her lunch. "Do you like gospel music?" I asked.

"Yes," she replied.

"Then I have something else for you. My sisters and I sing together, and I have some of our CDs in the car. If you don't mind following me outside, I'd like to give you one."

The girl went to put her food on a table, while I went to the soda machine. As I was filling my cup, two men got up and came over. "Ma'am, that was really cool—what you did. I don't know many people who would have done something like that."

The other admitted, "I'm kind of ashamed of myself. Wish I'd thought to do that. I will next time."

By now the young girl had joined us, and I motioned for her to follow me out to my car. As I handed her one of our CDs, I asked, "What's your name?"

"Charity," she replied.

I introduced her to Linda and then explained to Charity that she was an answer to our prayer. I mentioned that just a few minutes earlier, we had prayed that God would allow us to be a blessing to someone and lead us to someone who needed to know that Jesus loves them.

"Wow! You will never know how much I needed to hear that," Charity exclaimed.

I reached over and gave her a big hug, reminding her once again, "Jesus loves you." Tears filled her eyes.

"I can't even believe this! Things are really tough for me right now, and I can't believe God picked *me* to answer *your* prayer." She wiped the tears from her cheek. "You certainly blessed me, that's for sure. I don't know how to thank you. Meeting you like this means so much to me. I'm going to think of you every time I listen to this CD."

She turned to leave and then stopped and turned around. She could hardly speak. "I really mean it. You'll never know what this has done for me. You just don't know. Thank you!"

Linda and I looked at each other and shook our heads. "I can't believe it," I exclaimed. "It didn't even take ten minutes, and God has already answered our prayer to meet someone who needed to know about His love."

"Thank You, Jesus," I prayed. *"You guided us here. You knew Charity was in trouble, without enough money in her pockets. It was Your planning that brought us here right at this very moment. Therefore, we give You all the credit, praise, honor, and glory."*

Linda added, *"And please, precious Lord, if You have another soul You want us to witness to today, we would like to be a blessing to someone else."*

As we continued on our way, our hearts were bubbling over. There is no greater joy than bringing Jesus' love to one more precious soul. We turned up the CD player and sang at the top of our lungs. We knew and recognized that it was God who gave us this joy. And you know, His joy is the best gift in the world. It's a promise that He fulfills when we pray. You can find it in John 16:24: "Ask, and you will receive, that your joy may be full."

To be healthy, I know I need good food. But without the joy of the Lord—which comes through claiming His Word and experiencing the phenomenal way He works out His daily plan for my life—I would be merely existing. Until you experience the overwhelming joy of doing His will, you'll have no idea what I'm talking about. Jesus' Word to me is clear, "Brenda, you shall not live by bread alone, but by every word that proceeds from My mouth." (See Matthew 4:4.) My response is a song that David sang in the wilderness of Judah:

O God, You are my God;
Early will I seek You;
My soul thirsts for You;
My flesh longs for You . . .
Because Your lovingkindness is better than life,
My lips shall praise You.
Thus I will bless You while I live;
I will lift up my hands in Your name.
My soul shall be satisfied as with marrow and fatness,
And my mouth shall praise You with joyful lips (Psalm 63:1, 3–5).

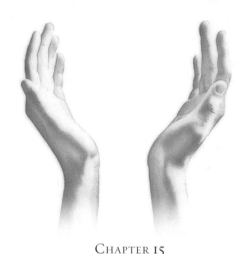

CHAPTER 15

DIVINE APPOINTMENTS

But sanctify the Lord God in your hearts,
and always be ready to give a defense to everyone who asks you.
—1 Peter 3:15

I've always been fascinated by divine appointments. There was the beautiful Rebekah who came to the well at exactly the same time Abraham's servant was praying, "I will ask one of the women for a drink, and if she says, 'Yes, and I will water your camels too,' then I will know she is the one You have chosen to be Isaac's wife." He looked up and saw Rebekah dipping her jug into the water. The servant ran over and asked for a drink. And Rebekah replied, "Yes, and I will water your camels too!" That's amazing—especially when you realize that it might have taken Rebekah over three hundred jugs of water to satisfy all those thirsty camels! (See Genesis 24.)

Then there was Esther, who won the Miss Medo-Persia beauty pageant and became King Xerxes' wife. Thus she was in a position of influence at exactly the time when the Jews in the kingdom were threatened with annihilation. A divine appointment? Her cousin Mordecai thought so when he said to Esther, "Who can say but that you have been elevated to the palace for just such a time as this?" (Esther 4:14, NLT).

God sent Philip on assignment to the middle of the desert in Gaza at the exact time the Ethiopian eunuch was trying to understand the text in Isaiah predicting the Messiah's death—and Philip was able to tell him all about Jesus. (See Acts 8.)

God must delight in divine appointments, but there must be an even greater delight in the hearts and emotions of the people who suddenly realize that they were brought together for a higher purpose. I know; I've been there. Here are just a few of the divine appointments that I've experienced. Each time I tell these stories, I'm reminded of just how much Jesus loves me to orchestrate people and situations in such amazing ways. I simply can't believe that these things happened by chance. They were miracles.

BETWEEN THE CHINA STAR AND ANGEL LANE

My sisters and I were working on our fourth CD project. From the beginning, we felt God was directing us. It all started when a friend urged us to do a CD of songs of hope and encouragement for hurting people. We prayed as we always do before starting a project, and all three of us felt we should move forward—if the same producer we had worked with on earlier projects would be willing to produce this CD. We knew he was super busy and had turned down quite a few requests from others, so we wondered what his response would be. When I called him, he didn't hesitate. "I'd love to do it!" he said. We had our answer.

Our next challenge was coordinating all of our schedules to find a time to record. We could find only one week that worked for all of us and that would make it possible to complete the CD before the marketing deadline.

Over the next couple of months, we selected the songs, worked with our producer, and practiced long hours until finally it was time to lay down our vocals at the recording studio. We drove to West Frankfort, Illinois, on Friday afternoon to be ready for the coming week. Because our schedules were so tight, we were not only recording our CD that week, we were taping two cooking programs for 3ABN, as well. We also had to get our pictures taken for the cover of our CD and had stopped on our way to 3ABN to purchase matching outfits—hoping they would fit. The only thing missing in our plan for the week was a photographer.

Our graphic designer for all our CD covers, Brenda McClearen from Nashville, had suggested an outside scene—preferably by water. We knew we had to get the photo taken when we were all together at 3ABN, and we were thinking the lake on Angel Lane, right across from our apartment, would be a perfect location. We thought we'd have time on Sunday for the photo shoot. There was only one problem. We didn't have a photographer nor did we have a lot of money to hire one. But we had gotten this far by faith, and we knew God would provide. What happened next I consider to be an amazing divine appointment.

The Micheff sisters have declared the food at the China Star restaurant to be the "world's greatest Chinese food." We eat there so often we have the restaurant's phone number on our speed dials! Qing Ping and Yan Lin, pictured here, are the owners and have become our special friends.

"Should we stop at the China Star and get something to eat?" I asked my sisters.

"I'd love to," Linda spoke up, "but we have all these groceries in the car for our cooking program, and we need to get them in the refrigerator. Besides, we all brought food from home, so we should be fine."

We had almost driven past the China Star when Cinda threw out the deciding vote. "Who cares how much food we have? This is going to be a horribly busy week. Let's treat ourselves to the best Chinese food in the world."

"That sounds good to me!" I agreed, as I turned into the parking lot.

"Count me in," Linda relented. "I'm hungry."

When we're busy taping at 3ABN, we rarely have much time to eat, much less to cook for ourselves, so we dine regularly at our favorite restaurant, the China Star. About ten minutes before we arrive, we call and ask for our "usual"—vegetable lo mein with extra cashews, sesame tofu with extra sauce on the side, and Chinese mixed vegetables—so by the time we arrive, our favorite waiters, Joe and Andre, are ready to serve us. We've been doing this for so long that "Miss Brenda's Menu" has become something that others have learned to ask for!

Joe and Andre greeted us. Since it had been a few weeks since we'd been at 3ABN, we asked Joe what was happening in his life and he shared that he and his fiancé had just had their photographs taken. We immediately exclaimed, "We want to see them!" Joe went out to his car to get the pictures. One look and we all knew that whoever had taken these pictures was an outstanding professional. "These are gorgeous!" "I love the beautiful outdoor scenes and the attractive poses!" "Who was your photographer?" we all said almost in unison.

"Oh," said Joe, "he's sitting right over there." He pointed to the back of the restaurant. "Would you like to meet him?"

"Yes, yes," the three of us responded.

"Hey, Ray, come on over. I want you to meet some of my special friends. They're on 3ABN."

Left to right: Yordan Apriyanto, Ray Pilot, and Andreas Kartika. Ray is the photographer we met through a "divine appointment," in answer to prayer, at the China Star. Our favorite waiters, "Joe" Yordan and "Andre," are serving Ray's dinner.

I saw a man look up with a big friendly smile, stand, and make his way toward us.

As soon as Joe made the introductions, I commented, "Ray, you did an awesome job on these photographs. They're absolutely beautiful. I love the way you captured the outdoor colors, and the poses are great."

"Thank you. It always helps when you have good subjects to photograph." He grinned as he nodded toward Joe, who then excused himself to help other customers.

"I don't know if we'd be good subjects, but we're in desperate need of a photographer," I told him.

"What did you have in mind?" Ray asked.

I explained that we needed a cover for our new CD project, and I told him about our time constraints. "The only time we will possibly have for the photo shoot is on Sunday or late Monday afternoon after taping the cooking show. Do you work on Sundays?"

"I mostly do weddings on Sundays, but I don't have one this Sunday."

"That's awesome!" I exclaimed. "I think God has arranged this meeting. I think God wants you to be our photographer!"

"Maybe not," he countered. "Girls, even though I'm free on Sunday, it's going to rain. I've looked at the forecast."

"Well, if it doesn't rain, will you do it? Besides," I added, "God can stop the rain."

"You think your God can stop the rain?"

"I *know* our God can stop the rain," I said emphatically. And then added, "But if God chooses to water the earth on Sunday, is it possible to do the photo shoot on Monday afternoon?"

He hesitated and replied, "Lighting is everything. At this time of the year, the best time of day for a photo shoot is between four-thirty and five-thirty in the afternoon. It's just a short window of time. Before that, the shadows are too intense, and afterwards, it's too dim."

"I have faith that we'll be able to do it on Sunday. We'll be too rushed on Monday after the cooking show. Besides, we'll be exhausted and will look terrible. So, let's plan on Sunday afternoon at four-thirty beside the lake on Angel Lane—just past the 3ABN Worship Center." Then I added, "This is no coincidence. God's hand is on this project. God knew you were going to be here. And He knew we needed you. That's why He put a yearning for Chinese food in our minds just as we were passing the restaurant!"

Ray seemed impressed. "That's pretty awesome!" he exclaimed.

We exchanged phone numbers. "See you Sunday," I told him.

We enjoyed the Sabbath services at the Worship Center. After sun-down, we prepared food samples for the cooking shows. Throughout the day we prayed, *Lord, please don't let it rain tomorrow!*

I was elated Sunday morning when I woke up to a clear blue sky brightened by rays of golden sun. "Do you think it looks like a good enough day for a photo shoot?" I teased Ray when I called him.

"I can't believe it!" he said. "I just knew it was going to rain!"

Ray arrived at the site early and had already decided the exact loca-tion. When we arrived he was blocking the shots to get the right angle of light and best background. We worked quickly. At five-thirty when the light was fading, Ray had taken over a hundred photographs. We prayed that he had captured something we could use, because we knew that Monday after the cooking show was the only time for a retake, and it would be very difficult to look vibrant and alive after spending all afternoon under hot lights in front of the TV cameras. And the chance of even being able to start at four-thirty was slim. *Lord, please give us one good photo so we don't have to retake!* was our prayer.

At one o'clock on Monday afternoon we started taping our cook-ing programs. Ray came by early and took a tour of the 3ABN head-quarters and studios. He was quite impressed by what God had built out in a cornfield in Thompsonville, Illinois.

Our newest CD project, Songs of Hope. *God sent photographer Ray Pilot at the very time we needed him to take the photo for the CD cover. Grandma Micheff always said, "God never gets in a hurry, but He always gets there on time."*

By four-thirty we had wrapped up our last cooking show; we were anything but "picture perfect" after spending the day running up and down stairs and preparing all that food. We quickly looked through Ray's pictures and exclaimed, "God got it right the first time!" We couldn't contain our joy! There were a number of shots suitable for the CD cover. (You can see the one we selected on the Micheff Sisters' *Songs of Hope* CD.) There was no need for a retake.

We didn't know it at the time, but God not only used Ray for the photograph on our *Songs of Hope* CD but also for the author's photo on the back of this book. Meeting Ray at the restaurant was no accident. It was a divine appointment. And it all happened between the China Star and Angel Lane!

The Knoxville News Sentinel

The *Knoxville News Sentinel* contacted my sister Cinda and me, wanting to write a feature story on our new cookbook, *Cooking Entrees With the Micheff Sisters.* The newspaper was interested in the story because both Cinda and I live in Knoxville, and 3ABN is on Channel 14 in Knoxville, so a lot of newspaper readers there watch our cooking program.

Cinda and I prayed about it and were impressed that this would be a wonderful way to witness to our local community. The paper sent out a photographer and a journalist. They explained that instead of posed pictures, they wanted action photos of us preparing food.

What they didn't explain was that the interview by Mary Constantine would also be informal—done at the same time as the photo shoot.

We had a great time with the photographer and Mary. We laughed. We shared our witnessing experiences. We goofed around. We talked about going to Russia and our trips to Belize and Japan. We told them all about being raised vegetarian. Mary asked if being a vegetarian was a requirement for our religion. We explained it was not, but that Seventh-day Adventists did follow God's directions in Leviticus 11 regarding "clean" and "unclean" meat. I even said, "Putting a dead cow inside of me isn't what God has in mind!" We explained that none of our recipes use any animal products. All the cooking programs at 3ABN feature entirely plant-based foods.

We told the interviewer about our childhoods. Our family was known for teaching people how to cook. We explained that we grew up in a Christian home where both Mom and Grandma were great cooks; we learned by working beside them. For example, every time Mom made bread, each of us girls would make a loaf in our own little pan.

We even told Mary about the time when we were visiting Russia and Cinda was demonstrating a recipe. A rather large woman got so excited when she sampled the food that she swung Cinda wildly around the room. Then she picked her up, threw her on her back like a sack of potatoes, marched up the aisle, dumped her off on the stage, and slapped her behind! The crowd roared! And to think, all

When we told Mary Constantine, reporter for the Knoxville News Sentinel, *the story of the Russian lady who had picked up Cinda, we had no idea she would actually include it in the printed interview. Here is the precious Russian lady we were talking about!*

this happened in front of a live audience! Mary thought this was hilarious, but never in a million years did we think she was going to print the story in the newspaper article.

When the photo shoot ended, Cinda and I sat down to do the interview. Mary and the photographer, however, started packing up their things to leave.

"Aren't we going to do the interview?" I asked.

"We just did," Mary explained.

Cinda and I looked at each other. *Oh no! We are in big trouble now!* we thought. *We're going to have to say a* BIG *prayer!* We had no idea what might be printed, but we certainly never realized that the interview was taking place all this time!

Oh, Lord, I pleaded, *please forgive me. If I had known Mary was interviewing us this whole time, I'd have asked her if we could start with prayer. And I would have been more careful! But now it is out of our hands. Lord, please direct Mary as she writes this article so that it will be* exactly what You want to have printed. Amen.

This photo appeared in the Knoxville, Tennessee, News Sentinel *accompanying our interview with newspaper reporter, Mary Constantine.*

The next Wednesday's food section of the newspaper featured a large picture of Cinda and me on the front page. I was rolling vegetarian meatballs, and Cinda had her head back laughing like crazy. It definitely wasn't the picture that we'd have chosen— and it certainly wasn't posed! What really surprised us about the article, however, was how much Mary wrote about our church and our love for Jesus. She mentioned that one's diet is important because it affects behavior. She captured the love that Christian parents have for their children and the blessing of being raised in a Christ-centered family. As we read the article our prayer was, *Lord, please use this to bless someone else.*

The day after the article was published the phone rang as I was sitting at my desk. "Is this Brenda Walsh of the Micheff sisters?" the woman asked. She introduced herself as Adriana Zoder and continued, "I'm a newlywed and a Seventh-day Adventist. My husband, Matt, was baptized and joined my church just before we were married. My father-in-law is a cantankerous man and thinks his son has married into a cult. I don't live in Knoxville, but my father-in-law sub-

Adriana and Matt Zoder. Because of the interview published in the Knoxville newspaper I was able to have a divine appointment with Adriana's father-in-law.

scribes to the *Knoxville News Sentinel,* and he happened to read the article about you in the paper.

"He couldn't resist calling his son and rubbing it in about him not being able to eat meat. He thinks we have the 'can't do' religion. He says things like, 'You can't go to the movies, can't dance, can't drink, can't do anything fun. The next thing you know, you'll have to stop eating meat!' My husband tried to tell Dad that he didn't have to give up meat to be a church member. Somehow what my father-in-law read in the paper confirmed his idea. I know you are a busy woman, but it would be so kind of you if you could take a few minutes and give him a call and explain that giving up meat is not a church requirement."

I asked for his name and number, and then Adriana and I prayed that I would say exactly the right words to this man. The last thing I wanted to do was make matters worse! *"Touch my lips, Lord. Through what I say let this man see that there is more joy in serving You then in doing anything else."* I continued to pray, *"Be with Adriana and her husband so that their faith will grow stronger. And let them be a mighty witness, so that when You come in the clouds of glory their family will be united. Amen.*"

I dialed the number. As the phone was ringing, I shot another prayer heavenward: *If I'm not suppose to talk with this man, Lord, don't let him be there. But if You want to use me to witness to him, let him answer the phone.* He answered!

"Hello, is Lin there?" I asked.

"This is Lin."

"Hi, this is Brenda Walsh from Three Angels Broadcasting Network."

"Oh, hi! I'm sitting here watching TV and drinking a beer." Adriana had warned me that he could be cranky and might even hang up on me. I didn't want to say anything to offend him. *OK, Lord, we're in for quite a ride. Please stay with me.*

What followed next was a most interesting conversation. I started by saying, "I heard you saw the article about us in the *Knoxville News Sentinel* and that you had some questions about whether not eating meat was a requirement for membership in our church. Actually being a vegetarian is not a requirement!"

"It's not?" he exclaimed.

He let me know he loved pork. I talked about Leviticus 11 and how God says in Deuteronomy 14:8 that pigs are so filthy He doesn't want us even to touch their carcasses. Then he let me know he loved lobster.

"You know what lobsters eat, don't you?" I asked.

"No," he replied.

"They gobble up the poop off the bottom of the ocean. You wouldn't want to put that in your body, would you?"

By now Lin was howling with laughter; he didn't sound as if he were going to hang up on me at all!

I told him that my husband had been a Seventh-day Adventist for more than twenty-seven years and that it had been only a few years ago that he had been impressed to give up eating meat. I explained that until that time, I never nagged him about it and that I lovingly cooked the meat dishes he enjoyed. I told Lin how these things had to be left with the Lord. He would impress people when it was time to remove animal products from their diets. "It happened for my husband," I said, "when he heard a gastro-intestinal specialist on the radio comment that if people were to give up meat and dairy products, it would put him out of a job! After that conversation, my husband came home and repeated what he had heard. 'Brenda, did you know that when you eat meat it has to rot inside you before it can be eliminated?' That was enough for him. No more meat!"

Then I said, "Lin, I would love to have a chance to fix you a vegetarian meal. I can guarantee you wouldn't even miss that old dead cow!"

We both laughed, and it wasn't until I hung up that I realized we had talked for almost an hour!

The next day Adriana was thrilled to learn about our conversation. "It's a miracle," she said. "I can't believe Lin was so nice and didn't hang up on you. Amazing! I believe God put that article in the paper at just the right moment for my father-in-law. It's almost like a divine appointment. If you knew my father-in-law, you'd know just how true that is! Thank you so much."

"You don't have to thank me," I said. "I thank you for calling me and allowing me to be a part of another witnessing opportunity. I just love divine appointments!"

AT WAL-MART'S CHECKOUT COUNTER

Now what am I going to do? I wondered. The paper I had glued to the top of the pillar had dried in a wrinkled mess instead of laying flat. *The camera will pick this up immediately, and we have only a couple of hours before we go live! What am I going to do?*

It was fall camp meeting time at Three Angels Broadcasting Network in Thompsonville, Illinois. My job was to decorate the stage each year, and I would have been finished except for one small detail. This was the first year there was a baptismal tank on stage, and it was positioned behind four small pillars. The top of the pillars had large holes in them so light could shine through. And because the jib camera would look directly down into the tank, the camera was certain to pick up the holes in the pillars.

Bobby Davis, the producer, had approached me earlier and asked if I could do something to cover the holes. I immediately found wallpaper the same color as the pillars and glued it in place, thinking I had fixed the problem.

Now, with just a couple hours before the meeting was to be broadcast live all over the world, I was staring at a wrinkled mess. *Lord, please show me how to fix this. You know that I don't have much time, and You can see that the glue didn't work. Please tell me what to do.*

Some people may think God is too busy to be bothered with something as small as covering unsightly holes in the pillars on a video broadcast. But, Jesus is my best Friend, and I talk to Him about everything! I had no sooner finished praying when the idea came. *I need double-sided tape. That should fix it!*

I spent five minutes asking everyone I could think of if they had any double-sided tape. All my attempts were unsuccessful. Realizing I couldn't afford to waste another minute, I ran to my car and began driving toward Marion, Illinois, thirty minutes away to Target, a variety store which carried just about everything. An added benefit—I knew exactly where they kept their double-sided tape. I figured if I hurried, I could run in, grab the tape, go through the checkout counter, and get back to 3ABN in time to fix the pillars. I knew timing was crucial and that I would have to make every second count!

I raced down Interstate 57 and got off at the Route 13 exit. Without realizing what I was doing, however, I found myself in the left-hand lane instead of the right one that would take me to Target. I looked quickly in my rearview mirror to see if I could safely make a lane change, but three giant semi trucks ruled out that option!

"Oh well," I muttered to myself. "I guess I'll just go to Wal-Mart because I don't have time to turn around, go back through the light, and cross the road to Target." I pulled into the Wal-Mart parking lot, found the closest space, and ran into the store. I thanked the Lord for directing me to the right aisle, as I quickly selected the tape and started for the checkout counter. Suddenly I thought, *I better get two rolls just in case.* Back I went and grabbed one more off the shelf. I looked to see which checkout counter had the shortest line.

Oh good. Thank You, Lord, no line, I thought as I made my way to the express checkout lane. The clerk had just finished with the man in front of me as I laid my tape on the counter.

She quickly scanned my purchases, placed them in a bag, and said, "That will be four dollars and twenty-three cents, please." I smiled at her and fumbled through my purse for my wallet. I removed a five-dollar bill and handed it to the clerk. Just as I was about to shut my purse, I glanced at my bookmarks. I always keep a supply to give away whenever God impresses.

"Whatsoever things are true, whatsoever things are honest, whatsoever things are just, whatsoever things are pure, whatsoever things are lovely, whatsoever things are of good report; if there be any virtue, and if there be any praise, think on these things."
† Philippians 4:8 KJV

But today, for a brief second, I hesitated because I was in a hurry and whenever I hand anyone a bookmark, it always generates a conversation about God. It was already after five o'clock, and the program went live at seven! Then in my mind I heard Jesus say, *"Brenda, you always have time for Me. What is more important—fixing those pillars or saving souls?"* I immediately pulled out the bundle of bookmarks and handed one to the clerk. "Here," I said, "I'd like to give you a gift. Do you read much?"

This is a photo of the actual bookmark that I gave Angela in Wal-Mart.

"Oh, this is beautiful," she said. "But I'll never get to keep it. My son is an avid reader, and he'll take this for sure."

"Oh no he won't. Here is one for him too! Now he can have his own."

The clerk seemed pleasantly surprised and thanked me. "Are you sure I can't pay you something for these?" she asked.

"No," I replied. "You can't pay for something when it's a gift. Besides you would steal my blessing!" I gave her a warm smile, and she thanked me again. Suddenly aware that I was in the express lane with people waiting, I turned to the woman behind me. I reached for another bookmark and quickly handed it to her. "Here, Ma'am, I don't want you to have that *left out* feeling. This one is for you."

She stared at the bookmark and then looked back at me. "This is so beautiful! Where can I buy more of these?"

"Oh, you can't buy them. They aren't for sale. I host and produce a children's program on 3ABN called *Kids Time*, and a group of ladies in Massachusetts make these for me. I send them all over the world to every child who writes to me." Her mouth was open, and she looked as if she had seen a ghost.

"Did you say 3ABN, as in Three Angels Broadcasting Network?"

"Yes," I replied. I started to explain but she interrupted. "You know, I've been listening to 3ABN radio for several months, and I've about decided they have it right on that Sabbath thing. Is there a Seventh-day Adventist church around here?"

Now, I was the one who was surprised. I swallowed hard and prayed, *Please, Jesus, tell me what to say.*

"Yes," I said, my excitement mounting. "There's a church in Thompsonville at the 3ABN Worship Center, and we're having camp meeting right now. Why don't you come to the meeting tonight?"

"Oh, I can't come tonight. I have to work," she explained. I glanced at her Dillard's name tag with "Angela" written on it. "Well, that's OK. How about tomorrow night? The meeting doesn't start until seven, and Doug Batchelor will be speaking."

"You've got to be kidding!" she exclaimed. Now she looked excited too. "He is the one that I've been listening to on the radio! I'd love to come and hear him. Did you say seven?"

"Yes," I nodded. "Let me give you directions." Angela searched in her purse and quickly found a pen and paper. All this time we were standing in the express lane. By now there was a line of people behind us. I was amazed that no one was complaining—not even the clerk, who was listening intently. Angela started writing down the directions, and I noticed that the man behind her started writing them down too.

I handed her my business card, "Angela, when you get there, be sure to call me on my cell phone, and I'll come out to the parking lot to meet you so we can sit together."

"That would be great," she said. "I'd like that very much."

I reached over and gave her a warm hug. "Meeting you today was no accident. It was a divine appointment." She nodded in agreement. I hugged her again and said, "I can't wait to see you tomorrow night." I walked to my car as if I were walking on air. *Thank You so much, Jesus, for using me today, for answering my prayer and placing someone in my path who needed to know about Your love! Please don't let the devil keep Angela away. Lord, I am pleading for Angela's soul that You will give her the courage to come tomorrow night. I am asking for a hedge of angels to surround her and protect her from Satan's snares. I know the devil would like nothing more than to discourage her from coming to hear Your word. But Lord, I know that You are so much stronger than the devil, and I know how much You love her, so don't let anything keep her away! Amen.*

I continued praying all the way to Thompsonville. I especially thanked God for bringing Angela into my life. Pulling into the parking lot of the 3ABN Worship Center, I glanced at the clock on my dashboard. *Oh no! I have less than an hour before the meeting starts.* I grabbed my bag of tape and raced for the stage. I quickly cut out new pieces of wallpaper to cover each pillar, and the tape worked perfectly. People were already filling the Worship Center. With ten minutes to

Here I am with Angela Piekarczyk, whom I met at Wal-Mart through another "divine appointment."

spare, I finished the task, hurried out the back door, and headed toward the Green Room, where program participants wait. Through the open door I noticed John Lomacang, pastor of the church.

"John! John! We have to pray for Angela!" The tone of my voice was so urgent that he stopped dead in his tracks with a look of real concern and panic on his face.

"What's happened to Angela?" he demanded. All at once I realized that he thought I was talking about his wife whose name is also Angela!

"No, not *your* Angela, *my* Angela!"

A look of relief swept over his face followed by a look of complete confusion. "*Your* Angela?"

I smiled and quickly told him the whole story, ending with, "Will you pray for Angela?"

"Let's pray right now," he said. And with that, we bowed our heads right there and then and poured out our hearts, pleading for God to intervene in Angela's life so that nothing would stand in her way of coming to the meeting the next night. I walked away thankful for a Christian friend like John who would stop and pray with me when he had just four minutes before he was to be out on the stage to open the live program. *He definitely has his priorities straight,* I mused to myself.

Just outside the Green Room I met a group of employees who worked at 3ABN radio. I raced over to give them the good news, and we prayed together for Angela. That night I asked everyone I met to pray for Angela. The next day was no different. All day long, I told people about Angela and asked them to pray that the devil would not keep her from coming to the meeting.

At six-thirty the next evening, I was in the back hall by the door to the parking lot, pacing back and forth, clutching my cell phone. But I wasn't just pacing—I was pacing and praying. There *is* a difference! I was pleading with the Holy Spirit to let Angela walk in that door. Seven o'clock came and went, but there was no sign of Angela. I continued praying, refusing to give up. At ten minutes after seven, still no Angela. Fifteen minutes after seven, the door swung open, and there she was!

I ran over and gave her a big hug. "Oh Angela, I'm so glad you made it!"

"I'm sorry I'm late," she apologized. "I got here early, but I was at the other 3ABN building across the road. I'm so sorry."

"That's no problem," I said, giving her another big hug. "I'm just so excited to see you. Let's hurry since the meeting has already started, and I don't want you to miss a thing."

As we were walking, I began to pray: *Lord, please help me find a seat next to someone who goes to this church, someone who can take a special interest in Angela and welcome her to the services.* I knew how important it is to "love someone to Jesus"! Being a pastor's daughter, I had learned never to let a visitor or stranger sit alone on a cold bench. I wanted someone to love Angela to Jesus! But I live in Knoxville and was home on weekends. *Lord, I need to find a member of this church to nurture her. Since the meeting has already begun and the place is packed, how am I going to find someone?*

Once inside the Worship Center, I looked across the crowded room. It seemed as if every chair was filled. *There must be fifteen hundred people here tonight,* I thought to myself. *Oh, dear Jesus, please help me find exactly where You want us to sit.*

Just then I noticed my friend, Mollie Steenson, and her husband, Hal, sitting along the wall at the back of the room. I walked up to her and introduced Angela, briefly explaining that I had just met Angela in Wal-Mart. Then I bent down and whispered in Mollie's ear, "I'm looking for two seats next to someone who goes to this church. Can you help me?"

Mollie gave me a knowing glance and looked around the room. Soon she smiled and pointed toward the second row. "There are two seats right by Shelley and JD." I squeezed her hand, thanked her, and we quickly made our way up front. Wintley Phipps was getting up to sing. His song spoke to my heart in such a personal way. I always love hearing Wintley sing, but tonight he sang as if the Holy Spirit were shining right through him. I glanced out of the corner of my eye and could see Angela was moved as well.

While Doug Batchelor was speaking there was no question in my mind that God was using him in a powerful way to speak to Angela's heart. I was praying. When the meeting was over I could see tears in Angela's eyes.

I introduced Angela to Shelley and JD Quinn, telling them the quick version of how we met and why Angela was here. I was thrilled at how warm and loving they were to her; Shelley even invited Angela to come to church with her the next Sabbath.

Then Angela said, "Now, I need to tell you the other side of the story. I have been listening to 3ABN radio for several months, and it seemed like every time I turned on the radio there was a sermon or program about the Saturday Sabbath. Realizing that God was trying to tell me something, I prayed, 'Lord, I already keep the Sunday Sabbath; isn't it just the same?'

"As clear as can be God spoke to my heart and said, 'I didn't say *a* sabbath, I said *the* Sabbath.' So I prayed again saying, 'Well, if it really means that much to You, if it really matters which day I worship, then please show me what I am supposed to do. Show me where I am to go. Please, Lord, give me a sign.'

"And God gave me my answer—the very next day, right there in Wal-Mart! The funny thing is, I didn't even know what I was doing there. I was buying a bicycle tire pump, which I don't even need and that I could have easily purchased at Target since it's in the same mall and just a three-minute walk from the store where I work. I didn't have a clue why I went to Wal-Mart. I was on my dinner break, so I didn't have much time, and I remember driving into the parking lot and saying to myself, *What are you doing here?* I was so upset with myself for even driving over there that I almost turned around, but something compelled me to go inside."

Angela turned and looked at me, "Brenda, I *had* to come tonight; I knew that if I didn't listen to God's voice, it would cost me my salvation." Tears ran down her cheeks and mine too. I gave her a hug and then pulled her through the crowd so I could introduce her to Doug Batchelor. I quickly told him about how we met, and he told Angela that he would be praying for her. I also introduced her to Danny Shelton, the president of 3ABN.

As I walked with Angela to the parking lot, I stopped and asked if I could pray with her before she left. We held hands and prayed right there under the stars. I thanked God for answered prayers and for Angela's decision to come that night. When we said our goodbyes, I gave her one last hug and said, "Angela, I want to be neighbors with you in heaven!"

The next day, before heading back to Knoxville, I stopped to talk with several people who I knew went to the Thompsonville church. I asked them to pray daily for Angela. As I was driving out of town, I called Pastor John on his cell phone and said, "John, please take care of *my* Angela."

He laughed and said, "Yes, I will."

Everywhere I went from that day forward, I asked people to pray for Angela. When I would speak at seminars or churches, I would tell Angela's story and ask for prayer warriors that would daily lift up Angela in prayer.

So you can imagine my excitement when a month or so later, while I was enjoying dinner with John and Angela Lomacang, John said, "By the way, the friend you met at Wal-Mart has been coming to church every Sabbath."

Angela Lomacang added, "She has even joined one of the groups to host fellowship dinners each week." My eyes lit up with excitement. I could hardly believe my ears! *Thank You, Jesus,* I prayed. *Thank You for answered prayers.*

A few weeks later John called with the good news, "Your Angela is in my baptismal class." Tears welled up in my eyes, and I couldn't speak. "Are you still there?" John asked.

"Yes," I managed to say. "I'm still here. I'm just so happy!" I reached for a tissue and wiped away my tears. Trying to compose myself, I said, "John, promise me one thing."

"What's that?" he asked.

"I want to be there."

"You've got it! Just keep on praying!"

"You don't have to worry about that! I've been praying for months, and I'm not going to stop now! Thank you so much for letting me know! You made my day, my week, and my whole year! There's no greater joy than serving Jesus and bringing others to Him!"

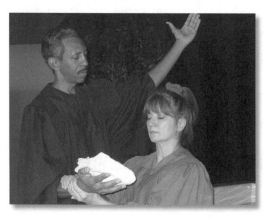

Pastor John Lomacang baptizes Angela Piekarczyk. This was a very special day for me— as well as for Angela.

John started to laugh. "You've got that right!" he agreed.

Just ten months from the time we met in Wal-Mart, Angela Piekarczyk had made her decision to be baptized. Angela Lomacang called me to give me the good news! I was beside myself and overcome with emotion. *God is so good!* There were only three weekends in the rest of the year when I wouldn't be traveling somewhere, and the weekend of Angela's baptism was one of those weekends I was free! *God's timing is perfect!*

The six hours driving from Knoxville, Tennessee, to Thompsonville, Illinois, felt like six minutes! And watching Angela being lowered into the baptismal tank was one of the highlights of my life. I wouldn't have missed it for anything! I can only imagine how God feels every time one of His precious children makes a decision to give their heart to Him! Oh how the angels in heaven must be singing and rejoicing!

Angela first heard of the three angels' messages on 3ABN Radio. Here Angela stands between Jay Christian, director of 3ABN Radio, and Mollie Steenson, general manager of 3ABN.

As Angela thanked me again for giving her the bookmark, she shared one more interesting detail that God had obviously planned. "Pansies are my favorite flower," she said. "I grow them and collect things that have pansies on them. Everyone who knows me knows I love pansies. I'm not sure you noticed, but the bookmark you gave me in Wal-Mart had a brilliant, dried pansy laminated on it. When I saw it, I knew it was a sign that meeting you in that checkout line was God-ordained. That's one of the reasons I had to go to the meeting that night."

When I heard "the rest of the story," I was amazed. That day in Wal-Mart, when I reached into my purse to give Angela a bookmark, I was in such a rush that I didn't even notice which one I gave her. I had no idea it was the last special bookmark that Margie Holden had made for me before she died. I had kept it in my purse as a reminder of her. She had made only two hundred bookmarks with dried flowers, and I had rationed them carefully, praying before I gave any of them away. That's how special they were. Margie had picked the flowers herself, dried them in the yellow pages of telephone books to preserve the colors, and then laminated them. Had I looked at the bookmark before I handed it to Angela, I probably would have exchanged it for another and kept the pansy as a reminder of the wonderful times

Ann Nuckles was one of many people who were praying for Angela. Ann believes in the power of prayer.

Margie and I had together. (See chapter 2.) Now, I rejoiced at how God used Margie's last bookmark to win a soul! That in itself was another direct answer to my prayer. I can hardly wait for that great resurrection day when I can share this story with Margie!

In the November 2006 issue of *3ABN World Magazine*, I wrote a short version of this story to let the 3ABN viewers know how the Holy Spirit is working today. Just as I was finishing the writing of this book, I received a letter from one of the individuals who was at the 3ABN camp meeting that very weekend when this story began. I was amazed, as I read Ann Nuckles's letter, to realize just how many people have been blessed by Angela's story. It is a testimony of the blessing that God has in store for those who will passionately pray for the salvation of others. I'd like to share Ann's letter with you.

Dear Miss Brenda,

I just wanted to write and let you know how much I appreciated your testimony in the November *3ABN World Magazine*.

It was my first time to be at a 3ABN camp meeting. You had just gotten back from Wal-Mart and were so excited about meeting this lady in line, and you asked me to pray for her. You gave me one of your bookmarks and signed my copy of your book *Battered to Blessed*.

I never knew if the lady came the next night or not, but I continued to pray for you and her. I was thrilled, as I'm sure many others were, to learn that Angela did come to that meeting and has since been baptized. I thought and prayed for Angela often, wondering, how the "divine appointment" would affect her life. You see, this story will continue till Jesus comes to take His children home. I know my life has been changed by this experience.

I have been blessed by your testimony and your book.

Sincerely,

Ann Nuckles

After reading Ann's letter, I was reminded once again of how God always sees the bigger picture. Angela's story is one that will keep on blessing others and winning even more souls for the kingdom! Throughout this entire miracle you can see God's plan. It's another example of His incredible love for each one of us.

I marvel at all the details God designed to make certain Angela recognized that the encounter with me at Wal-Mart was orchestrated by Him! Oh how important it is that we always give God the glory! I thank our Lord and Savior for answered prayers and the miracle that took place in Angela's heart and life, and I can't wait to see what He has planned next!

I pray passionately every day, "Please, dear heavenly Father, please give me another divine appointment!"

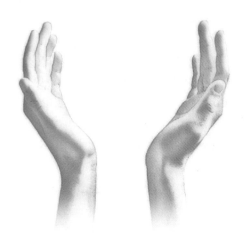

CHAPTER 16

MORE PASSIONATE PRAYER

For the eyes of the Lord are over the righteous,
and His ears are open unto their prayers.
—1 Peter 3:12

*M*y sisters and I were at 3ABN taping cooking shows, and it had been a particularly stressful week. We were shooting four programs in only two days, which was double what we usually did. Our friends Sandy Lee, Corrine Jones, and Rosalie Peters had volunteered to help us with food preparation. They would make finished samples, set up trays for each show, and help with clean-up. Even my *Kids Time* Production Assistant, Brenda Abbott, came to help. She is blessed with a gift of organization and has a way of keeping everything running smoothly!

We were in the middle of taping our last program with only two recipes left to demonstrate, when our director, Halima Martin, stopped taping and called my name over the studio intercom. "Brenda, can you please come to the control room?"

I gave my sisters a quick glance to see if they knew what this was all about. They shrugged their shoulders, letting me know they were as clueless as I was.

When I reached the studio door, Halima was waiting for me. "Brenda, you have an emergency phone call from your husband. He needs you to call him right away. You can use the phone here in the Green Room."

My heart was pounding, and a thousand horrible thoughts were racing through my mind as I dialed Tim's number. As soon as he answered, I blurted "Honey, what's the matter? Are you OK? They told me there was an emergency!"

"It's Jason," Tim's voice cracked with emotion. "He's been rushed to the hospital in Winchester in critical condition. The doctor said he has bacteria in his blood and that he is septic." Then the line went silent.

"Honey, are you there?" My hand shook so much I could barely hold the phone.

Gaining his composure at last, Tim continued, "Yes, I'm here. Oh, Brenda, it doesn't look good! I think you need to get there as soon as possible."

Bursting into tears, I hung up the phone trying to process what I had just learned. My nineteen-month-old grandson, Jason, was critically ill. Just the thought of this precious little boy suffering for a single moment was more than I could bear. Of course, none of us are immune to family tragedies or medical crises, but when they come, we're never prepared! Just then, Linda and Cinda came running into the room. Seeing me in tears, they threw their arms around me.

Between sobs I told them about Jason and immediately, with our arms tightly around each other, Linda began to pray. *"Precious heavenly Father, We come to You with tears and heavy hearts, knowing that You are the only One who can help little Jason. Please take him on Your lap and bless him. We are claiming the promise in Jeremiah chapter thirty-three, verse three, where You have said, 'Call on Me and I will answer you and show you great and mighty things that you know not of.' We place our trust in You for Jason and ask You to be his Great Physician. Thank You for hearing and answering us. We love You. In Jesus' name, Amen."*

When Linda finished praying, there was a knock on the door of the Green Room, and Halima poked her head inside. Cinda quickly filled her in on what had happened.

"Brenda, don't worry about anything," Halima said. "You just go and be with your grandson. We don't have to finish this program."

I reached for a tissue and wiped my eyes. "No, Halima. I'll be OK. We can pray our way through this. It shouldn't take long to tape the last two recipes and close the show. I won't be able to get a flight to Boston until morning anyway. With God's help, I'll get through it."

"Are you sure? You don't have to do this."

"Yes, I'm sure. Just give me a minute to pull myself together. I want to talk with Brenda Abbott to see if she can go online while we're taping and find a plane ticket for me to Boston. Once I know she has started working on getting a reservation, we can finish the taping."

Halima gave me a hug and said, "OK, then. Just tell me when you're ready and we'll try to get through without any edits." I had worked with Halima many years, not only on cooking programs but also on *Kids Time*. I knew she is a serious prayer warrior and that I could count on her to pray us through this program!

In order to get to Boston, I would have to drive the six-hour trip home to Knoxville, Tennessee and then take the earliest flight to Boston from there. Brenda Abbott began searching all the airlines for the fastest and cheapest ticket.

Before heading back to the set, my sisters and I closed the door of the Green Room and went to the Lord in prayer once more. This time we prayed not only for Jason, but also for ourselves that we would be able to smile our way through the rest of the taping. We asked Jesus to give us His joy in our hearts.

The crew was so supportive. I could feel their prayers. But before the cameras could start rolling, we needed a pot of water to come to a boil! That's right, a *pot* of water! You know what they say about a watched pot—that it never boils? Well, I was starting to believe it as we waited and waited for what seemed forever!

The recipe we were about to demonstrate was for Tuscan Eggplant Roll-ups. Because there is not time to finish every recipe on the show, we prepare certain parts of the recipe off camera. For this particular recipe, the eggplant had to be cut in strips and partially boiled before rolling. We had time to demonstrate only the filling and rolling processes, which meant the boiling had to be done ahead of time.

Standing there, waiting for the water in that pot to boil, was sheer agony. My mind drifted back to Jason. I had a very clear image of him lying in the hospital helpless, burning up with fever. I could almost hear him whimpering in pain.

Cinda took one look at me and instantly sensed I was about to burst into tears again. Immediately she swung into action and began to clown around. She did everything but stand on her head to keep the mood light. I knew what she was doing, and I loved her for it. She had a migraine headache all day, so putting on a comedy show was the last thing she felt like doing. She is a doting "Auntie" and loves Jason with all her heart and was just as worried as I was, yet she was doing this for me. I will never forget her precious act of love and how God used her to help me through the rest of that program.

When the cameras were rolling at last, we all managed to put on a smile and joke and tease like we always do. Amazingly, we finished in record time without any edits! When the floor director announced "all clear," I literally ran from the studio, my eyes brimming with tears. Brenda Abbott had already packed my things, and we jumped into the car to race home to Knoxville. As soon as we were on our way, I called my daughter, Becky, on my cell phone to get more details. When she heard my voice, she broke down in tears.

"Oh, Mom, I'm so scared. Jason looks terrible. He's burning up with fever and has projectile vomiting and diarrhea. He is so dehydrated that his little veins have collapsed. The nurses almost couldn't start his IV. He screamed as they had to stick him over and over again. They finally found a vein in his foot that they could use. He is so weak he can hardly turn over. It's breaking my heart to see him in such a pitiful condition."

"Oh, Becky, I'm so sorry. I want you to know I'm coming to help you. I'm taking the next possible flight; it will put me in Boston by nine o'clock in the morning."

"You are? You'll be here tomorrow?" I could hear Becky sobbing on the phone.

"Yes, Honey. I'll be there tomorrow. Please don't worry, because Jesus loves that little boy even more than you do!"

"Oh, Mom, thank you for coming. I need you so much."

At eleven o'clock that night, as Brenda Abbot and I were nearing Knoxville, Dee Hilderbrand, a production coordinator at 3ABN, called. "Hi Brenda, this is Dee. I just wanted to make sure you are safe. I don't want you to fall asleep driving. Are you doing OK?"

"Yes, I'm wide awake. Brenda Abbott is with me."

"Oh, that's good. I'm glad you're not driving alone. I want you to know that Hal Steenson has put Jason on the 3ABN prayer list. Not only is everyone here at 3ABN praying for Jason, but there are literally millions of prayers going up for Jason around the world right this very moment!"

I started crying again. "I'm so very grateful," I managed to say.

"Remember how much Jesus loves that little boy. I'll be praying for him, too."

"Thank you, Dee. It means a lot to me that you called. Please tell Hal that I thank him as well. Having so many people praying for Jason is the best thing anyone could have done for him—or for me!"

I arrived home just after midnight and quickly unpacked and re-packed for my trip. There was no time for sleep; I had to leave for the airport at four-thirty that morning. When I arrived in Boston, David, my son-in-law, was there to pick me up and we raced to the hospital. Nothing could have prepared me for what I saw.

I looked at little Jason, lying there in the hospital crib. He held his little arms out to me and managed to say "Gwamma," and then he screamed out in pain. I ran to Becky and held her in my arms as she burst into tears.

"Oh, Mom, I can't believe you're really here. Look at him; just look at him!" Jason was so weak that most of the time he could only whimper softly, occasionally crying out in agony.

Please dear Jesus, let me be strong for my daughter, I prayed silently. Jason had on a little hospital gown that tied

David and Becky Coffin.

in the back, and I could see all the bruises from the numerous attempts to draw blood.

Just about that time, the doctor arrived for morning rounds. After she examined Jason, I listened as she told Becky and David that she still didn't have a clue what was wrong with their son.

"The good news is that he does not have a bacteria in his blood," she told them. "I believe our earlier test showed a false positive from a contaminated blood sample. But the bad news is that we don't know what *is* going on with him. He is obviously a very sick little guy. I expected him to have perked up by now after receiving this much IV fluid."

The doctor paused to look at her chart and then continued. "I've reviewed his history and see that he has basically stopped growing for the past three months and has no appetite."

"Yes, that's right," Becky replied. "I've offered him every kind of food, and he just hits it out of my hand. He went from a normal healthy boy, eating everything in sight, to wanting nothing! I've taken him to his regular doctor every week, and he told me to give him formula in a sippy cup, but to be honest, he hasn't even taken much of that. I'm so worried about him."

"Well, quite frankly, I'm worried too. I don't want to lie to you. I don't know what is wrong. I'm not sure if his lack of growth is related to this acute episode or not. I suspect that we are dealing with two different things. I'll increase his fluids today and see how he does. Other than that, there isn't much we can do. We can't treat something if we don't know what we're treating."

"May I ask you a question?" I asked. The doctor looked at me and nodded. "How long will you continue to let him stay in this condition before transferring him to Children's Hospital in Boston? I'm concerned that he has already been like this for three days, and he's getting worse, not better."

"If he hasn't improved significantly by tomorrow, I'll transfer him. Right now, I'm testing him for everything. I've ordered tests on his liver function, thyroid, and a host of other things. We will do everything we can to figure this out."

When the doctor left, I went over and put my arms around Becky. She was trying so hard to be strong, and my heart was breaking for her as well as for little Jason.

"Mom, can you get Michael? My friend, Kristin, came to the ER and picked him up when Jason was admitted, but she has her hands full with her own three kids. I called Michael this morning to tell him you were coming, and he is counting the minutes until he sees you. There's nothing you can do here. As you can see, we can only wait. I would worry a lot less if you could take care of Michael. I'm sure he's confused and worried about his brother."

"Absolutely! I'll make sure Michael has a fun day, so don't worry, OK?"

As soon as I drove into Kristin's driveway, Michael bounded out of the house with an abundant supply of six-year-old energy. I picked him up and swung him in my arms!

"Oh Gramma! I can't believe you're here! I'm so excited!"

I hugged him tightly, giving him lots of kisses. Becky's friend, Kristin Safford insisted that it had been "no trouble at all," as we gathered his things and headed for the car. I was so thankful that Becky had such a precious, Christian friend.

We spent the day shopping at Toys "R" Us and sightseeing at all his favorite places. For dinner I took him to The Rainforest Café. When we were leaving, the staff were giving the children helium-filled balloons. Michael indicated that green was his favorite color, so they handed him a big green balloon. After saying thank you, Michael gently pulled on the sleeve of the man giving out the balloons. "Excuse me, Sir."

"Yes, young man?"

"May I have another balloon for my brother. He's in the hospital, and he's very sick."

"Why, of course you can. Here's a yellow one just for him, and you tell him to get well quick, OK?"

"Thank you," Michael called back again as we made our way out the door with Michael holding tightly to the balloons.

"Gramma, do you think we could buy a present for Jason? He loves monkeys, and I think a present would make him feel better."

"Michael, I think that's an awesome idea." After searching several stores, we finally found a cute stuffed monkey. Then with the monkey tucked under Michael's arm, we made our way to the car.

Michael and me.
He is my little "prayer warrior"!

Becky had called earlier and asked if I would bring Michael by the hospital before taking him home. When we pulled into the hospital parking lot, he quickly unfastened his seat belt. But before opening the door, he handed me his green balloon.

"Gramma, I'm not going to keep my balloon."

"Why not, Honey? I thought you loved balloons, and this one is your favorite color."

"I do love balloons. But I want to give this one to Jesus. Will you say a special prayer for Jason? Then I'm going to let it go to heaven."

"Oh, Michael, I think that's a wonderful idea! Yes, let's pray right now. *Dear Jesus, please be with Jason tonight. You know how sick he is. The doctor doesn't know what is wrong with him, but You do. So please be with him and heal him if it is Your will. Thank You for taking care of Jason. We love You, Jesus. Amen.*"

Michael and I got out of the car, and he lovingly held that green balloon. Then he gently kissed it and let it go. We stood and watched as it rose higher and higher in the sky. It was a crisp, clear night, and all the stars were shining. We stood quietly there for several minutes until we could no longer see the balloon as it disappeared among the stars.

"OK, Gramma, we can go. I think Jesus has it now."

"Yes, I'm sure of it," I said. I could feel the tears welling up inside me as I thought of this unselfish act of love and the faith of my precious grandson.

Michael was so excited to give Jason the new stuffed monkey. He seemed disappointed that Jason was too sick to enjoy it. Michael patiently placed the monkey in the corner of Jason's crib and gave me a wink. I bent down so I could hear him whisper, "It's OK, Gramma. He can play with it when he feels better."

Becky gave Michael a squeeze and assured him that Jason would love the present when he was a little stronger. I could see Michael looking at everything in a quizzical manner. He went over and inspected the IV in his brother's foot and checked out the IV pump. He seemed fascinated by all the equipment and was very quiet.

I was worried about how Michael was feeling; I didn't want him to be afraid. As we walked out of the hospital hand-in-hand, I asked, "Honey, are you worried about your brother?"

I'll never forget his answer for as long as I live! He looked up at me with the most confused look on his face. "Of course not, Gramma! What are you thinking? We prayed to Jesus, didn't we? Jesus will take care of Jason!"

Oh, if we all could have that kind of faith! I was so choked up I could hardly speak! After tucking Michael into bed, I decided I'd get some sleep myself. At this point I had been awake for thirty-eight hours, and my body was feeling it. I think the devil works hardest when we are weakest, and discouragement was beginning to set in.

After a long prayer for Jason, I got up from my knees and sat on the edge of my bed and began to sob. All the emotions that I had been forced to hold in all day were now erupting, and not even the Hoover Dam could have stopped their flow. *How much should one little boy have to suffer?* All of a sudden, I heard the "beep-beep" of my Blackberry, announcing I had an e-mail. It was from someone I didn't even know! I couldn't believe my eyes. I read:

Dear Miss Brenda, I am praying for Jason as well as the rest of your family. I hope Hal keeps us informed of his condition. Dear Jesus: As You look down and see Jason suffering, You know who is behind all of this. Please send help—extra angels to come to the family and encircle them with Your loving arms. Please show the doctors how they can help Jason. Please touch Jason with Your special healing touch. Above all, may Jesus be glorified and the family know that You are the Healer of broken bodies and hearts! I pray this in Jesus' name and for His sake only! Amen. Love to you, Yvette Stuart, prayer warrior in Redding California.

Before I could even hit the reply button, another e-mail popped up and then another and another. There must have been a hundred emails an hour coming in from all over the world! I couldn't believe what was happening, and yet here it was, right in the palm of my hand! Even though I was completely exhausted, I sat there and read e-mails for over an hour. These messages were so faith building, so spiritually sustaining, that I was overwhelmed with God's goodness and mercy!

One man wrote: *Dear Sister, Life has its ups and downs. It's important when we are facing the down side to read the Word of God. In Hebrews 13:5 God has promised, "I will never leave you nor forsake you." Sister, you chose to serve the Lord in your line of work. Romans 8:28 tells us "we know that all things work together for good to those who love God, to those who are the called, according to His purpose." And 2 Corinthians 1:3, 4 says; "Blessed be the God and Father of our Lord Jesus Christ, the Father of mercies and God of all comfort, who comforts us in all tribulation, that we may be able to comfort those who are in any trouble with the comfort with which we ourselves are comforted by God." Dear Sister, put all your trust in the Lord. Remember Ephesians 1:8. "For by Grace you have been saved through faith and that not of yourselves it is the gift of God" And Philippians 4:19: "My God shall supply all your need according to His riches in glory by Christ Jesus." May our dear Lord and Savior keep you and your grandson in His safety and love. May He protect and cure your grandson. I ask this in the Master's name, Jesus Christ, Amen. Your servant in Christ, Nader Dahan.*

Wow! He had given me so many uplifting promises and Bible texts to hang on to. Surely, God had heard my cry and was pouring out blessings from the windows of heaven!

Another lady wrote: *Just wanted you to know that I am praying. It is so difficult for your kids or grandkids to be ill, but God hears and answers our prayers. "Where two or more are gathered in my name, there I am also." Know that you are very special—both to God and to me! Love and prayers, Sister Kathy S.*

From India an e-mail read: *Dear Brenda, I pray and place Jason in the hands of Jesus. No better or more comfortable place can I see than the hands of Jesus. May God hear our prayers. Love Nirobindu Das, Calcutta, India.*

No longer able to keep my eyes open, I dropped to my knees to thank my heavenly Father for all His goodness and mercy. *Thank You precious heavenly Father for so many blessings. Thank You for reminding me how much You love me. Thank You for the precious promises in Your Holy Word. I believe in You, and I do know that You always keep Your promises. I am entrusting Jason to Your loving care for I know there is no better place for him to be. Thank You, Jesus, for being the awesome God that You are. My heart is overflowing with love for You!*

The e-mails continued coming in all night long—not only to my personal email address, but to my *Kids Time* email address as well. In order to sleep I had to actually turn off my Blackberry so I wouldn't hear them when they came in. In the morning I read this precious e-mail from my friend, Hal Steenson, who works in the pastoral department at 3ABN.

Brenda, I just sent out an Urgent Prayer Request to our prayer warriors around the world, askng for prayers for you, Becky, and Jason. Currently, we have 530 prayer warriors from 186 countries that will be praying twenty-four hours a day. Great and mighty is the Lord our God. Hal.

I read Hal's e-mail and then read it again. I don't know how to describe the peace that came over me. I had such a calm and a sense of assurance that Jason was going to be just fine! I knew that with so many prayers going toward heaven in Jason's behalf, that he would be OK. This little boy was bathed in so much prayer that the devil didn't stand a chance! I actually felt a sense of joy inside me in spite of the situation.

My joy was even greater when I arrived at the hospital that morning. Jason was sitting up and smiling! He called out to me, "Gwamma, play toys?" Tears of gratitude welled up in my eyes.

"Oh, Mom, you just missed the doctor. She said Jason has tested positive for the Rotavirus, which causes severe abdominal cramping. That is why he was in such pain. She told us that once we get him hydrated, she thinks he's going to be OK. She still doesn't know why he isn't growing or eating, so he'll have to go through a

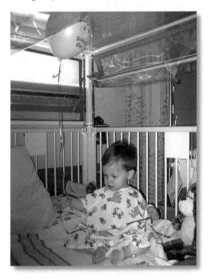

After so many prayers going up to heaven on Jason's behalf, he awoke the next morning, and you could hardly tell he had been sick at all. Here he is ready to play with his yellow balloon and the monkey Michael gave him!

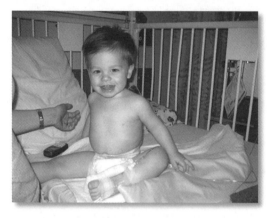

Jason Patrick Coffin is all smiles because he is getting ready to leave the hospital! The nurse has not yet removed the IV from his foot, but he is excited to be going home!

bunch of tests to find out what's wrong, but she feels like that issue is not related to this one. Doesn't he look so much better?"

"Oh, Honey, yes. He looks amazing! Becky, you have no idea how many people are praying for Jason! And not just one or two prayers! There are prayer warriors literally praying twenty-four hours a day for him. I'm telling you, Becky, I *know* Jason is going to be OK. The doctors can test him all they want, but I don't think they will find a thing! I believe God has healed this little boy!"

"Oh, Mom, I sure hope you're right. God has already worked a miracle. Just seeing Jason smiling and sitting up like this is a gift to me!"

The next day we took Jason home from the hospital, and except for the bruises from all the needle sticks, you would never be able to guess that he had been sick at all! He was soon running around the house, laughing and playing and asking "Gwamma" to play "horsie" with him.

You can imagine our joy the next morning when I made homemade waffles for Michael, and Jason begged for some too. He ate not one, but two big waffles all by himself! His appetite had returned! He ate more in this one meal than he had eaten in the last two months! Unbelievable! The next meal was the same. In fact, he was eating like I had never seen him eat before!

This experience happened just as I am completing the writing of this book, so it is too soon for me to tell you how much Jason has grown and continued to flourish. I believe, however, that God has something special planned for this little boy and that Jesus has taken him on His lap and blessed him.

When I think about the miracle God performed in my grandson's life, I am overwhelmed with gratitude. But I am also filled with awe and amazement when I think of the power of prayer. I'm talking real *passionate prayer!* It's mind boggling to me to think that literally hundreds of people—maybe even thousands, or millions—from 186 countries around the world were all praying for little Jason at the same time! Prayer doesn't get more passionate than that!

Jason Patrick is all smiles just one week after being in the hospital! We are praising God for His goodness and mercy!

Oh how our heavenly Father rejoices when His children come to Him in prayer! He has told us so many times to come to Him and that He will be there for us. He has promised in Hebrews 13:5 that He will never leave us or forsake us. So many times during a crisis we think we are all alone. The truth is, we are never alone! When things are the toughest, God is the closest. I remember what my Grandma Micheff always told me, "If things were easy, we would never know we needed Jesus."

Let's not forget God's blessings. He can turn evil into good. He can take the darkest moments of our lives and turn them into the most brilliant moments. I also know that God never performs a miracle in order for us to keep it to ourselves. He wants miracles to be used to glorify His name so that others will know the incredible God that we serve!

That is why I believe God wanted Jason's story in this book. You may be surprised when I tell you that this book had already gone to my publisher when Jason became ill. The book was ready for the final formatted copy to be sent to me for approval before printing. I called Russ Holt, my book editor at Pacific Press, and told him about Jason's miracle. "Russ, I believe God wants this story in the book. Is it too late to add one more chapter? Is there even room to add one more chapter?"

"For a praise report like this, we'll make room!" he replied. "You're right. Jason's story needs to be in the book."

Our God whom we serve is such an awesome God. He never does anything halfway! His way is always the best way! And His timing is always perfect. I can't wait to see how much Jason has grown for his check-up next month, and I wish I could tell you about it. Maybe God will have me share the rest of Jason's miraculous story in another book, *More Passionate Prayer!*

Grandma and her "two boys"!
Michael, Jason, and I are always happy when we
are together! Being their grandmother is one of
my favorite gifts from God!

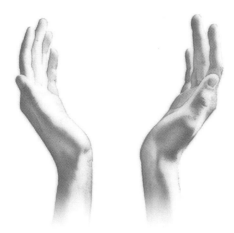

EPILOGUE
Just One More Thing . . .

You are about to close this book, and I hope that it will cause you to ponder what God has been trying to say to you through the stories and teachings of its pages. There is only one more thing I should emphasize. I would like to expand the reason for *passionate prayer*.

Passionate prayer isn't just for miracles to happen—even though we need them. It's not just for getting out of trouble—although that's probably the biggest reason we cry to God for help. It's not just for winning souls, as important as that is since God has commissioned us to "go into all the world . . ."

The real reason for *passionate prayer* is to develop an intimate relationship with Jesus. It's to get to know Him so deeply that you trust Him explicitly with your life; that your will becomes His will. All this, I hope, you have found in the pages of this book.

Before I close, however, I want to expand for just a moment on why it is so important to have *an intimate relationship with Jesus.*

Why? Because when Jesus lives in you, you become changed. You have power over temptation that was impossible when you were going it alone. You are God's will in action—defeating the enemy with courage and confidence. You see life from the perspective of the

Cross. You know that the battle has already been won and therefore you experience joy regardless of what the devil is trying to throw your way.

Because Jesus lives in you, you don't have to wait until heaven to begin living the abundant life that Jesus promises and the "thief" has been trying to steal from you! (See John 10:10.)

In other words, through *passionate prayer*, **You have victory in Jesus!** It's that simple!

My sister Linda often forwards me gems that float around the Internet—gems whose authors have long been forgotten, but the wisdom of the messages strike a responsive chord. Here is one such gem that has made a significant impact on my life. It's titled: "Victory in Jesus."

Victory in Jesus

When you are forgotten, or neglected or purposefully ignored, and you do not sting or hurt at the oversight; when your heart is happy being counted worthy to suffer for Christ . . . *that is victory!*

When your good is evil-spoken-of; when your wishes are crossed, your advice disregarded, your opinions ridiculed and you refuse to let anger rise in your heart or even defend yourself, but take it all in patient loving silence . . . *that is victory!*

When you lovingly and patiently bear any disorder, any irregularity, any unpunctuality, or any annoyance; when you stand face-to-face with waste, folly, extravagance, spiritually insensibility, and endure it as Jesus endured it . . . *that is victory!*

When you are content with any food, any offering, any climate, any society, any solitude, and interruption by the will of God . . . *that is victory!*

When you never care to refer to yourself in conversation or to record your own good works or smile inwardly after a compliment; when you can truly love to be unknown and allow Jesus only to be known . . . *that is victory!*

When you receive correction and reproof from one of less stature than yourself and can humbly submit inwardly as well as outwardly, finding no rebellion or resentment rising up in your heart . . . *that is victory!*

That's what I want every day of my life. *I want victory in Jesus!* That's why I passionately pray. And that's what I want for you, too! That's why I urge you to begin today a more vital, meaningful, *passionate prayer* life.

I pray for victory in Jesus every day. And He's answered my prayer in so many ways. Years ago, before I started every day with *passionate prayer,* I'd get upset over the injustice of what I was experiencing or the sting of malicious rumors. But when I turn my will over to Jesus and ask Him to replace the hurt and anger with His love, He rewards my prayer for victory. He fills my heart with peace and joy, and all resentment just melts away. There are no feelings of revenge, only love.

This incredible peace comes when you are willing to surrender to Christ and let Him fight your battles. Jesus longs for each one of us to experience His abundant, overwhelming, extravagant love.

Years ago I found the following prayer taped to the bathroom mirror in my sister Linda's house. I jotted it down, and I keep it in the back of my Bible, reading it almost daily. It's a prayer for victory. As you close this book, perhaps you would like to make this prayer your first prayer of a *passionate prayer* journey with Jesus.

"Lord, please order my steps today. Make me strong—not for the sake of possessing strength, but to make me sufficient for the crisis moments in my life and in the lives of others who reach out to me. Please keep me close to You and remove all selfishness from my heart. Precious heavenly Father, give me victory."

My Own Prayer Requests

My Answers to Prayer

My Prayer Promises

IF YOU'VE BEEN INSPIRED BY THIS BOOK, YOU'LL WANT TO READ THESE, ALSO.

Battered to Blessed
Brenda Walsh with Kay D. Rizzo
This is the gripping and powerful story of Brenda Walsh's painful secret and the healing power of love. While just eighteen years old, she found herself entangled in a web of deception and cruelty—trapped in a marriage to a man she hardly knew and did not love. Her husband's rage and escalating violence threatened her very life and endangered the safety of her baby. As events spiraled downward into a pit of despair, from which there seemed no escape, Brenda cried out to God.
Paperback, 224 pages   0-8163-2067-5

Between Hell and High Water: Survival Stories From Hurricane Katrina
Kay Kuzma and Brenda Walsh
Imagine yourself in the hell that was Katrina. Follow a former NFL player as he struggles to keep his mother alive—on life support—in a New Orleans hospital as the water rises. Put yourself in the place of the man who is buried under putrid water for thirty minutes with only a PVC pipe to breathe through. Hold on with Pat as she's swept away by the violent flood, frantically grabbing on to tree branches while attempting to shake off the rats clinging to her back. Meet Red, whose addictive habits had destroyed his will to live—until he starts helping those who had lost everything.
Paperback, 256 pages   0-8163-2153-1

Discovering God's Will
Troy Fitzgerald
You can know God's will and live happily in it. Part one of this important book will teach you principles of guidance. Part two points you to Scripture to discern and to do God's will. Part thee will show you how to live God's will for you each day.
Paperback, 144 pages   0-8163-2180-9

Order from your ABC by calling **1-800-765-6955,** or get online and shop our virtual store at **http://www.AdventistBookCenter.com.**
• Read a chapter from your favorite book
• Order online
• Sign up for e-mail notices on new products